SPIRITUAL SECRET OF HUDSON TAYLOR

SPIRITUAL SECRET OF HUDSON TAYLOR

Dr. and Mrs.
HOWARD TAYLOR

Publisher's note:
This new edition from Whitaker House has been updated for the modern reader. Words, expressions, and sentence structure have been revised for clarity and readability.

Unless otherwise indicated, all Scripture quotations are taken from the King James Version of the Holy Bible. Scripture quotations marked (RV) are taken from the Revised Version of the Holy Bible.

SPIRITUAL SECRET OF HUDSON TAYLOR

ISBN-13: 978-0-88368-387-3
ISBN-10: 0-88368-387-3
Printed in the United States of America

Whitaker House
1030 Hunt Valley Circle
New Kensington, PA 15068
www.whitakerhouse.com

LCCN: 2003010104

3 4 5 6 7 8 9 10 11 𝖜 17 16 15 14 13 12 11

Contents

Chapter 1

The Beginning of a Life Lived for God

James Hudson Taylor was a sensitive, thoughtful little fellow from the first, though bright and winsome as any heart could wish. He was a child of many prayers, born to God-fearing parents in Barnsley, England on May 21, 1832. It almost seemed as though he brought more love than usual into the world with his great capacity for loving and the frailty of health that drew forth all the tenderness of those about him. For he was delicate, unusually so, as his parents soon discovered. This was no little sorrow and added difficulty to the task of bringing him up to be a brave and faithful follower of the Lord Jesus Christ. As time went on, he was often so far from well that it seemed almost impossible to insist upon obedience and self-control. Yet the very difficulty only made it all the more necessary. For nothing in the life after, his parents realized, could ever compensate for the injury of an undisciplined childhood. But they knew where to turn for strength and grace. Were they not workers together with God in molding this little life for His holy service? If they lacked wisdom for so high a task, as indeed they did, would He not give it liberally according to His promise?

At no time is there greater capacity for devotion or more pure, uncalculating ambition in the service of God than in early childhood when the heart is full of love for Christ. Little Hudson, for example, was deeply impressed at four or five years of age by what he heard about the darkness of heathen lands.

"When I am a man," he would often say, "I mean to be a missionary and go to China."

Was it only a childish impulse? Yes, but he meant it with all his heart, and meant it because he loved the Lord and wanted to please and follow Him.

Though he took life seriously from the first, he was sunny and bright by nature and dearly loved boyish fun. He had eyes and a heart for everything and retained to the end a capacity for enjoyment that was remarkable. Nature was his great delight, and he had the patience, sympathy, and power of observation needed for entering into its secrets. He would take any amount of trouble to cultivate a little fern or flower brought home from the woods, or to learn about the ways of birds, animals, and insects. All living, growing things seemed to possess a charm for him that years only increased.

Thus Hudson grew in body, mind, and spirit as the days went on. He was still too delicate to go to school, but the education he received at home more than made up for this loss. Not only were his studies systematic and his general intelligence developed, but the conversation of his parents and their visitors awakened thought and purpose to which the average schoolboy is a stranger. Hudson's childhood, therefore, was filled not only with boyish games and pleasures but with learning things that would be needed for his extraordinary life to come.

The Finished Work of Christ

Childhood's years passed by, and all unconsciously Hudson Taylor was drawing near to the crisis of his life. Outwardly he was now a bright lad of seventeen, with few anxieties or cares, but inwardly he was passing through a period of trial. Events had brought him into contact with the world as it is beyond the shelter of a Christian home. Under the stress of new experiences, he had begun to think for himself and live his life more or less independently of others, and a difficult business he found it until he learned to trust a higher strength than his own.

He had traveled far in those difficult years from the love and faith of childhood. And there yet had to be sad revelations of his own heart before he was to know that wonderful rest of faith into which he was privileged to lead so many others. Meanwhile, the unrest deepened, and he began to prove how little the world has to give in exchange for the presence and blessing of God.

Needless to say, this state of things marred the happiness of home and overclouded his naturally sunny disposition. He was all wrong, and his parents could not help seeing it. His father tried to help him but found it hard to be patient with the phase through which he was passing. His mother understood him better and redoubled her tenderness and prayers. But it was his sister Amelia, thirteen years of age, who was nearest to him and best able to win his confidence.

To her he could speak more freely than to grown-up people, and his indifference and unhappiness so affected her that she determined to pray about him three times every day until he was really converted. This she did for some weeks, going alone to plead with God for the salvation of her brother and even making a note in her journal that she would never cease to pray for him until he was brought into the light, and that she believed her petitions would be answered before long.

Thus wearied by failure, harassed by doubt, disappointed in all he had most wished to do and be, Hudson Taylor drew near to the crisis of his life, held by the faith and prayers of a few loving hearts that did know their God. He said in later years:

> It may seem strange, but I have often felt thankful for this time of skepticism. The inconsistencies of Christian people who, while professing to believe the Bible, were yet content to live just as they would if there were no such book, had been one of the strongest arguments of my skeptical companions, and I frequently felt at that time, and said, that if I pretended to believe the Bible I would at any rate attempt to live by it, putting it fairly to the test, and if it failed to prove true and reliable, would throw it overboard altogether. These views I retained when the Lord was pleased to bring me to Himself. And I think I may say that since then I have put God's Word to the test. Certainly it has never failed me. I have never had reason to regret the confidence I have placed in its promises or to deplore following the guidance I have found in its directions.
>
> And now let me tell you how God answered the prayers of my mother and of my beloved sister for my conversion.
>
> On a day I can never forget...my dear mother being absent from home, I had a holiday, and in the afternoon looked through my father's library to find some book with which to while away the unoccupied hours. Nothing attracting me, I turned over a basket of pamphlets and selected from amongst them a Gospel tract that looked interesting, saying to myself: "There will be a story at the commencement and a sermon or

moral at the close. I will take the former and leave the latter for those who like it."

I sat down to read the book in an utterly unconcerned state of mind, believing indeed at the time that if there were any salvation it was not for me and with a distinct intention to put away the tract as soon as it should seem prosy. I may say that it was not uncommon in those days to call conversion "becoming serious," and judging by the faces of some of its professors it appeared to be a very serious matter indeed! Would it not be well if the people of God had always telltale faces, evincing the blessings and gladness of salvation so clearly that unconverted people might have to call conversion "becoming joyful" instead of "becoming serious"?

Little did I know at the time what was going on in the heart of my dear mother, seventy or eighty miles away. She rose from the dinner table that afternoon with an intense yearning for the conversion of her boy, and feeling that, absent from home and having more leisure than she could otherwise secure, a special opportunity was afforded her of pleading with God on my behalf. She went to her room and turned the key in the door, resolved not to leave the spot until her prayers were answered. Hour after hour that dear mother pleaded, until at length she could pray no longer but was constrained to praise God for that which His Spirit taught her had already been accomplished, the conversion of her only son.

I in the meantime had been led in the way I have mentioned to take up this little tract, and while reading it was struck with the phrase: "The finished work of Christ."

"Why does the author use this expression?" I questioned. "Why not say the atoning or propitiatory work of Christ?"

Immediately the words, "It is finished," suggested themselves to my mind.

"What was finished?"

And I at once replied, "A full and perfect atonement and satisfaction for sin. The debt was paid for our sins, and not for ours only, but also for the sins of the whole world."

Then came the further thought, "If the whole work was finished and the whole debt paid, what is there left for me to do?"

And with this dawned the joyful conviction, as light was flashed into my soul by the Holy Spirit, that there was nothing in the world to be done but to fall down on one's knees and, accepting this Savior and His salvation, praise Him for evermore.

Thus while my dear mother was praising God on her knees in her chamber, I was praising Him in the old warehouse to which I had gone alone to read at my leisure this little book.

Several days elapsed ere I ventured to make my beloved sister the confidante of my joy, and then only after she had promised not to tell anyone of my soul secret. When Mother returned a fortnight later, I was the first to meet her at the door and to tell her I had such glad news to give. I can almost feel that dear mother's arms round my neck as she pressed me to her heart and said,

"I know, my boy. I have been rejoicing for a fortnight in the glad tidings you have to tell."

"Why," I asked in surprise, "has Amelia broken her promise? She said she would tell no one."

My dear mother assured me that it was not from any human source she had learned the tidings, and went on to tell the incident mentioned above. You will agree with me that it would be strange indeed if I were not a believer in the power of prayer.

Nor was this all. Some time after, I picked up a pocketbook exactly like my own and, thinking it was mine, opened it. The lines that caught my eye were an entry in the little diary belonging to my sister, to the effect that she would give herself daily to prayer until God should answer in the conversion of her brother. One month later the Lord was pleased to turn me from darkness to light.

Brought up in such a circle and saved under such circumstances, it was perhaps natural that from the commencement of my Christian life I was led to feel that the promises were very real, and that prayer was, in sober matter of fact, transacting business with God, whether on one's own behalf or on the behalf of those for whom one sought His blessing.

Here I Am; Send Me

It was the month of June 1849 when this definite apprehension of the atoning work of Christ changed the whole of life for Hudson Taylor. Hence forward he rejoiced in the conscious acceptance of God, not on the ground of anything he could do or be, but simply because of what the Lord Jesus is and has done. "Not I, but Christ" (Gal. 2:20) brought freedom, joy, and rest. It was the turning point in his experience, the commencement of a new order of things that, little as he realized it at the time, meant for him—China.

And now the unspeakable value of early training such as he had received and years of steady discipline in a Christian home became apparent. He was in a position to make rapid progress. The Bible was no strange book to him but familiar territory, a land of promise waiting to be possessed. Prayer was no unaccustomed effort but the natural outgoing of a heart long used to turning to God. There was much yet to learn, but mercifully there were few habits or memories of evil to erase. The Holy Spirit had, comparatively, a free field in his heart. And at seventeen years of age, all life was yet before him in which to "spend and be spent" (2 Cor. 12:15) for the Lord he loved.

Very manifest for one thing is the joy that overflowed those summer days, as Hudson Taylor realized himself to be indeed a child of God. He was happy. He found it to be a glad life, full of heart rest and satisfaction. For "the Spirit itself beareth witness with our spirit, that we are the children of God" (Rom. 8:16). And the sweetness of this fellowship could never be forgotten. It embraced all who were dearest to him on earth. For he found that being right with God put things right with those around him. It restored the happiness of home, made him a better son and more useful assistant to his father, and deepened especially the love that bound him to the dear sister whose prayers for him had been unfailing. Well may we doubt the reality of any blessing that does not make us easier to get along with, sweeter, and more loving, especially to those at home.

Another outcome of the change that had taken place was a longing every true child of God must know, the longing to give all in return for all that has been given. In the spirit of the Hebrew bondman this young heart cried, "I love my master…I will not go out free" (Exod. 21:5). He longed for some work to do for God, some service that might prove his gratitude, some suffering, even, that might bring him into deeper fellowship with the Lord he loved. An afternoon of leisure gave opportunity for prayer, and with this desire filling his heart he went up to his room to be alone with God. And there in a special way the Lord met him. He wrote about this long after:

> Well do I remember that occasion, how in the gladness of my heart I poured out my soul before God, and again and again confessing my grateful love to Him who had done everything for me—who had saved me when I had given up all hope and even desire for salvation—I besought Him to give me some work for Him, as an outlet for love and gratitude; some self-denying service, no matter what it might be, however trying or however trivial; something with which He would be pleased, and that I might do for Him who had done so much for me. Well do I remember, as in unreserved consecration I put myself, my life, my friends, my all upon the altar, the deep solemnity that came over my soul with the assurance that my offering was accepted. The presence of God became unutterably real and blessed, and I well remember...stretching myself on the ground, and lying there before Him with unspeakable awe and unspeakable joy. For what service I was accepted I knew not. But a deep consciousness that I was not my own took possession of me, which has never since been effaced.

It was an hour that left its mark on life, an hour in which the soul began to apprehend "that for which also" it was "apprehended of Christ Jesus" (Phil. 3:12). The lad who closed his door that day to be alone with God was a very different being from the lad who rejoined the family circle some hours later. A purpose and a power possessed him, unknown before. He had given himself to

God. His offering had been accepted. And though he did not know for what special service the Lord had need of him, he knew that he was no longer his own and must be ready for the call whenever it might come.

One result of this definite consecration is that he began to care about the welfare of others. Hitherto he had been concerned chiefly with his own growth in grace; now he must be about his Master's business, which was the salvation of those around him. He was not deterred by the fact that he could do but little, nor did he excuse himself on the ground of unworthiness. If he could not preach or lead a class as yet, he could at any rate give away tracts and invite people to the house of God. Busy from morning until night in his father's shop, it was not easy to make time for this work. But he found that by denying himself one of his chief pleasures on Sunday, he could gain a few hours just when people would be most accessible. The enjoyment that had to be forgone was the Sunday evening service to which he had been accustomed from childhood. But as much as he loved those helpful seasons, he could no longer be satisfied to feed his own soul continually and do nothing to carry the Bread of Life to the perishing around him. It was "a day of good tidings" (2 Kings 7:9). He was rejoicing in wealth and blessedness untold. And like the lepers in the Syrian camp, he and his sister Amelia felt as they talked it over, "we do not well" to "hold our peace" (2 Kings 7:9).

Instead of attending chapel therefore on Sunday evenings, they went out as soon as tea was over and made their way to the poorest parts of the town. Tracts were handed to all who would receive them, and the message of salvation was simply given as opportunity offered. Even the poorest lodging houses were not passed over. And though it cost an effort to go down those dark, narrow passages into the crowded kitchens, they were more than rewarded by a sense of His approval, whose they were and whom they sought to serve.

But joy in the Lord and in His service was not the only experience as summer passed away. There were also times of painful deadness of soul and much conflict. The heart that had so gladly accepted the finished work of an all-sufficient Savior now knew what it was to be wearied and disappointed in its struggles with sin. Somehow there seemed a gap between the power of the Lord Jesus to save "to the uttermost" (Heb. 7:25) and the needs of everyday life in shop and home. He found himself yielding to temptation, ease-loving, self-indulgent, and often disinclined for private prayer and study of the Word of God. Nothing could have been more real than his consecration; nothing could have been plainer than the disappointment that followed when he discovered his inability to do and be what he would. It even seemed to make matters worse instead of better. For things that before would not have troubled him were now intolerable. He had given himself to God without reserve, longing to be always and only His. And yet he could not maintain that attitude. Coldness of heart crept in, forgetfulness, indifference. The good he longed to do he did not, and the evil he hated too often had the mastery. He did "delight in the law of God after the inward man" (Rom. 7:22), but there was that other law bringing him into captivity to sin with all its deadening influences. (See Romans 7:19–23.) And he had not yet learned to cry: "Thanks be to God, 'the law of the Spirit of life in Christ Jesus hath made me free from the law of sin and death' (Rom. 8:2)."

At such times two courses are open to tne perplexed and troubled soul. One is to abandon the ideal and gradually sink down to a low-level Christian life in which there is neither joy nor power. The other is just to go on with the Lord, and because of His "exceeding great and precious promises" (2 Pet. 1:4), to claim complete deliverance not from the guilt only, but also from the mastery of sin, just to go on with the Lord, trusting His strength and faithfulness to pardon, loose and cleanse, sanctify us wholly, and make our own every blessing promised in the eternal covenant.

Nothing less than this could satisfy Hudson Taylor. Conversion with him had been no easy-going assent of the mind to an abstract creed. No, it was a change deep and real. The cross of Christ had cut him off forever from the old life and from rest in anything the world could give. Nothing could satisfy him now but genuine holiness, unbroken fellowship with God who was his life, his all. Hence, times of spiritual lethargy and indifference were alarming. Deadness of soul was painful beyond endurance. He could not take backsliding easily. Thank God, even the beginnings of backsliding were worse to him than death.

Moreover, he recognized that he was saved to serve, and that a work was waiting for which a life of inner victory and power would be essential. He had had his unsatisfactory experiences and deeply knew how little a man has for others, who is not himself walking at liberty within. During his skeptical days he had seen that the only logical position for the Christian is to go all lengths with God. He had then determined to throw off religion altogether, unless it were possible to obtain in actual reality the promises held out to simple faith. There could be no middle course for him. If his life were to be of any use to God or man he must have that love "out of a pure heart, and of a good conscience, and of faith unfeigned" (1 Tim. 1:5) which is sanctification indeed. This was the only power to make even the most wholehearted consecration practical and enduring.

And this was a gift from above, like the fire that fell in answer to Elijah's prayers; the supernatural, divine response to a heart that, having laid all upon the altar, would not be denied the cleansing, sanctifying power.

It is not to be wondered at that in seeking this promised blessing the Barnsley lad should have times of conflict and defeat. In comparing his experience with that of other men of God one is surprised, rather, that he did not suffer more from the opposition and assault of the Devil. For it was nothing less than full deliverance upon which he had set his heart; that was the point: real holiness and daily victory over sin.

Absorbed in his own need, the lad was longing for true holiness, the life that is "no longer I, but Christ" in everything. (See Galatians 2:20.) The Lord with wider needs in view was seeking him for this, but not for this only. In His great purposes the time had come when the Gospel could no longer be withheld from the "uttermost parts of the earth" (Ps. 2:8). China even must be opened, and its most distant provinces gladdened with tidings of a Savior's love. There it lay in agelong darkness, its teeming millions—a quarter of the human race—living, dying without God. It was of China the Lord was thinking, may we not say it reverently, as well as of Hudson Taylor. But the lad was not ready yet to hear the call, "Whom shall I send, and who will go for us?" (Isa. 6:8). The work of the convicting Spirit needed to go deeper before he could be fully blessed and brought into harmony with the mind of God. Thus his sense of sin and need became more intense as he wrestled for the deliverance without which he could not, dared not go on.

What was it that was keeping him from the life for which he longed? What was the secret of his frequent failure and backsliding in heart? Was there something not fully surrendered, some disobedience or unfaithfulness to light? Fervently he prayed that God would show him the hindrance, whatever it might be, and enable him to put it away. He had come to an end of self, to a place where only God could deliver, where he must have His succor, His enlightenment, His aid. It was a life and death matter. Everything seemed at stake. Like one of old he was constrained to cry, "I will not let thee go, except thou bless me" (Gen. 32:26).

And then, alone upon his knees, a great purpose arose within him. If only God would work on his behalf, would break the power of sin and save him spirit, soul, and body for time and for eternity, he would renounce all earthly prospects and be utterly at His disposal. He would go anywhere, do anything, suffer whatever His cause might demand, and be wholly given to His will and service. This was the cry of his heart, nothing held back—if only God would deliver him and keep him from falling. He wrote:

> Never shall I forget the feeling that came over me then. Words can never describe it. I felt

I was in the presence of God, entering into covenant with the Almighty. I felt as though I wished to withdraw my promise, but could not. Something seemed to say, "Your prayer is answered, your conditions are accepted." And from that time the conviction never left me that I was called to China.

For distinctly, as if a voice had spoken it, the command was given: "Then go for Me to China."

Silently as the sunrise over a summer sea, this new day dawned upon his waiting soul. China? Yes, *China*. That was the meaning of his life—past, present, and to come. Away beyond himself, outside the little world of his own heart experience, lay the great, waiting world, those for whom no man cared, for whom Christ died. *"Then go for Me to China."* Your prayer is answered; your conditions are accepted. All you ask and more, far more, will be given. There will be deeper knowledge of the Lord; fellowship in His sufferings, His death, His resurrection; a life of inner victory and power.

> *For I have appeared unto thee for this purpose, to make thee a minister and a witness both of these things which thou hast seen, and of those things in the which I will appear unto thee; delivering thee from the people, and from the Gentiles, unto whom now I send thee, to open their eyes, and to turn them from darkness to light, and from the power of Satan unto God.* (Acts 26:16–18)

A little slip of paper tells the rest—all, that is, that can be told—a brief postscript to his letter written that very night, the outpouring of a heart so full that it must overflow.

> Bless the Lord, O my soul, and all that is within me shout His praise! Glory to God, my dear Amelia. Christ has said, "Seek, and ye shall find" (Matt. 7:7), and praise His name, He has revealed Himself to me in an overflowing manner. He has cleansed me from all sin, from all my idols. He has given me a new heart. Glory, glory, glory to His ever blessed Name! I cannot write for joy. I open my letter to tell you.

Yes, it was done. From that day onward life was on another plane. The Lord had met him, satisfied his soul, and spoken again the sweet, compelling command, "Follow Me." Outwardly it was manifest that a great change had come over him. His mother wrote:

> From that hour, his mind was made up. His pursuits and studies were all engaged in with reference to this object, and whatever difficulties presented themselves his purpose never wavered.

For inwardly there was a deep subjection to the will of God, resting upon a profound and unalterable sense of what that will was for him. And with this came new purity and power, a steady growth in grace, and fullness of blessing that carried him through all the testing and preparation of the next few years.

"Faithful is he that calleth you, who also will do it" (1 Thess. 5:24).

That was what made him and kept him, the real beginning of his walk with God as a man set apart.

Chapter 2

Preparation for China

Thus closed the old year and the old life, and with the dawn of 1850 came a new beginning of things for Hudson Taylor. He was seventeen and a half years of age and employed in his father's shop. Good prospects were opening before him as a chemist, and the powers he afterwards displayed in the development of a great mission would have made him successful in this or any other line of business. But now all was changed. A work of which he knew next to nothing claimed him, a work that must absorb every energy of his being and might require the sacrifice of life itself. How to set about it he had no idea; how even to make preparation was difficult to discover. But the call of God had come, and there could be no looking back. Whatever might be involved, the future held but one thing for him: to do his Master's will in and for China.

But what problems faced him as he thought of it! He, a mere lad, a chemist's assistant in a provincial town, what could he do for China? Wrapped in the proud exclusiveness of centuries, there it lies, that mightiest empire of the East, vast in size and population, shrouded in mystery, fascinating, repellent; appalling in its need, inaccessible in its seclusion. How could he hope to forward there the coming of the kingdom of God? *"Then go for Me to China."* That was definite and final. So he began at once to pray for guidance and to learn all he could as to his future field.

His purpose went deep, and from the first he realized that a call to missionary work in China involved the beginning of true missionary life at home. "A voyage across the ocean," he often said in later years, "does not make any man a soulwinner." So to humble, loving efforts for the good of those around him, he gave himself with renewed diligence, and especially to the practice of his life calling as a fisher of men.

Another form of preparation entered upon with ardor was the study of Chinese, that formidable task requiring, as Milne put it, "bodies of iron, lungs of brass, heads of oak, hands of spring-steel, eyes of eagles, hearts of apostles, memories of angels, and lives of Methuselah." Courageous in his inexperience, Hudson Taylor set to work despite the fact that he had neither teacher nor books, with the exception of that one little volume of the writings of St. Luke. A grammar would have cost no less than four guineas, and a dictionary could hardly have been purchased for fifteen. Needless to say he had neither. But hard work and ingenuity accomplished wonders, as may be judged from the fact that within a few weeks he had found out the meaning of over five hundred characters. Besides this, he also prepared himself in other ways:

> I have begun to get up at five in the morning and so find it necessary to go to bed early at night. I must study if I mean to go to China. I am fully decided to go and am making every preparation I can. I intend to rub up my Latin, to learn Greek and the rudiments of Hebrew, and to get as much general information as possible. I need all your prayers.

No Good Thing Will He Withhold

Hudson Taylor was very busy at this time, rising early every morning for study. Latin, Greek, theology, and medicine occupied every available moment even during business hours, and Sunday brought opportunities of ministry to others. Sharing a room with his cousin made it difficult to obtain much privacy, but, as he wrote to his sister:

> I go into the warehouse, stable, or anywhere to be alone with God. And some most precious seasons I have....Do your best to keep hold of Jesus. And if in an unguarded moment you should fall, humble yourself before God....We cannot be perfect as angels who have never sinned, nor as Adam before he fell. Sin always has had and always will have a power over us, if we look not to the Lord for strength. Yet, though we are vile in ourselves, we may be made "pure in heart" (Matt. 5:8) through the all-prevailing blood of Jesus. Washed in His blood we are even now "whiter than snow" (Ps. 51:7). But it must be constant washing. Grace we every moment need. Oh, seek this grace, strive for it, and may God bless you with "a pure heart" for Christ's sake.

Meanwhile, prayers for guidance were being answered through an opening that occurred in Hull for an assistant to one of the busiest doctors there. An aunt on his mother's side was married to a brother of this Dr. Hardey, and it was probably her influence that secured the position for her nephew in Barnsley. Thus the quiet years of life at home drew to a close, and it was on his nineteenth birthday that, after a brief visit to his grandparents in Hull, the new apprentice took up his duties with Dr. Hardey.

In what was called the surgery, Hudson Taylor found himself at home. His knowledge of bookkeeping also proved of value to Dr. Hardey, who had much work of that sort on hand and was glad to leave it to so competent a helper. Thus the doctor's relations with the Barnsley lad soon came to be of a cordial character. He was so bright and eager to learn, so willing and good-tempered, that to work with him was a pleasure, and before long the busy doctor found that it was a help to pray with him too. Many were the quiet times, after that, from which the older man came away refreshed and strengthened. Needless to say, there was no familiarity or presuming on these relations. The young assistant respected himself and his employer far too much for that. He did his work faithfully, as in the sight of God, and Dr. Hardey showed his appreciation by giving him opportunities for study and by directing his reading as much as possible.

But there were drawbacks to the life at Charlotte Street, of which Hudson Taylor himself was largely unconscious. For one thing it was too comfortable, too easygoing in certain ways, and failed on that account to afford some elements needed in a missionary's training. Quite in another part of Hull amid very different surroundings was a little prophet's chamber, bare in its furnishings and affording neither companionship nor luxury, where a stronger if a sterner life could be lived, apart with God. Moses at the backside of the wilderness, Joseph in Pharaoh's prison, and Paul in the silence of the Arabian desert all lived that sort of life and came out to do great things for men in the power of God. That was the life Hudson Taylor needed and to which he was being led. He did not choose it for himself, at any rate not at first or consciously. The Lord chose it for him and so ordered circumstances that he was brought to see and to embrace it, finding in self-denial and the daily cross a fellowship with his Master nothing else can yield.

So there came a day, providentially, when the young assistant could no longer be domiciled at Dr. Hardey's. His room was needed for a member of the family, and as the surgery was not provided with sleeping accommodation, he had to seek quarters elsewhere. But it was too much, perhaps, of a transition to that other, better life that awaited him, without some intermediate experience, and for the time being Hudson Taylor found himself welcomed by his aunt, Mrs. Richard Hardey, into her pleasant home.

But though happy in outward circumstances he was anything but free from anxiety and unrest. Life was opening before him, and away from the scenes of childhood, dependent for the first time upon his own earnings, he was feeling the seriousness of his position as never before. He had taken, as he thought, a step toward China, and yet his hope of getting there, his ideal of a life devoted to its evangelization, seemed more and more remote as time went on. He had come to Hull eager to fit himself for medical work, but his busy days with Dr. Hardey left little time for study, while they showed him with increasing clearness how far he was from the end in view. Though he said little about it, the call of God was as a fire burning within him. The thought of perishing souls in China was ever present. Day and night he pondered the problem of how to prepare for and enter upon his lifework. To his youth and inexperience no answer seemed forthcoming, yet how hard it was to wait in patience, to wait for God alone. Generally, he did, as before leaving Barnsley, rest in the Lord and count upon His working. Yet the quiet surgery witnessed many an hour of anxious thought as well as many an hour of prayer, and all through that summer and autumn there was a good deal of unnecessary exercise of heart.

His work helped him, not only the daily round of duties in the surgery but the service he had undertaken, in addition, for the Lord. A little to the west of Dr. Hardey's stood the Royal Infirmary, the largest hospital in the city, about which lay a network of squalid streets culminating in the Irish quarter. Here drinking saloons and tramps' lodging houses abounded, and the police hardly ventured to appear in less force than three or four at a time. Riots and drunken brawls were of frequent occurrence, and nothing was more common than for the priest to be called in to thrash his tipsy parishioners. Garden Street, one of the larger thoroughfares through this district, and West and Middle Streets close to the infirmary seemed especially the haunts of misery and vice. It required courage, as Hudson Taylor found, to go among that bigoted population as a preacher of the Gospel, but a little knowledge of medicine with a great deal of love and prayer opened the way and gave access to many a heart.

Settled in the home of his relatives on Kingston Square, Hudson Taylor's every want was anticipated, and pleasant companionship was afforded to him outside of working hours. But this was not all His love had planned, He who was molding this young life in view of China. Already, through discipline of heart, the lad was learning lessons of patience and submission to the will of God. But something more was needed, something even of outward trial to prepare him for the lifework that was to be. Away in an unfrequented suburb, that little home was waiting—a single room in which he could be alone as never before, alone with God. He wrote:

> After much thought and prayer I was led to leave the comfortable home and pleasant circle in which I resided, and engage a little lodging in the suburbs, a sitting room and bedroom in one, undertaking to board myself. I was thus enabled to tithe the whole of my income, and while one felt the change a good deal, it was attended with no small blessing. More time was given in my solitude to the study of the Word of God, to visiting the poor, and to evangelistic work on Sunday evenings than would otherwise have been the case. Brought into contact in this way with many who were in distress, I soon saw the privilege of still further economizing, and found it possible to give away much more than I had at first intended.

"Drainside," as the neighborhood was termed, could not under any circumstances have been considered inviting. It consisted of a double row of workmen's cottages facing each other across a narrow canal. The canal was nothing but a deep ditch into which Drainside people were in the habit of casting their rubbish, to be carried away in part whenever the tide rose high enough. It was separated from the town by desolate spaces of building land, across which ran a few ill-lighted streets ending in makeshift wooden bridges. The cottages, like peas in a pod, were all the same size and shape down both sides of the long row. They followed the windings of the drain for half a mile or more, each one having a door and two windows, one above the other. The door opened straight into the kitchen, and a steep stairway led to the room above. A very few were double cottages with windows to the right and left of the door and two rooms overhead.

On the city side of the canal, one of these larger dwellings stood at a corner opposite The Founder's Arms, a countrified public house whose lights were useful as a landmark on dark nights, shining across the mud and water of the drain. The cottage was tenanted by the family of a seafaring man whose visits home were few and far between. Mrs. Finch and her children occupied the kitchen and upper part of the house, and the downstairs room on the left as one entered was let at a rental of three shillings a week. It was too high a charge, seeing the whole house went for little more. But the lodger in whom we are interested did not grudge it, especially when he found how much it meant to the good woman, whose remittances from her husband came none too regularly.

Mrs. Finch was a true Christian and delighted to have "the young doctor" under her roof. She did her best no doubt to make the little chamber clean and comfortable, polishing the fireplace opposite the window and making up the bed in the corner farthest from the door. A plain pine table and a chair or two completed the furnishings. The whole room was less than twelve feet square and did not need much furniture. It was on a level with the ground and opened familiarly out of the kitchen. From the window one looked across the narrowest strip of "garden" to the drain beyond, whose mud banks afforded a playground for the children of the neighborhood.

Whatever it may have been in summer, toward the close of November, when Hudson Taylor made it his home, Drainside must have seemed dreary enough, and the cottage far from attractive. To add to the discomforts of the situation, he was boarding himself, which meant that he lived upon next to nothing, bought his meager supplies as he returned from the surgery, and rarely sat down, with or without a companion, to a proper meal. His walks were solitary across the unlighted waste region on the outskirts of the town; his evenings solitary beside the little fire in his otherwise cheerless room; and his Sundays were spent alone, but for the morning meeting and long hours of work in his district or among the crowds that frequented the Humber Dock. He wrote:

> Having now the twofold object in view of accustoming myself to endure hardness, and of economizing in order to be able more largely to assist those amongst whom I spent a good deal of time laboring in the Gospel, I soon found that I could live upon very much less than I had previously thought possible. Butter, milk, and other luxuries I ceased to use, and found that by living mainly on oatmeal and rice, with occasional variations, a very small sum was sufficient for my needs. In this way I had more than two-thirds of my income available for other purposes, and my experience was that the less I spent on myself and the more I gave to others, the fuller of happiness and blessing did my soul become.

For the Lord is no man's debtor, and here in his solitude Hudson Taylor was learning something of what He can be to the soul that leaves all for Him. In these days of easygoing Christianity, is it not well to remind ourselves that it really does cost to be a man or woman God can use? One cannot obtain a Christlike character for nothing; one cannot do a Christlike work save at great price.

Much prayer, as we have seen, was going up for China, and countless hearts were stirred more or less deeply for its evangelization. But when disappointment and unexpected failure came, the great majority ceased to help or care. Prayer meetings dwindled to nothing, would-be missionaries turned aside to other callings, and contributions dropped off to such an extent that more than one society in aid of the work actually ceased to exist. But here and there in His own training schools were those the Lord could count upon: little and weak perhaps, unknown and unimportant, but willing to go all lengths in carrying out His purposes, ready through His grace to meet the conditions and pay the price.

Here in his quiet lodging at Drainside was such a man. With all his youth and limitations, Hudson Taylor desired supremely a Christlike character and life. As test after test came that might have been avoided, he chose the pathway of self-emptying and the Cross, not from any idea of merit in so doing, but simply because he was led by the Spirit of God. Thus he was in an attitude that did not hinder blessing.

> *Behold, I have set before thee an open door, and no man can shut it: for thou hast a little strength, and hast kept my word, and hast not denied my name.* *(Rev. 3:8)*

A great door and effectual is opened unto me, and there are many adversaries.

(1 Cor. 16:9)

Adversaries there certainly were to oppose Hudson Taylor's progress at this time. He was entering upon one of the most fruitful periods of his life, rich in blessing for himself and others. Is it any wonder that the tempter was at hand? He was alone, hungry for love and sympathy, living a life of self-denial hard for a lad to bear. It was just the opportunity for the Devil, and he was permitted for a while to do his worst, that even that might be overruled for good.

For it was just at this juncture, when he had been a few weeks at Drainside and was feeling his position keenly, that the dreaded blow fell, and the one he loved most in all the world seemed lost to him forever. For two long years he had hoped and waited. The very uncertainty of the future had made him long the more for her presence, her companionship through all changes. But now the dream was over, and how bitter the awakening! Seeing that nothing could dissuade her friend from his missionary purpose, the young music teacher made it plain at last that she was not prepared to go to China. Her father would not hear of it, nor did she feel herself fitted for such a life. This could mean but one thing, though the heart that loved her best was well-nigh broken.

It was not only an overwhelming sorrow; it was a tremendous test of faith. The tempter, naturally, did everything in his power to call in question the love and faithfulness of God. Only break down his trust, make him give up the struggle now, and the usefulness of all his later life would be marred.

"Is it all worthwhile? Why should you go to China? Why toil and suffer all your life for an ideal of duty? Give it up now, while you can yet win her. Earn a proper living like everybody else, and serve the Lord at home. For you can win her yet."

Love pleaded hard. It was a moment of wavering and peril. The Enemy came in like a flood. But enough! The Spirit of the Lord lifted up a standard against him. Hudson wrote the next day:

> Alone in the surgery I had a melting season. I was thoroughly softened and humbled and had a wonderful manifestation of the love of God. "A broken and a contrite heart" (Ps. 51:17) He did not despise, but answered my cry for blessing in very deed and truth. May He keep me softened and thoroughly impress on me the seal of His own nature. I see this to be my privilege. Oh, may I be filled with His Spirit and grow in grace until I reach "the measure of the stature of the fulness of Christ" (Eph. 4:13).
>
> I am happy, not without trial, anxiety, or care, but by the grace of God I no longer bear it all myself. "The LORD gave, and the LORD hath taken away" (Job 1:21).

And he also wrote:

> Yes, He has humbled me and shown me what I was, revealing Himself as a present, a very present help in time of trouble. And though He does not deprive me of feeling in my trial, He enables me to sing, "Yet I will rejoice in the LORD, I will joy in the God of my salvation" (Hab. 3:18). Thus I do rejoice by His grace and will rejoice and praise Him while He lends me breath.

> Now I am happy in my Savior's love. I can thank Him for all, even the most painful experiences of the past, and trust Him without fear for all that is to come.

From Faith to Faith

"I never made a sacrifice," said Hudson Taylor in later years, looking back over a life in which to an unusual extent this element predominated. But what he said was true. For as in the case in point, the first great sacrifice he was privileged to make for China, the compensations that followed were so real and lasting that he came to see that giving up is inevitably receiving when one is dealing heart to heart with God.

It was so, very manifestly, that winter. In the hour of trial, a step of faith had been taken and a victory won that made it possible for the Holy Spirit to lead him on. Not outwardly only, but inwardly, he had accepted the will of God, giving up what seemed his best and highest, the love that had become part of his very life, that he might be unhindered in serving and following Christ. The sacrifice was great, but the reward far greater. A new tone is perceptible about his letters, which are less introspective from this time onward and more full of missionary purpose. China comes to the front again in all his thinking, and there is a quickened longing for likeness to Christ and unbroken fellowship with Him. Jesus Himself was filling the empty place and drawing His servant on to deeper love and closer following. He wrote to his sister early in the New Year, 1852:

> I feel my need of more holiness and conformity to Him who has loved us and washed us in

> His blood. Love so amazing should indeed cause us to give our bodies and spirits to Him as living sacrifices....Oh, I wish I were ready! I long to be engaged in the work. Pray for me, that I may be made more useful here and fitted for extended usefulness hereafter.

And again a few weeks later:

> I almost wish I had a hundred bodies. They should all be devoted to my Savior in the missionary cause. But this is foolishness. I have almost more than I can do to manage one, it is so self-willed, earthly-minded, fleshly. Constantly I am grieving my dear Savior who shed for me His precious blood, forgetting Him who never has relaxed His watchful care and protection over me from the earliest moment of my existence. I am astonished at the littleness of my gratitude and love to Him, and confounded by His long-suffering mercy. Pray for me that I may live more and more to His praise, be more devoted to Him, incessant in labors in His cause, fitted for China, ripened for glory.

This was no mere emotion, no superficial interest that might give place to considerations of personal advantage. It was not that he had taken up missionary work as a congenial branch of Christian activity, but that the need of the perishing in heathen lands, the need and longing of the heart of Christ—"them also I must bring" (John 10:16)—had gripped him and held him fast. He believed that the heathen are perishing, and that without a knowledge of the one and only Savior they must be eternally lost. He believed that it was in view of this, and because of His infinite love, that God had given "his only begotten

Son, that whosoever believeth in him should not perish, but have everlasting life" (John 3:16). And these convictions pledged him to the only life possible in view of such stupendous facts, a life wholly given to making that great redemption known especially to those who had never heard.

Yet as much as he longed to go, and go at once, there were considerations that held him back. He wrote of his thoughts that winter:

> To me it was a very grave matter to contemplate going out to China, far from all human aid, there to depend upon the living God alone for protection, supplies, and help of every kind. I felt that one's spiritual muscles required strengthening for such an undertaking. There was no doubt that if faith did not fail, God would not fail. But what if one's faith should prove insufficient? I had not at that time learned that even "if we believe not, yet he abideth faithful: he cannot deny himself" (2 Tim. 2:13). It was consequently a very serious question to my mind, not whether He was faithful but whether I had strong enough faith to warrant my embarking in the enterprise set before me.
>
> "When I get out to China," I thought to myself, "I shall have no claim on anyone for anything. My only claim will be on God. How important to learn, before leaving England, to move man through God by prayer alone."

He knew that faith was the one power that could remove mountains, conquer every difficulty, and accomplish the impossible. But had he the right kind of faith? Could he stand alone in China? As much as he longed to be a missionary, would such faith as he possessed be sufficient to carry him through all that must be faced? What had it carried him through already, here at home?

He thankfully realized that faith, the faith he longed for, was a "gift of God" (Eph. 2:8), and that it might grow exceedingly. But for growth, exercise was needed, and exercise of faith was obviously impossible apart from trial. Then welcome trial; welcome anything that would increase and strengthen this precious gift, proving to his own heart, at any rate, that he had faith of the sort that would really stand and grow.

And here it should be remembered that in taking this attitude before the Lord, Hudson Taylor was wholly earnest and sincere. He was bringing "all the tithes into the storehouse" (Mal. 3:10), a most important consideration, living a life that made it possible for him to exercise faith to which God could respond in blessing. In a word, there was no hindrance in himself to the answer to his prayers, and experiences followed that have been made an encouragement to thousands the wide world over.

The following story illustrates the only principle of growth in spiritual things: "From faith to faith" (Rom. 1:17), the law reiterated by our Lord Himself that, "He that hath, to him shall be given" (Mark 4:25).

"To learn, before leaving England, to move man through God by prayer alone." This and nothing less was the object Hudson Taylor had before him now, and it was not long before he came to see a simple, natural way of practicing this lesson:

> At Hull my kind employer, always busy, wished me to remind him whenever my salary

became due. This I determined not to do directly but to ask that God would bring the fact to his recollection and thus encourage me by answering prayer.

At one time as the day drew near for the payment of a quarter's salary, I was as usual much in prayer about it. The time arrived, but Dr. Hardey made no allusion to the matter. I continued praying. Days passed on, and he did not remember, until at length, on settling up my weekly accounts one Saturday night, I found myself possessed of only one remaining coin, a half crown piece. Still, I had hitherto known no lack, and I continued praying.

That Sunday was a very happy one. As usual my heart was full and brimming over with blessing. After attending divine service in the morning, my afternoons and evenings were taken up with gospel work in the various lodging houses I was accustomed to visit in the lowest part of the town. At such times it almost seemed to me as if heaven were begun below, and that all that could be looked for was an enlargement of one's capacity for joy, not a truer filling than I possessed.

After concluding my last service about ten o'clock that night, a poor man asked me to go and pray with his wife, saying that she was dying. I readily agreed, and on the way to his house asked him why he had not sent for the priest, as his accent told me he was an Irishman. He had done so, he said, but the priest refused to come without a payment of eighteen pence which the man did not possess, as the family was starving. Immediately it occurred to my mind that all the money I had in the world was the solitary half crown, and that it was in one coin; moreover, that while the basin of water gruel I usually took for supper was awaiting me, and there was sufficient in the house for breakfast in the morning, I certainly had nothing for dinner on the coming day.

Somehow or other there was at once a stoppage in the flow of joy in my heart. But instead of reproving myself I began to reprove the poor man, telling him that it was very wrong to have allowed matters to get into such a state as he described, and that he ought to have applied to the relieving officer. His answer was that he had done so and was told to come at eleven o'clock the next morning, but that he feared his wife might not live through the night.

"Ah," thought I, "if only I had two shillings and a sixpence instead of this half crown, how gladly would I give these poor people a shilling!" But to part with the half crown was far from my thoughts. I little dreamed that the truth of the matter simply was that I could trust God plus one and sixpence but was not prepared to trust Him only, without any money at all in my pocket.

My conductor led me into a court, down which I followed him with some degree of nervousness. I had found myself there before, and at my last visit had been roughly handled. My tracts had been torn to pieces and such a warning given me not to come again that I felt more than a little concerned. Still, it was the path of duty and I followed on. Up a miserable flight of stairs into a wretched room he led me, and oh, what a sight there presented itself! Four or five children stood about, their sunken cheeks and temples all telling unmistakably the story of slow starvation, and lying on a wretched pallet was a poor, exhausted mother, with a tiny infant thirty-six hours old, moaning rather than crying at her side, for it too seemed spent and failing.

"Ah!" thought I, "if I had two shillings and a sixpence, instead of half a crown, how gladly should they have one and sixpence of it." But still a wretched unbelief prevented me from obeying the impulse to relieve their distress at the cost of all I possessed.

It will scarcely seem strange that I was unable to say much to comfort these poor people. I needed comfort myself. I began to tell them, however, that they must not be cast down, that though their circumstances were very distressing there was a kind and loving Father in heaven. But something within me cried, "You hypocrite! Telling these unconverted people about a kind and loving Father in heaven and not prepared yourself to trust Him without a half a crown."

I was nearly choked. How gladly would I have compromised with conscience, if I had had a florin (two shillings) and a sixpence! I would have given the florin thankfully and kept the rest. But I was not yet prepared to trust in God alone, without the sixpence.

To talk was impossible under these circumstances, yet strange to say, I thought I should have no difficulty in praying. Prayer was a delightful occupation in those days. Time thus spent never seemed wearisome, and I knew no lack of words. I seemed to think that all I should have to do would be to kneel down and pray, and that relief would come to them and to myself together.

"You asked me to come and pray with your wife," I said to the man, "let us pray." And I knelt down.

But no sooner had I opened my lips with "Our Father who art in heaven," than conscience said within, "Dare you mock God? Dare you kneel down and call Him Father with that half crown in your pocket?"

Such a time of conflict then came upon me as I have never experienced before or since. How I got through that form of prayer I know not, and whether the words uttered were connected or disconnected I cannot tell. But I arose from my knees in great distress of mind.

The poor father turned to me and said, "You see what a terrible state we are in, sir. If you can help us, for God's sake do!"

At that moment the word flashed into my mind, "Give to him that asketh [of] thee" (Matt. 5:42). And in the word of a King there is power.

I put my hand into my pocket, and slowly drawing out the half crown, gave it to the man, telling him that it might seem a small matter for me to relieve them, seeing that I was comparatively well off, but that in parting with that coin I was giving him my all; what I had been trying to tell them was indeed true—GOD really was a FATHER and might be trusted. The joy all came back in full flood tide to my heart. I could say anything and feel it then, and the hindrance to blessing was gone—gone, I trust, forever.

Not only was the poor woman's life saved, but my life, as I fully realized, had been saved too. It might have been a wreck—would have been probably, as a Christian life—had not grace at that time conquered and the striving of God's Spirit been obeyed.

I well remember how that night, as I went home to my lodgings, my heart was as light as my pocket. The dark, deserted streets resounded with a hymn of praise that I could not restrain. When I took my basin of gruel before retiring, I would not have exchanged it for a prince's feast.

I reminded the Lord as I knelt at my bedside of His own Word, "He that giveth to the poor lendeth to the Lord"; I asked Him not to let my loan be a long one, or I should have no dinner next day. And with peace within and peace without, I spent a happy, restful night.

Next morning for breakfast my plate of porridge remained, and before it was finished the postman's knock was heard at the door. I was not in the habit of receiving letters on Monday, as my parents and most of my friends refrained from posting on Saturday, so that I was somewhat surprised when the landlady came in holding a letter or packet in her wet hand covered by her apron. I looked at the letter but could not make out the handwriting. It was either a strange hand or a feigned one, and the postmark was blurred. Where it came from I could not tell. On opening the envelope I found nothing written within, but inside a sheet of blank paper was folded a pair of kid gloves, from which, as I opened them in astonishment, half a sovereign fell to the ground.

"Praise the Lord," I exclaimed. "Four hundred percent for twelve hours' investment—that is good interest! How glad the merchants of Hull would be if they could lend their money at such a rate." Then and there I determined that a bank that could not break should have my savings or earnings, as the case might be—a determination I have not yet learned to regret.

I cannot tell you how often my mind has recurred to this incident, or all the help it has been to me in circumstances of difficulty in afterlife. If we are faithful to God in little things, we shall gain experience and strength that will be helpful to us in the more serious trials of life.

But this was not the end of the story, nor was it the only answer to prayer that was to confirm his faith at this time. For the chief difficulty still remained. Dr. Hardey had not remembered, and though prayer was unremitting, other matters appeared entirely to engross his attention. It would have been so easy to remind him. But what then of the lesson upon the acquirement of which Hudson Taylor felt his future usefulness depended: "to move man through God by prayer alone"?

> This remarkable and gracious deliverance was a great joy to me as well as a strong confirmation of faith. But of course ten shillings, however economically used, will not go very far, and it was none the less necessary to continue in prayer, asking that the larger supply which was still due might be remembered and paid. All my petitions, however, appeared to remain unanswered, and before a fortnight elapsed I found myself pretty much in the same position that I had occupied on the Sunday night already made so memorable. Meanwhile, I continued pleading with God more and more earnestly that He would Himself remind Dr. Hardey that my salary was due.
>
> Of course it was not the want of money that distressed me. That could have been had at any time for the asking. But the question uppermost in my mind was this: "Can I go to China? Or will my want of faith and power with God prove so serious an obstacle as to preclude my entering upon this much-prized service?"
>
> As the week drew to a close I felt exceedingly embarrassed. There was not only myself to consider. On Saturday night a payment would be due to my Christian landlady, which I knew she could not well dispense with. Ought I not, for her

sake, to speak about the matter of the salary? Yet to do so would be, to myself at any rate, the admission that I was not fitted to undertake a missionary enterprise. I gave nearly the whole of Thursday and Friday, all the time not occupied in my necessary employment, to earnest wrestling with God in prayer. But still on Saturday morning I was in the same position as before. And now my earnest cry was for guidance as to whether I should still continue to wait the Father's time. As far as I could judge, I received the assurance that to wait His time was best and that God in some way or other would interpose on my behalf. So I waited, my heart being now at rest and the burden gone.

About five o'clock that Saturday afternoon, when Dr. Hardey had finished writing his prescriptions, his last circuit for the day being taken, he threw himself back in his arm-chair as he was wont, and began to speak of the things of God. He was a truly Christian man, and many seasons of happy fellowship we had together. I was busily watching, at the time, a pan in which a decoction was boiling that required a good deal of attention. It was indeed fortunate for me that it was so, for without any obvious connection with what had been going on, all at once he said,

"By the by, Taylor, is not your salary due again?"

My emotion may be imagined. I had to swallow two or three times before I could answer. With my eye fixed on the pan and my back to the doctor, I told him as quietly as I could that it was overdue some little time. How thankful I felt at that moment! God surely had heard my prayer and caused him in this time of my great need to remember the salary without any word or suggestion from me. He replied,

"Oh, I am so sorry you did not remind me! You know how busy I am. I wish I had thought of it a little sooner, for only this afternoon I sent all the money I had to the bank. Otherwise I would pay you at once."

It is impossible to describe the revulsion of feeling caused by this unexpected statement. I knew not what to do. Fortunately for me the pan boiled up, and I had a good reason for rushing with it from the room. Glad indeed I was to get away and keep out of sight until after Dr. Hardey had returned to his house, and most thankful that he had not perceived my emotion.

As soon as he was gone I had to seek my little sanctum and pour out my heart before the Lord for some time before calmness and, more than calmness, thankfulness and joy were restored. I felt that God had His own way and was not going to fail me. I had sought to know His will early in the day, and as far as I could judge, had received guidance to wait patiently. And now God was going to work for me in some other way.

That evening was spent as my Saturday evenings usually were, in reading the Word and preparing the subject on which I expected to speak in the various lodging houses on the morrow. I waited perhaps a little longer than usual. At last about ten o'clock, there being no interruption of any kind, I put on my overcoat and was preparing to leave for home, rather thankful to know that by that time I should have to let myself in with the latchkey, as my landlady retired early. There was certainly no help for that night. But perhaps God would interpose for me by Monday, and I might be able to pay my landlady early in the week the money I would have given her before had it been possible.

Just as I was about to turn down the gas, I heard the doctor's step in the garden that lay between the dwelling house and surgery. He was laughing to himself very heartily, as though greatly amused. Entering the surgery he asked for the ledger and told me that, strange to say, one of his richest patients had just come to pay his doctor's bill. Was it not an odd thing to do? It never struck me that it might have any bearing on my own case, or I might have felt embarrassed. But looking at it simply from the position of an uninterested spectator, I also was highly amused that a man rolling in wealth should come after ten o'clock at night to pay a bill which he could any day have met by a cheque with the greatest ease. It appeared that somehow or other he could not rest with this on his mind and had been constrained to come at that unusual hour to discharge his liability.

The account was duly receipted in the ledger, and Dr. Hardey was about to leave, when suddenly he turned and, handing me some of the banknotes just received, said to my surprise and thankfulness:

"By the way, Taylor, you might as well take these notes. I have no change but can give you the balance next week."

Again I was left, my feelings undiscovered, to go back to my little closet and praise the Lord with a joyful heart that after all I *might go to China.* To me this incident was not a trivial one, and to recall it sometimes, in circumstances of great difficulty, in China or elsewhere, has proved no small comfort and strength.

It is perhaps hardly to be wondered at that in the light of these experiences the importance of something far higher than money, in relation to the service of God, began to impress Hudson Taylor. His quiet life at Drainside was working a change in his attitude toward many things. There were memorable hours that winter in which he saw from the divine standpoint as never before.

But ready though he was for the sacrifice involved, Hudson Taylor was not to work his way out to China before the mast. "He was not to be tried thus far," wrote his mother, recalling with thankfulness the guidance given in answer to their prayers. For it was evident to those whose opinions he valued most that the time had not yet come for him to go forward. He was too young as yet. Further training and experience in the things of God were needed. It was well, no doubt, that it was in his heart to leave all and follow wherever the Master led. But was He leading just at that time to China? To his parents and friends it seemed not. He had been much in prayer that if it were the Lord's will for him to go without delay, they might recognize it and bid him Godspeed. But all advised against it. He could not have taken the step without disregarding the counsel of Christian friends in Hull as well as of his own circle in Barnsley. And this he would not do, for he was dealing with God, who can overrule second causes.

He gathered therefore that the Lord's time had not yet come. It might be that He was leading to some other step in preparation for the future, but evidently it was not His purpose that he should leave immediately for China. The conclusion was not come to lightly. It was hard to give up his carefully thought-out plans, and he learned that there may be self-will even in what looks like devotion. It was an opportunity, however, for putting into practice the important principle, "To obey is better than sacrifice" (1 Sam. 15:22), and he embraced it cheerfully, handing over all results to the Lord.

Now came a time long to be remembered in his experience, a time that would have been one of painful anxiety had not the grace of God turned it all to joy and peace. For the clearer his conviction of what the Lord would have him do became, the greater seemed the difficulties in the way of carrying it out. He felt quite sure that the right thing was to give notice to Dr. Hardey without delay and go forward to his medical studies in London. But all his efforts to find suitable employment proved unavailing. With no means to fall back upon, save the small sum laid by to provide an outfit for China, with few friends in the great city, and no home open to him there, he might well have been discouraged. But the very reverse was the case. Instead of wasting time and strength in anxious thought, he was enabled to leave it all in the hands of God, praying with childlike trust, "Make *thy* way [plain] before my face" (Ps. 5:8, italics added). How things would work out for him he could not tell, but he gave himself the more to prayer, confident that at the right time guidance would be given.

The way then began to clear before him. His uncle in London offered a temporary home; the Chinese Evangelization Society, with whom he had been corresponding about serving in China, made an arrangement with him regarding his hospital fees; and the meeting he attended in Hull gave him introductions to a few Christian friends who would be accessible from his Soho quarters. Other offers of help reached him which, though not accepted, confirmed his assurance that he was being guided aright.

The Lord Will Provide

As Hudson Taylor came into London in September 1852, how new it was, and how great his need of the strength that comes from God alone, no one had any idea but himself. Not to his mother or even to the sister who spent the last days with him at Drainside had he spoken of the decision he had taken before leaving Hull that now filled his mind as he finished his journey to the city. His friends and parents knew that he was going up to London to support himself, if possible, while completing his medical studies. They knew that the Chinese Evangelization Society had offered financial help, and concluded that as he had declined similar offers from home, he must be sufficiently provided for. And so he was—by nothing more and nothing less than all the promises of God. He had a little money in his pocket and a few pounds laid by toward an outfit for China. He had a promise also of help with his hospital fees and an invitation to be the guest for a few days or weeks of his bachelor uncle while looking for a situation. But beyond this there was nothing, humanly speaking, between him and want in the great city in which he was almost a stranger.

Yet this caused him no anxiety as he faced the coming winter. For the future, near as well as distant, he had one all-sufficient confidence. If that could fail, it would be better to make the discovery in London than far away in China. Deliberately and of his own free will he had cut himself off from possible sources of supply that he might make full proof, under difficult circumstances, of the promised care of God alone. It was God, the living God, he needed, a stronger faith to grasp His faithfulness, and more experience of the practicability of dealing with Him directly about every need. Comfort or discomfort in London, means or the lack of means, seemed to him a small matter compared with deeper knowledge of the One on whom everything depended. And now had come an unexpected opportunity for putting that knowledge to the test, and he was going forward, strong in the assurance that the Lord who had already responded so graciously to his little faith would see and would provide.

Of the way in which he had been led to this position just before leaving Drainside, the following is his own account:

> By-and-by the time drew near when it was thought desirable that I should leave Hull to attend the medical course of the London Hospital. A little while spent there, and then I had every reason to believe that my lifework in China would commence. But much as I had rejoiced at the willingness of God to hear and answer prayer and to help His half-trusting, half-timid child, I felt that I could not go to China without having still further developed and tested my power to rest upon His faithfulness, and a marked opportunity for doing so was providentially afforded me.
>
> My dear father had offered to bear all the expense of my stay in London. I knew, however,

that, owing to recent losses, it would mean a considerable sacrifice for him to undertake this just when it seemed necessary for me to go forward. I had recently become acquainted with the committee of the Chinese Evangelization Society, in connection with which I ultimately left for China, and especially with its secretary, my esteemed and much-loved Mr. George Pearse, then of the Stock Exchange but now and for many years himself a missionary. Not knowing of my father's proposition, the committee also kindly offered to bear my expenses while in London. When these proposals were first made to me, I was not quite clear as to what I ought to do, and in writing to my father and the secretaries, told them that I would take a few days to pray about the matter before deciding any course of action. I mentioned to my father that I had had this offer from the society, and told the secretaries also of his proffered aid.

Subsequently, while waiting upon God in prayer for guidance, it became clear to my mind that I could without difficulty decline both offers. The secretaries of the society would not know that I had cast myself wholly on God for supplies, and my father would conclude that I had accepted the other offer. I therefore wrote declining both and felt that without anyone having either care or anxiety on my account, I was simply in the hands of God, and that He who knew my heart, if He wished to encourage me to go to China, would bless my effort to depend upon Him alone at home.

And so Hudson Taylor was to find this blessing; although, his London experiences were not without trial: walking eight miles a day to and from the hospital, living on nothing but brown bread and apples for months at a time, and being uncertain as to his connection with the only society willing to send him to China without university training. These trials, however, helped to strengthen his faith and gave him the necessary preparation for China.

Then, the way cleared suddenly for him to go to China. All had seemed uncertain before him, and he had scarcely been able to see a step ahead. Very earnestly had he been in prayer for guidance, longing with all his heart to know and do the will of God. And now the light shone suddenly and in the way he had least expected, because the time had come, and there is behind events, as the old prophet tells us, "a God...which worketh for him that waiteth for Him" (Isa. 64:4 RV).

In the room of the C.E.S. sat one of the secretaries writing a letter. Events had succeeded one another in China with startling rapidity. Since their conquest of Nanking, the Taipings had carried all before them, sweeping over the central and northern provinces until Peking itself was almost within their grasp. Nothing, it seemed, could save the tottering dynasty, unless foreign powers could be persuaded to intervene. Sir George Bonham, the British representative, after a visit to Nanking, had brought back a report very favorable to the Taipings. "The insurgents are Christians," wrote the *North China Herald* on May 7, and the religious aspect of the movement seemed to keep pace with the increase of the power.

This could mean but one thing: if Peking surrendered, the seclusion of ages was at an end and China would forthwith be thrown open to the Gospel. The very possibility, imminent as it was, proved a powerful stimulus to missionary effort.

Christian hearts everywhere were aflame. Something must be done, and done at once to meet so great a crisis! And for a time, money poured into the treasuries.

In the light of these new developments, the committee of the C.E.S. had been reconsidering their position. The only representative they had in China was the German missionary Lobscheid, laboring near Canton. They had long wished to supply him with a fellow worker and now decided to send two men to Shanghai also, to be ready for pending developments. Money was not the difficulty, their income having considerably increased within the last few months, but men, suitable men, would not be easy to find.

Thus it was that on June 4, 1853, Mr. Bird of the C.E.S. sat in his office writing as follows to one in whom they had every confidence, the young medical student, Hudson Taylor.

> My Dear Sir—As you have fully made up your mind to go to China, and also not to qualify as a surgeon, I would affectionately suggest that you lose no time in preparing to start. At this time we want really devoted men, and I believe your heart is right before God and your motives pure, so that you need not hesitate in offering...If you think it right to offer yourself, I shall be most happy to lay your application before the board. It is an important step, and much earnest prayer is needed. But guidance will be given. Do all with thy might, and speedily.

The suggestion made was a great surprise to Hudson Taylor. Constantly as China had been before his mind for three and a half years, it seemed rather overwhelming to think of sailing as soon as a vessel could be found. Besides, there were all those questions about the future and his uncertainty as to whether he ought to connect himself with any society. Mr. Bird was evidently sympathetic and helpful, and the younger lad had much to lay before the Lord.

How strange the difference that had come over everything. Could it be possible that all that had formerly blocked his way to China had indeed vanished, that the society was not only willing but anxious to send him out? Then God's time surely must have come, and he could not hold back. He wrote to his mother the following day:

> Mr. Bird has removed most of the objections and difficulties I have been feeling, and I think it will be well to comply with his suggestions and at once propose myself to the committee. I shall await your answer, however, and rely upon your prayers. If I should be accepted to go at once, would you advise me to come home before sailing? I long to be with you once more, and I know you would naturally wish to see me; but I almost think it would be easier for us not to meet, than having met to part again forever. No, not forever!
>
> A little while: 'twill soon be past!
> Why should we shun the promised cross?
> Oh let us in His footsteps haste,
> Counting for Him all else but loss:
> Then, how will recompense His smile
> The sufferings of this little while!
>
> I cannot write more, but hope to hear from you as soon as possible. Pray much for me. It is easy to talk of leaving all for Christ, but when it comes to the proof—it is only as we stand

> "complete in him" (Col. 2:10) we can go through with it. God be with you and bless you, my own dear, dear mother, and give you so to realize *the preciousness of Jesus,* that you may wish for nothing but to "know him"...even in "the fellowship of his sufferings" (Phil. 3:10).

He continued later to his sister:

> Pray for me, dear Amelia, that He who has promised to meet all our need may be with me in this painful though long-expected hour. When we look at ourselves—at the littleness of our love, the barrenness of our service, and the small progress we make toward perfection—how soul-refreshing it is to turn and gaze on Him, to plunge afresh in the "fountain opened...for sin and for uncleanness" (Zech. 13:1), to remember that we are "accepted in the beloved" (Eph. 1:6)..."who of God is made unto us wisdom, and righteousness, and sanctification, and redemption" (1 Cor. 1:30). Oh the fullness of Christ: *the fullness of Christ!*

Chapter 3

Arrival and First Experiences in China

It was a foggy Sunday off Gutzlaff Island, cold with occasional rain, as might be expected at the end of February (1854), and the *Dumfries,* on which Hudson Taylor traveled to China, lay at anchor waiting for a pilot to take her up to Shanghai. It seemed as if ages had passed since he and his mother had knelt together in prayer right before beginning his long voyage from Liverpool. She and Hudson's father had come up to see him off, though delays in sailing meant that his father was obliged to go home before the ship set sail. Through months of travel and numerous times of stormy weather the ship had held her way, driven out of her course at times by gales, caught in a cyclone and blinding snowstorms, but now the last stage of her long journey was reached, and the yellow, turbid water surging around her told that they were already in the estuary of a great river.

Muffled in his heaviest wraps, Hudson Taylor paced the deck, doing his best to keep warm and be patient. It was a strange Sunday, this last at sea. For days he had been packed and ready to leave the ship and, hindered by storm and cold from other occupations, had given the more time to thought and prayer.

Not until the next day was he able to land in Shanghai, and then it was quite alone and without his belongings, the *Dumfries* being still detained by adverse winds.

My feelings on stepping ashore, I cannot attempt to describe. My heart felt as though it had not room and must burst its bonds, while tears of gratitude and thankfulness fell from my eyes.

Then a deep sense of the loneliness of his position began to come over him: not a friend or acquaintance anywhere, not a single hand held out to welcome him, or anyone who even knew his name.

Mingled with thankfulness for deliverance from many dangers, and joy at finding myself at last on Chinese soil, came a vivid realization of the great distance between me and those I loved and that I was a stranger in a strange land.

I had three letters of introduction, however, and counted on advice and help from one especially to whom I had been commended by mutual friends, whom I knew well and highly valued. Of course I inquired for him at once, only to learn that he had been buried a month or two previously, having died of fever while we were at sea.

Saddened by these tidings, I asked the whereabouts of a missionary to whom another of my introductions was addressed, but only to meet with further disappointment. He had recently left for America. The third letter remained, but it had been given me by a comparative stranger, and I expected less from it than from the others. It proved, however, to be God's channel of help.

This letter then in hand, he left the British Consulate near the river to find the London Mission compound at some distance across the settlement. On every side strange sights, sounds, and smells now greeted him, especially when the

European houses gave way to Chinese shops and dwellings. Here nothing but Chinese was to be heard, and few if any but Chinese were to be seen. The streets grew narrower and more crowded, and overhanging balconies above rows of swinging signboards almost hid the sky. How he found his way for a mile or more is not clear, but at length a mission chapel came in sight, and with an upward look for guidance, Hudson Taylor turned in at the ever-open gateway of the London Mission compound.

Several buildings stood before him, including a hospital and dwelling houses, at the first of which he inquired for Dr. Medhurst, to whom his letter was addressed. Sensitive and reserved by nature, it was no small ordeal to Hudson Taylor to have to introduce himself to so important a person, the pioneer as well as founder, along with Dr. Lockhart, of Protestant missionary effort in this part of China, and it was almost with relief he heard that Dr. Medhurst was no longer living on the compound. He too, it seemed, had gone away!

More than this Hudson Taylor was unable to make out, as the Chinese servants could not speak English, nor could he understand a word of their dialect. It was a perplexing situation until a European came in sight, to whom the new arrival quickly made himself known. To his relief he found he was talking with Mr. Edkins, one of the junior missionaries, who welcomed him kindly and explained that Dr. and Mrs. Medhurst had moved to the British Consulate, as the premises they had occupied were within sight and sound of constant fighting at the North Gate of the city. Dr. Lockhart, however, remained, and while Mr. Edkins went to find him, he invited the stranger into one of the mission houses.

It was quite an event in those days for an Englishman, and especially a missionary, to appear in Shanghai unannounced. Most people came by the regular mail steamers once a month, and their arrival caused general excitement. None was expected then, and even the *Dumfries* was not yet in port, so that when another of the London Missionary Society people came in during Mr. Edkin's absence, Hudson Taylor had to explain all over again who and what he was. It did not take long for these new friends to understand the situation, and then there was nothing for it but to receive the young missionary into one of their own houses. They could not leave him without a home, and the settlement was so crowded that lodgings were not to be had at any price. Dr. Lockhart, happily, had a room at his disposal. He was living alone, Mrs. Lockhart having been obliged to return to England, and with genuine kindness welcomed Hudson Taylor as his guest, permitting him to pay a moderate sum to cover board expenses.

This arrangement made, Mr. Edkins took him to see Mr. and Mrs. Muirhead, who completed the L.M.S. staff in Shanghai, and introduced him also to Mr. and Mrs. Burdon of the Church Missionary Society, who had rented an unoccupied house on the same compound. The Burdons invited him to dinner that evening. They were young and newly married, having only been a year or two in China, and from the first they were drawn to Hudson Taylor in a sympathy he warmly reciprocated.

Here then was an answer to many prayers, the solution of many ponderings. For the moment he was provided for under favorable circumstances, and though he could not long trespass upon the doctor's hospitality, it would afford him at any rate a little while in which to look about and make permanent arrangements. With good courage, therefore, he arose next morning to see what could be done, and then procure the necessary books and a teacher to commence as soon as possible the study of the language. It was his first whole day in China.

As he had his belongings brought up to Dr. Lockhart's, it was a peculiar sensation to be marching at the head of a procession of coolies through the crowded streets, all his belongings swinging from bamboo poles across their shoulders, while at every step they sang or shouted "Ou-ah Ou-ay" in varying tones, some a third above the rest. They were not really in pain or distress, although it sounded like it, and by the time some of the copper cash he had received in exchange for a Mexican dollar had been distributed among them, he had had his first lesson in business dealings with the Chinese.

Then came the daily service in the hospital, conducted on this occasion by Dr. Medhurst, and Hudson Taylor listened for the first time to gospel preaching in the tongue with which he was to become so familiar. In conversation afterwards, Dr. Medhurst advised him to commence his studies with the Mandarin dialect, the most widely spoken in China, and undertook to procure a teacher. Evening brought the weekly prayer meeting when Hudson Taylor was introduced to others of the missionary community, thus ending, with united waiting upon God, a day full of interest and encouragement.

But before the week closed he began to see another side of Shanghai life. The journal tells of guns firing all night, and the city wall not half a mile away covered with sentry lights; of sharp fighting seen from his windows, in which men were killed and wounded under his very eyes; of a patient search for rooms in the Chinese part of the settlement, only emphasizing the fact that there were none to be had; of his first contact with heathenism; and of scenes of suffering in the native city which made an indelible impression of horror upon his mind.

Of some of these experiences he wrote to his sister ten days after his arrival:

> On Saturday I took a walk through the market, and such a muddy, dirty place as Shanghai I never did see! The ground is all mud, dry in dry weather, but one hour's rain makes it like walking through a clay field. It scarcely is walking—but wading! I found that there was no probability of getting a house or even apartments and felt cast down in spirit.
>
> The following day, Sunday, I attended two services at the L.M.S. and in the afternoon went into the city with Mr. Wylie. You have never seen a city in a state of siege or been at the seat of war. God grant you never may! We walked some distance round the wall, and sad it was to see the wreck of rows upon rows of houses near the city. Burnt down, blown down, battered to pieces—in all stages of ruin they were! And the misery of those who once inhabited them, and now at this inclement season are driven from house, home, and everything, is terrible to think of.... By the time we came to the North Gate they were fighting fiercely outside the city. One man

> was brought in dead, another shot through the chest, and a third whose arm I examined seemed in dreadful agony. A ball had gone clean through the arm, breaking the bone in passing. We could do nothing for him unless he would come to the hospital, for, as Dr. Lockhart said, who came up just at the moment, they would only pull our dressings off....It makes one sad indeed to be surrounded by so much misery, to see poor creatures so suffering and distressed, and not be able to relieve them or tell them of Jesus and His love. I can only pray for them. But is not He almighty? He is. Thank God we know He is! Let us then pray earnestly that He may help them.

Trial and hardship Hudson Taylor had looked for, of the kind usually associated with a missionary's lot, but everything was turning out differently from his anticipation. External hardships there were none, save the cold from which he suffered greatly, but distress of mind and heart seemed daily to increase. He could hardly look out of his window, much less take exercise in any direction, without witnessing misery such as he had never dreamed of before. The tortures inflicted by the soldiery of both armies upon unhappy prisoners from whom they hoped to extort money and the ravages perpetrated as they pillaged the country for supplies harrowed him unspeakably. And over all hung the dark pall of heathenism, weighing with a heavy oppression upon his spirit. Many of the temples were destroyed in whole or part and the idols damaged, but still the people worshipped them, crying and praying for help that never came. The gods, it was evident, were unable to save. They could not even protect themselves in these times of danger. But in their extremity, rich and poor, high and low, turned to them still, for they had nothing else.

Seeing this, it can be easily imagined how Hudson Taylor longed to tell them of One mighty to save. But not a sentence could he put together so as to be understood. This enforced silence was a keen distress, for he was accustomed to speaking freely of the things of God. Ever since his conversion five years previously, he had given himself as fully as possible to the ministry of the Gospel. And now for the first time his lips were sealed, and it seemed as if he never would be able in that appalling tongue to tell out all that was in his heart. This again could not but help affecting his own spiritual life. The channels of outflow to others were sealed, and it was a little while before he realized that they must be kept all the more clear and open toward God. His eagerness to get hold of the language made him devote every moment to study, even to the neglect of prayer and daily feeding upon the Scriptures. Of course the great Enemy took advantage of all this, as may be seen from early letters to his parents in which he unburdened his heart:

> My position is a very difficult one. Dr. Lockhart has taken me to reside with him for the present, as houses are not to be had for love or money....No one can live in the city, for they are fighting almost continuously. I see the walls from my window...and the firing is visible at night. They are fighting now, while I write, and the house shakes with the report of cannon.
>
> It is so cold that I can hardly think or hold the pen. You will see from my letter to Mr. Pearse how perplexed I am. It will be four months before I can hear in reply, and the very

kindness of the missionaries who have received me with open arms makes me fear to be burdensome. Jesus will guide me aright....I love the Chinese more than ever. Oh to be useful among them!...

The cold was so great and other things so trying that I scarcely knew what I was doing or saying at first. Then, what it means to be so far from home, at the seat of war, and not able to understand or be understood by the people was fully realized. Their utter wretchedness and misery, and my inability to help them or even point them to Jesus, powerfully affected me. Satan came in as a flood, but there was One who lifted up a standard against him. Jesus is here, and though unknown to the majority and uncared for by many who might know Him, He is present and precious to His own.

Make It A Place of Springs

It may seem exaggerated, at first sight, to dwell much upon the trials of Hudson Taylor's position. True he was at the seat of war, but as far as circumstances permitted he was living in safety and even comfort. He was so well off, apparently, that one wonders at the undertone of suffering in his letters, until a little consideration reveals another side of his experiences. The assistance he received from Dr. Medhurst and other L.M.S. missionaries was of the greatest value, and yet it gave rise to a distressing situation. If he had belonged to their society and had been preparing to work with and for them, nothing could have been better. But as it was, he felt almost like an unfledged cuckoo, an intruder in another bird's nest. That his companionship at every meal in solitary tête-à-tête was somewhat wearisome to his generous host, he could not but feel. Not that he received anything but kindness from Dr. Lockhart and his associates. But he was not as they were, highly educated and connected with a great denomination and important work. The preparation providentially ordered for him had been along different lines, and his religious views made him singular, while his position as a missionary was isolated and open to criticism.

He had been sent out, almost hurried out, by his society before his medical course was finished, in the hope of reaching the rebels at Nanking. Misled by optimistic reports about the Taiping movement, the secretaries of the C.E.S. had taken a position that to practical men on the field seemed wholly absurd. It is just as natural for missionaries to be critical, apart from restraining grace, as for others, and it was not long before Hudson Taylor discovered that the Chinese Evangelization Society, with its aims and methods, was the butt of no little ridicule in Shanghai.

He realized the weaknesses of the C.E.S., or was coming to, no less clearly than they did; however, he knew and respected many members of the committee, and to some, including the secretaries, he was attached with grateful love. This put matters in a very different light. Fellowship with them in spiritual things could never be forgotten, and even when feeling their mistakes most keenly, he longed for their atmosphere of prayer, their love of the Word of God, and their earnest zeal for souls.

Hudson Taylor was not entirely in accord with the current conception of what a missionary should be. He was bright and fairly educated but had no university or college training, had taken no medical degree, and disclaimed the title "Reverend" given him at first on all hands. That he was good and earnest could easily be seen, but he was connected with no particular denomination and was not sent out by any special church. He expected to do medical work, but he was not a doctor. He was accustomed, evidently, to preaching and to an almost pastoral care of others, and yet he was not ordained. And strangest perhaps of all, though he belonged to a society that seemed well supplied with funds, his salary was insufficient and his appearance shabby compared with those by whom he was surrounded.

That Hudson Taylor felt all this, and felt it increasingly as time went on, is not to be wondered at. He had come out with such different expectations! His one longing was to go inland and live among the people. He wanted to keep down expenses and continue the simple, self-denying life he had lived at home. To learn the language that he might win souls was his one ambition. He cared nothing, nothing at all about worldly estimates and social pleasures, though he did long for fellowship in the things of God. With a salary of eighty pounds a year, he found himself unable to manage upon twice that sum. So he was really poor, poor and in serious difficulty before long, and there was no one to impress the fact upon the committee at home or make them understand the situation.

Then too he was lonely, unavoidably lonely. The missionaries with whom he lived were all a good deal older than himself, with the exception of the Burdons who were fully occupied with their work. He could not trespass on their kindness too frequently, and having no colleague of his own, he found it impossible to speak of many matters connected with the society and future developments that were on his heart. Soon he learned to mention such affairs as little as possible, but he did long for someone with whom to bring them before the throne of grace.

Letters, of course, were a great comfort, and much time was given during his first year in China to correspondence. Strangely enough, the months of June and July brought him the peculiar trial of hearing nothing from home, mail after mail, when he was especially longing for news. How this happened never quite appeared, for he had been written to regularly, but the letters never reached him, or if they did it was out of their proper order and long after they were due. This, combined with the great heat and the effects of a brief but serious illness, tried him to a degree that can only be understood by those who have been in similar circumstances.

And just then, to add to his perplexity, news reached him in a roundabout way that seemed a climax to his troubles. The society was sending another missionary to Shanghai, and not a bachelor like himself, but a married man with a family. Dr. Parker, a Scottish physician who had applied to the C.E.S. before Hudson Taylor left England, was already on his way to join him and might be expected in a few months. Glad as the young missionary would have been of such tidings under other circumstances, with Shanghai in the condition in which it was, the outlook was cause indeed for concern. Dependent himself for shelter upon the generosity of others, what arrangements could he make for a married couple with three children? He hardly dared mention it to those with whom he was living, and yet the news would soon be the talk of the settlement whether he kept silent or not.

Anxiously he awaited letters from the committee explaining the situation. Surely they would send him notice, in view of all he had written, of such an addition to their staff, and instruct him fully how to act. But mail after mail came in with no reference to Dr. Parker's coming. Repeated requests for directions as to how to arrange for himself had as yet received no answer, and before summer was over, Hudson Taylor saw that he must act on his own initiative.

Meanwhile, comments and questions were not wanting, which made the position more trying. "Is it true that a medical man is about to join you, with a wife and family? When did you hear it? Why did you not tell us? Have you bought land? Why do you not begin to build?" And so forth! To all of which no satisfactory reply was forthcoming. At first, in his perplexity, Hudson Taylor suffered as only a sensitive nature can, but when the talk was at its worst and the summer heat almost unbearable, the Lord himself drew near and went with him.

The more he thought over the situation, the more he felt that there was nothing for it but to seek a native house in the Chinese part of the settlement in which to receive the travelers who were drawing nearer every day. So, in spite of overpowering heat and his lack of a sedan chair, he set about the weary search once more. It was four or five months now since he had hunted for quarters on his first arrival without finding even a room available, and if anything the conditions seemed worse than before. Nothing he could begin to think of was to be found, and but for a growing rest of heart in God, Hudson Taylor would have been almost in despair. As it was, he was learning precious lessons of his own helplessness and of almighty strength.

To his sister Amelia he wrote:

> I have been puzzling my brains again about a house, etc., but to no effect. So I have made it a matter of prayer and have given it entirely into the Lord's hands, and now I feel quite at peace about it. He will provide and be my Guide in this and every other perplexing step.

It must have seemed almost too good to be true when only two days after the preceding letter was written, Hudson Taylor heard of a house, and before the month was over he found himself in possession of premises large enough to accommodate his expected colleagues. Five rooms upstairs and seven down seemed a spacious residence indeed, and though it was only a native house, built of wood and very ramshackle, it was right among the people, near the North Gate of the Chinese city.

It did not all come about, however, as easily as the statement is made. In less than a month, he learned many a lesson of patience, for in China these arrangements are compassed with difficulty. The house first heard of was not the one finally obtained, nor was the price first demanded one that he could or would give; between the two lay much weary negotiation that had to be carried on through interpreters, and deepened the debt he was already under to his missionary friends.

As autumn weather set in, forecasting the bitter cold of winter, Hudson Taylor was driven to see that the house he had secured in view of the arrival of the Parkers would not be a place they could come to even for a night. This house was not only unwarmed but unwarmable, drafts sweeping through it mercilessly from unnumbered cracks and crevices. The location also added to the unsuitableness of the house.

> As to my position, it certainly is one of great peril. On two successive nights, recently, bullets have struck the roof over my head. How little difference in the direction of the gun might have rendered them fatal to me. But "as the mountains are round about Jerusalem" (Ps. 125:2), so the Lord is on every side to protect and support me and to supply all my need, temporal as well as spiritual. I can truly say my trust is in Him. When I hear guns fired near me and the *whizz* of the balls as they pass the house, I do feel alarmed sometimes, but a sweet, still voice says inwardly, "O thou of little faith, wherefore didst thou doubt?" (Matt. 14:31)....But "Lo, I am with you alway" (Matt. 28:20), has quieted the troubled waters and restored peace to my soul.

Three weeks later matters were even worse, and he wrote again to the secretaries:

> There is a great deal of firing going on here now, so much so that...I am seldom able to get half a night's sleep. What Dr. Parker and his family are to do, I do not know. Their coming here as things are now is out of the question. This constant anxiety for them as well as myself, together with another still more trying (the expense I am unable to avoid) is by no means a desirable addition to the difficulties of language and climate....Pray for me, for I am almost pressed beyond measure, and were it not that I find the Word of God increasingly precious and feel His presence with me, I do not know what I should do.

But the Lord knew, and He had not forgotten His tried servant. At that very moment, the Lord had a home in view into which to receive the Parkers and their children. He was not limited to the house on the North Gate Street, though Hudson Taylor was, and just in time, when lessons had been learned that He saw were needed, the way was opened to a safer residence.

On the London Mission compound, through the coming of a great sorrow, a little house stood empty, that in comparison with Hudson Taylor's quarters offered a haven of security and peace. Shadowed as it was with the suffering of his dearest friends in China, he had not thought of it as other than their home. There he had found them in their early married life, rejoiced with them in the gift of a precious child, and shared the bereavement that in so short a time left her motherless. Then he had helped Mr. Burdon to leave the home from which the light had fled and take his infant daughter to the care of the chaplain's household. And still the little house in the London Mission compound stood empty.

A Way of Escape

It is put before us as an evidence of the faithfulness of God that for those who trust Him He always has a way of escape, that no trial may be greater than they can bear. Strong consolation this was for the troubled soul! And Hudson Taylor was to make full proof of it now in his extremity.

For extremity it really was. Where to go and what to do he did not know, and the Parkers were drawing nearer every day. Without authorization from the committee or instructions from Dr.

Parker himself, how could he venture upon the expense of Mr. Burdon's house? And yet it was just what they needed and might be lost by delay. He had no money to furnish the house, nor did he know where the rent was coming from, but at the end of October, looking to the Lord for help and guidance, he obtained at least the first opportunity of the premises.

Meanwhile the situation of the native city was becoming desperate. The French, in defiance of international law and treaty obligations, were openly taking part in the siege. Their soldiers, "bloodthirsty as tigers," seemed bent on slaughter, and the house at the North Gate daily witnessed scenes of almost fiendish cruelty. It became unendurable at last. The premises next door were deliberately set on fire, with the intention of driving the foreigner out, and just at this juncture another offer was made for Mr. Burdon's house. Word was sent to Hudson Taylor that if he wanted it he must take it at once. And so, paying the rent out of his own meager resources, a home was secured for the family so soon to arrive in the settlement.

And then, providentially no doubt, he was urged to sublet half the premises. Another missionary was in distress, not knowing where to take his wife and children for safety, and for three rooms was thankful to pay half the rent. True, the house was very small for two families, but it was a relief to have his financial obligations lessened and a comfort to be able to help somebody else.

When he was again at the North Gate to remove the last of his belongings, he was recalled by a message from Dr. Lockhart. Hurrying back with many conjectures as to what the summons might mean, he found the doctor at lunch with a pleasant-looking stranger—none other than his own long-expected colleague, Dr. Parker. So they had come at last! And he was only just in time with arrangements for their accommodation.

At first, in the joy of meeting and all the excitement of bringing up their belongings from the ship, Hudson Taylor hardly had time to realize how the narrowness of their quarters would strike his newfound friends. But when they were all in them, including the little baby whose first appearance had been made at sea, the three rooms seemed even more crowded than he had feared they would be. Strong, sensible Scottish people, the Parkers were quite prepared to put up with hardships and accommodated themselves to the situation as well as could be expected. But to Hudson Taylor it was a painful experience to have to reveal the pitifulness of his preparations.

If the rooms had been suitably furnished, it would have been another matter, but his Chinese bed, two or three square tables, and half a dozen chairs seem to have been all that he possessed. He had only just moved in on Saturday night and had not had time to get into working order. Now the sudden advent of a family with all their paraphernalia made confusion worse confounded, and the despair of a thrifty housewife with three little children to provide for may be better imagined than described.

Oh, the trying, difficult days that followed; could they ever be forgotten! For, to make matters worse, the Shanghai community began to call upon the new arrivals, and those with whom Hudson Taylor was acquainted were not sparing in their comments upon what seemed his negligence.

It was all very well for him to live in Chinese style, if he liked, and put up with a hundred and one discomforts. But people who knew what was what could not be expected to fall in with such ways. Why had he not furnished their rooms properly and provided warm carpets and curtains? Did he not know that children must be protected from the bitter cold of winter? Had he no stoves in readiness, no proper supply of fuel? Had he not written to tell them that they would need warm clothes and bedding on their arrival in November? And as to unpacking and getting settled, how could it be done without shelves or cupboards, chests of drawers or bookcases in which to bestow their belongings?

All of which was true, no doubt, and unanswerable, for how could the young missionary let it be known that he had gone far beyond the limits of authorized expenditure in taking the house at all, that he had done it entirely on his own responsibility, and that after paying the first installment of rent he had been left with only two or three dollars in hand, not enough to cover a week's expenses?

His hope was, of course, that Dr. Parker would be supplied with all that was necessary, and would be the bearer of instructions from the society about mission headquarters in Shanghai or elsewhere, as well as some more satisfactory arrangement for financial transactions in the future. The very reverse, however, was the case. Dr. Parker had nothing with him but a few dollars for immediate use. He was expecting a letter of credit to be awaiting him in Shanghai, which he understood had been sent off before he left England. As to supplies, they had an abundance of clothing for the tropics, but had not been at all prepared for cold weather, so the children then were in immediate need of winter outfits. And for the rest, nothing had been said about how they were to live and work in Shanghai or in what way their salary was to reach them. All this they seem to have taken for granted that Hudson Taylor would be able to arrange.

No special anxiety was felt as yet, however. A large mail was waiting their arrival, and among the letters would doubtless be one containing the document on which so much depended. The secretaries had assured Dr. Parker while he was still in London that his letter of credit, if not already on its way to Shanghai, would be there long before his own arrival. But on going through his mail no trace of it appeared. Carefully they read and reread the letters, but although it was taken for granted that he would be at the end of his journey when they reached him, there was no mention whatever of money matters or how his needs were to be supplied. The letter of credit had evidently been overlooked and forgotten.

Happily, another mail was due within a day or two, and that no doubt would put matters right. In the meanwhile, they were thankful for the little preparation Hudson Taylor had been able to make, and with his few dollars and their own they laid in a small supply of what was indispensable.

The mail came in. Yes, there were letters from the secretaries dated September 15, more than three months after the Parkers had left London. There seemed to be no enclosures, but perhaps they had sent the letter of credit directly to their Shanghai agents and would mention having done so. No, nothing was said about it. There was positively no allusion to the matter. What could be the meaning of such an omission? To Dr. Parker it seemed inexplicable. But Hudson Taylor, with more experience of the working of things, was not altogether surprised and found it less easy to be hopeful, though he acceded to the only suggestion that could be made: that they should go at once to the agents and inquire. Dr. Parker was satisfied that this must bring a conclusion to their difficulties, so with a light heart, as far as he was concerned, they presented themselves at the office of Messrs. Gibb, Livingston, and Company.

Hudson Taylor had had dealings before with the manager of this firm, and though he had found him a friend in need on more than one occasion, it was not possible to forget the sarcasm of some of his remarks, nor the emphasis with which he said, "The management, or rather mismanagement, of your society is very bad." It was with some trepidation, therefore, that he introduced Dr. Parker and asked if any advice had been received as to his letter of credit.

"No," answered the manager promptly, "none."

"Is it possible," queried Dr. Parker, "that you have heard nothing from the society as to the amount I am entitled to draw?"

"It is more than possible," replied the manager, "to judge by past experiences"; though when he saw how this information was received, he was inclined to be more sympathetic.

Painful as the position was in itself, it was rendered still more so by the necessity they were under of explaining matters to this comparative stranger, with his prompt, efficient, businesslike ways, upon whom for the time being they were dependent. If he had not seen fit to advance them money, upon such evidence of their genuineness as they could afford, they would have been reduced to sore straights indeed. But his friendliness, both then and after, was the Lord's way of answering their prayers and providing for them in the absence of the letter of credit that for long months did not make its appearance.

Dr. Parker said little about all this, but he must have felt it keenly, and probably all the more so as he came to realize the tempting possibilities opened to him as a medical man in China. How easily he could have supported his family in comfort, had he been willing to turn aside from missionary work. But in spite of poverty and many privations, prolonged all through the winter, spring, and following summer, he and Mrs. Parker held on their way with quiet self-sacrifice that never wavered.

Difficulties notwithstanding, they tackled their work bravely, and between long, busy Sundays among the people, they settled down as well as they could to study. It was almost impossible to concentrate attention upon the language at this time, for the condition of the people around them was heartrending. Hundreds were dying of cold and starvation, and there seemed no hope of relief until one side or other could win a decisive victory.

Ever since the arrival of Dr. Parker, the open interference on the part of the French had been rousing the hatred of the soldiery. Their attitude was becoming menacing, and the Chinese who favored their cause, both in and around the settlement, were plotting revenge upon the whole European community. This made evangelistic work both difficult and dangerous and might not unreasonably have formed an excuse for lessened activity for the time being. But as far as the missionaries on the L.M.S. compound were concerned, it had no such effect. Dr. Medhurst and his colleagues still planned and carried out their excursions to the interior, as well as constant evangelization in the neighborhood of Shanghai, and Dr. Parker made many visits in company with Hudson Taylor to towns and villages within a radius of ten or fifteen miles, everywhere searching out serious and intelligent persons with whom to leave Scriptures and tracts. In this way, in the month of December alone they distributed many hundreds of New Testaments and Gospels, together with a still larger number of tracts explaining the way of life.

Chapter 4

Evangelistic Journeys

It was with no little interest, as may well be imagined, that Hudson Taylor made preparation for the first inland journey. In addition to clothes and bedding, a good supply of drugs and instruments had to be packed, for there was no knowing what demands might be made upon him as a medical man. Then there were food baskets to be stored with provisions; a stove, cooking utensils, and fuel to be provided; and last but not least, an ample assortment of books and tracts were needed.

Usefulness was what they desired most of all, and it was natural that, as the year drew to a close, they should consult together and work out careful plans to this end. Dr. Parker, an able, experienced man, had a family to think of, and Hudson Taylor, young as he was, was becoming an efficient missionary. Nothing had yet been heard of the missing letter of credit, so that their perplexity with regard to money matters was extreme, and tidings that new missionaries of the L.M.S. were about to sail for China reminded them that even the premises they now occupied would have to be vacated before long. This it was that gave urgency and definiteness to their consultations and resulted in several letters setting forth plans of usefulness that for the next few months largely occupied their thoughts.

A permanent center was needed and had to be obtained without delay. Of the five treaty ports open to the residence of foreigners, none was more suitable than Shanghai, which was within reach of many important cities and held a strategic position with regard to mid-China. In Shanghai, therefore, their headquarters should be located. And the next step was equally plain: in Shanghai they must have suitable premises, and that at once.

This again necessitated a certain adequacy of method and equipment, for other missions were there before them and had established precedents that could not be ignored. Plan as simply as they might, they would at least require a doctor's house and a school building, in addition to a hospital and dispensary. For a chapel they could wait, using meanwhile the receiving room of the hospital, specially adapted for meetings. From this central station, their plan was to visit the surrounding country and establish branch schools and dispensaries wherever possible. These would be regularly supervised by one or other of the missionaries and would become in their turn centers of Christian effort.

It was all admirable no doubt, and the estimate of a thousand pounds for land and buildings was not immoderate. But it was based upon conclusions that in their case were misleading, and, just because the good is often the enemy of the best, would have thwarted their real life usefulness, foreordained in the purposes of God.

But the letters were sent off, and the New Year (1855) was given to prayer with these thoughts specially in mind. It was now the depth of winter and exceptionally cold. Hudson Taylor had bought a native boat for half its value, and on frequent excursions to the country was able to purchase fuel and provisions at a lower rate than in Shanghai. This, with Mrs. Parker's thrifty housekeeping, made such means as they had, last as long as possible, but even so it was with difficulty that they could keep one room warm enough for study. Hudson Taylor was working hard at two dialects; a Shanghai teacher came to him in the daytime, and his Mandarin-speaking pundit at night. He was also carrying on a school, encouraged to find himself well understood by the children.

Eager as he was to make progress with his studies, it was all the more remarkable that the need of the unevangelized regions round about should press so heavily upon his heart. Certainly it was not the season of the year that tempted him to another journey, nor was it pleasant companionship, for he had to go alone. The condition of affairs, politically, might in itself have been sufficient to hold him back, for a crisis could not long be delayed in the siege of the native city. But little as he realized what it foreshadowed, Hudson Taylor found himself unable to disregard the appeal of the unreached. The ice was broken. He had been on one evangelistic tour already and had seen how such work could be done. Perhaps it was this that drew him on? Perhaps it was something deeper, more significant.

* * * * *

Three months had elapsed since their plans had been laid before the society, and communications that had crossed their own had not been encouraging. Old objections had been raised against building in the treaty ports, and arguments reiterated in favor of opening new fields to the Gospel. But how they were to live and work until this was possible the letters did not suggest. The missionaries themselves could not believe that this point of view was unalterable. They had stated their case so clearly that its importance must be felt, and surely when their well-considered scheme was laid before the committee, it would be seen to forward the very ends they themselves had in view.

Meanwhile, it was more and more difficult to continue waiting in uncertainty. The American missionary who shared their little house was building premises of his own, but with no hope of completing them before summer. Dr. Parker's letter of credit had not come, nor did the society seem to remember that he had any financial needs. If their privations through the winter had been severe, what would the hot season mean—the dreaded months of summer—in those crowded rooms?

When all these circumstances are considered, and it is further taken into account that missionaries, even the most devoted, are only human after all, it will not be wondered at that Hudson Taylor said and felt some things that hardly seem in keeping with his simple faith in God. He was passing through a period of peril for his spiritual usefulness and was under the influence of friends called to a line of things entirely different from his own. But side by side with this, which one cannot but see was unlike him, went another, very different development. Strangely the currents mingled at this time—one drawing him to the settled life of the ports, the other carrying him far afield to regions beyond any that had yet been reached. He could not even wait for the expected reply of the committee, so eager was he to set out upon another evangelistic journey. The local rebellion was at an end, Dr. Parker needed a change from study, their boat was lying in the creek—was it not just the opportunity for a preaching tour which should include a good deal of medical work?

Emptied from Vessel to Vessel

Summer was now in possession of the settlement, and it was a warm welcome Hudson Taylor received in more ways than one on his return there after his evangelistic journey with the Parkers. The little house was still as crowded as ever, and there seemed no prospect of relief for this season at any rate, but grace was found sufficient for daily needs, even when these extended into long, breathless nights when sleep was well-nigh impossible because of the heat. If only the rats had not been so lively, the nights would have been less trying. But whether the temperature excited them or not, they were aggressive in the extreme, running all over the room and even jumping on the beds in their nocturnal carousals.

Yet, how thankful Hudson Taylor and his fellow workers were for the shelter of even these indifferent quarters! Anything better, indeed anything they could live in at all, was still unattainable, in spite of the reconstruction that was quickly going on. Worse than staying on in those three rooms all summer would be having to leave them when they were needed for reinforcements expected by the L.M.S.

One evangelistic trip indeed had been attempted since the beginning of June, which, though cut short by illness, was to have an important bearing on his future as well as on that of Dr. Parker. Accompanied by Mr. Burdon, they had set out on a preaching tour that was to include a visit to Ningpo for a partial rest and change. Missionaries of several societies were at work in that important city, and the blessing of God was manifestly resting upon their labors. Hudson Taylor and his colleague looked forward, therefore, to much help from this visit, far though they were from realizing all it was to bring into their lives.

The next two months were spent, then, in and around the settlement. But though this temporary work was encouraging and full of promise, it was accompanied by no little trial as to their position and prospects. Gradually it was becoming evident that the society was not prepared to endorse their suggestion with regard to mission headquarters in any of the treaty ports. It was a matter of principle with the committee not to put money into bricks and mortar, even though it seemed that their representatives could be housed in no other way. But their veto upon the carefully thought-out scheme laid before them did not come all at once, and meanwhile the faraway missionaries were not forgotten by Him who sees the end from the beginning.

It is easy enough now for us to realize that the Shanghai idea, as far as they were concerned, was a mistaken one, but it was anything but easy for them. Dr. Parker had not yet received the invitation to Ningpo, and Hudson Taylor, eager though he was to go inland, knew all too well the seriousness of such an undertaking and the need for a good home base, as evidenced in the following letter written to his sister:

> It is hard to be ever on the move and to have no settled dwelling. I have some thought of buying a set of Chinese garments soon, and seeing

> how I could get on with them. If I could get a little place somewhere in the interior, perhaps I might settle down and be useful. As things are at present, we cannot hope to see much fruit—for we have no station, no chapel, no hospital, no house even of our own....The future is in the hands of God....There we must leave it....Pray for me, for I am very weak and unworthy and have been a good deal tried of late.

And no wonder, when one considers the conditions under which they were living and the exhausting heat of summer! But the point especially worthy of notice is the changed attitude of the writer since a previous letter on the subject. Then it had been: Our plans are laid before the society; if they do nothing, we mean to try and carry them out ourselves; if they oppose, it may become a question as to which we will dispense with, the society or our plans for usefulness. Now it was: Chinese dress, a little place somewhere in the interior, and, above all, a future left in the hands of God. How great a difference! The Lord had had time to work. And as always in His providence, the molding force came not only from outward circumstances but from the development of His life within.

How little could Hudson Taylor have imagined that, even before the answer to those January letters could be received, his own outlook would be so changed that he would no longer cling to what had then seemed desirable? How little could Dr. Parker have foreseen that before summer was over he would be called to a more important and congenial sphere? And how little can we tell all we are being delivered from by our very limitations or the wider service to which the Lord is leading in ways beyond our reach? So let us thank God from our hearts for trials that are not removed, though brought before Him in believing prayer, and praise Him for answers that seem long in coming, knowing the delay is needed to make us ready to receive them.

Thus Hudson Taylor and his colleague were really being led of God, though the month of August only seemed to bring a climax to their difficulties. The Parkers were being called to Ningpo, and Hudson Taylor had to decide where he felt he belonged. What was the Lord's guidance in it all? That was the question. Regarding all of this, Hudson Taylor wrote:

> Many reasons make me desire to go to Ningpo with the Parkers, but there are also many against it. There are already fourteen missionaries there...and they are working the field well and in much peace and unity. Shanghai is not nearly so well worked, with more than double the number of missionaries. The Ningpo dialect, I must confess, is no attraction, though once learned, it would no doubt increase my opportunities of usefulness. There may be something of laziness in it, but I do feel this is an objection against going to a new district. ...Expenses are less there than in Shanghai. If I stay here I shall certainly have to move, for our cotenants are leaving in about a month (their new house is just finished), and the whole rent of these premises would be far more than I can afford.
>
> So you see that I am as unsettled as to my future prospects as the first day I landed in China. I am waiting on the Lord for guidance. Meanwhile, my thought is to stay on here in

> Shanghai if possible, at any rate for the present. I feel as if my work here were not done. But eventually I may go to Ningpo, if my efforts to obtain a footing in the interior should fail in this district. It does seem as if I never should be settled! I do long for a helpful companion with whom I could take counsel and have real sympathy of mind and feeling, and to be fixed somewhere in good, regular work.

But there was something more important still, if his prayers for usefulness were to be answered as fully as the Lord was able and willing to answer them. Moab, we are told, was "at ease from his youth...settled on his lees...hath not been emptied from vessel to vessel" (Jer. 48:11)—referring to a poor, inferior quality of wine of which nothing could be made. "Therefore his taste remained in him, and his scent is not changed" (Jer. 48:11). But the life that was to be made a blessing the wide world over had to pass through a very different process, including much of that emptying and reemptying "from vessel to vessel," so painful to the lower nature from which we are being refined.

It was August when the long-expected came at length, and Hudson Taylor and his colleague received notice that the house they were occupying must be vacated by the end of September. Two new missionaries were on the way from England and would require the premises.

And just then, strangely enough, further letters from their own committee put a final veto upon their plans for Shanghai as a permanent center. No, they were not to build, though permission was given to Dr. Parker to rent rooms for a dispensary. How or where they were to live was left a matter of uncertainty, the committee apparently having no suggestion to make. Well was it for the much-tried missionaries that the Lord had not overlooked this important detail, but was caring for His workers as well as for the best interests of His work.

Another letter, also received early in August, gave full proof of this. Several weeks previously, the unanimous invitation of the missionaries in Ningpo had reached Dr. Parker, earnestly requesting that he go and settle among them. He had replied that he could not feel justified in doing so unless he was assured that it would open to him a wider door of usefulness. For a home and practice of his own, no matter how attractive, he could not sacrifice missionary work. But if in connection with such a position he could be assured of the support of a hospital for the Chinese, the expense of which would be at least eight hundred dollars per annum, the matter might look very different. And now the answer reached him. Just when he was ready for it—eight months in the country having given him some familiarity with the people and language—then, and not before, the opening came that was to determine his lifework.

The resolution, which had been come to so opportunely, while it cleared the way for Dr. Parker and his family, only left Hudson Taylor the more cast upon God. Now he would be lonely indeed, bereft of companionship as well as home. Feeling so definitely, as he did, that his work in Shanghai was not yet finished, he had at once to set about seeking quarters to which he might remove his belongings. But, as before, the search proved useless. Nothing was to be had at a price within his means.

Day after day went by in weary trampings up and down the city, and at the end of three weeks the hope of finding what he needed seemed farther off than ever. Many thoughts had been in his mind during this time, some idea of which may be gathered from a note to his sister:

> Dr. Parker has accepted the invitation to Ningpo, and will be going down in a few days to arrange accommodation for his family. Nearly the whole of last week I spent in seeking a house to move into here myself, but I have not found one. They all want heavy deposits that I am not able to pay. It is wearisome work, and if I do not succeed soon I shall adopt Chinese dress and seek a place in the country....These changes are not easy. Do pray much for me.

Chinese dress and a home somewhere in the country—the thought was becoming familiar. But it was a recourse that was almost unheard-of in those days. Sometimes, on inland journeys, a missionary would wear the native costume as a precautionary measure, and Dr. Medhurst himself had suggested to Hudson Taylor that he might find it helpful. But it was invariably discarded on the traveler's return, and he would have been careless of public opinion indeed who would have ventured to wear it always and in the settlement.

But it was on nothing less than this that the young missionary was meditating, driven to it by his longing to identify himself with the people and by the force of outward circumstances. If he could not find quarters in Shanghai, he must go to the interior, and why add to his difficulties and hinder the work he most desired to accomplish by emphasizing the fact that he was a foreigner?

Another week went by in almost incessant house hunting, and the time drew near when Dr. Parker was to leave for Ningpo. Hudson Taylor had promised to escort him as far as Hangchow Bay, to see him through the more difficult part of the journey. They were to start on Friday morning the twenty-fourth, and up to Thursday afternoon, the search for premises had been in vain.

Yes, it was growing clearer. For him, probably, the right thing was a closer identification with the people: Chinese dress at all times and the externals of Chinese life, including chopsticks and native cookery. How much it would simplify traveling in the interior! Already he had purchased an outfit of native clothing. If, after all the prayer there had been about it, he really could not get accommodation in Shanghai, it must be that the Lord had other purposes. He would send his few things down to Ningpo with Dr. Parker, who had offered to store them, and, living on boats, would give himself to evangelistic work until his way opened up somewhere in the interior.

Thursday night came, and Dr. Parker was to leave the following morning. It was useless to seek premises any longer, so Hudson Taylor went down to engage the junk that was to take them to Hangchow Bay with their belongings. His Chinese dress was ready for the following morning when he expected to begin a pilgrim life indeed.

And this, apparently, was the point to which it had been necessary to lead him. He had followed faithfully. It was enough. And now on these new lines could be given the answer to weeks and months of prayer.

As he was on his way to make arrangements for their journey, a man met him. Did he want a house in the Chinese city? Would a small one do, with only five rooms? Because near the South Gate there was such a house, only it was not quite finished being built. The owner had run short of money and hardly knew how to complete the work. If it suited the foreign teacher, no deposit would be asked; it could be had in all probability for an advance of six months' rent.

Feeling as though in a dream, Hudson Taylor followed his guide to the southern quarter of the city, and there he found a small, compact house, perfectly new and clean, with two rooms upstairs and two down and a fifth across the courtyard for the servants. It was just the very thing he needed, in the locality that suited him best, and all for the moderate sum of ten pounds to cover a half year's rent.

What it must have been to him to pay the money over that night and secure the premises is more easily imagined than described. The Lord had indeed worked on his behalf. Prayer was being answered. He had not missed or mistaken the guidance for which he had waited so long. It almost seemed as if the Lord had broken silence to confirm and encourage His servant at this critical time. And best of all was the wondering consciousness that He Himself had done it when, humanly speaking, it seemed impossible: "I being in the way, the LORD led me" (Gen. 24:27).

That night he took the step he had been prayerfully considering—called in a barber and had himself so transformed in appearance that his own mother could hardly have known him. To put on Chinese dress without shaving the head is comparatively a simple matter, but Hudson Taylor went to all lengths, leaving only enough of the fair, curly hair to grow into the *queue* of a Chinese man. He had prepared a dye, moreover, with which he darkened this remaining hair to match the long, black braid that at first must do duty for his own. Then in the morning he put on, as best he might, the loose, unaccustomed garments and appeared for the first time in the gown and satin shoes of a "Teacher," or man of the scholarly class.

Some Better Thing

How it all opened up after this step had been taken! Returning alone from Hangchow Bay, Hudson Taylor hardly knew himself as the same person who had so often been tried by the petty annoyances and more serious hindrances to his work by curious and excited crowds. Plenty of people still followed him whenever he became known as a foreigner, and it was not difficult to gather an audience to listen to the Gospel. But the rowdy element seemed somehow to have disappeared with his European dress, and if he wished to pass unnoticed he was able to do so, even in the busiest streets. This, of course, greatly lessened the strain of being much alone among the people, and at the same time gave him access to a more respectable, serious-minded class.

Not suspected even of being a European until his speech betrayed him, he had a far truer, more natural point of view from which to study conditions around him, and found himself coming into touch in a new way with people and things Chinese. It was natural now to adopt their point of view, as he could not before, and instinctively he began to identify himself with those toward whom he had hitherto occupied the position of a foreigner.

Now he was one of them in all outward respects—dressing, living, eating as they did, and greatly lessening the cost and difficulty of providing for his needs by doing so. Altogether, the change was one for which he found himself increasingly thankful and which made his following journeys more interesting and productive.

When he returned to Shanghai, he took up in the old surroundings a very different life. For the change he had made after so much prayer was soon found to affect more than his outward appearance. The Chinese felt it, Europeans felt it, and above all he felt it himself—putting an intangible barrier between him and foreign associations, and throwing him back as never before upon the people of his adoption. This, while he rejoiced in it for his work's sake, was not without its sting.

The covert sneer or undisguised contempt of the European community he found less difficult to bear than the disapproval of fellow missionaries. But this also had to be faced, for he was practically alone in his convictions and certainly the only one to carry them into effect. The more he suffered for them, however, the more they deepened; the more he gave himself to the Chinese in consequence, the more a new and wonderful joy in the Lord flooded his soul.

Yet his surroundings were far from attractive within the walls of the native city, and his arrangements of the simplest, providing only for the bare necessaries of life. Chinese food and cooking were something of a trial at first, especially when the weather continued to be warm, and so were the sights and smells that could not be avoided amid that teeming population which was devoid of the most elementary ideas of sanitation. But the principal remains the same throughout the ages: "As the sufferings of Christ abound in us, so our consolation also aboundeth by Christ" (2 Cor. 1:5), and the consolation, or "encouragement," as it may be read, far exceeds the loneliness and sacrifice.

A Parish of a Million

Could it really be true? A home of his own in the interior, and he himself in Chinese dress, quietly living among the people, a day's journey from the nearest treaty port? Often during those autumn days of 1855, it must have seemed like a dream. Yet the dream lasted, with most encouraging results.

It was all in answer to prayer no doubt, but the Chinese dress he was wearing had had a great deal to do with it. As soon as he could leave the South Gate house, he had set out on another evangelistic journey, which was to include a visit to the island of Tsungming. But he had gotten no further than the first place at which he landed, for there, within two or three days of his arrival, he found himself in possession of another little house of his own.

The people simply would not hear of his leaving. Clothed like themselves and living much as they did, he did not seem like a foreigner, and when they heard that he must have an upstairs room to sleep in, on account of the dampness of the locality, they said, "Let him live in the temple, if no other upper room can be found."

And quite willingly the young missionary would have done so, if the semidiscarded idols could have been cleared out of one of the silent, dusty chambers looking down upon the court. But in this the priests foresaw a difficulty. Most of the idols, they said, were old and unimportant, but there were some, even upstairs, that it would not do to interfere with. Could not the foreign teacher allow them to remain? But when he explained that it was a question of his God—the true and living God, Creator of earth and heaven, who could not be asked to company with idols, the work of men's hands, and dependent for power, if they had any, upon the presence of evil spirits—both priests and people saw the reasonableness of his position. But even so they dared not dispossess a certain number of those idols.

What made them want so much to have him is not clear. Perhaps it was the medicine chest. Perhaps it was the preaching. At any rate, there was nothing in his outward appearance to frighten them away, and the difference between this experience and anything he had met with on previous journeys taught him afresh the value of Chinese dress.

The second day of his stay there was a Sunday, and already a house with some sort of an upper story had been discovered, whose owner was quite willing to receive the missionary. Indeed he could rent the entire premises, if they pleased him, for a moderate sum. But keen as he was to secure the place, Hudson Taylor would not go to see it on Sunday, and the people watching him received their first impressions of the day God calls His own.

The delay did but forward Hudson Taylor's interests, however, and before Monday was half over, the agreement was concluded that gave him possession of his first home in "inland China."

Busy indeed were the days that followed, one of the hardest-worked and happiest times the young missionary had ever known in his life. The house needed cleaning, not to speak of furnishing, before it could be considered habitable even from a Chinese point of view. But more important than all this was the stream of visitors who had to be received with courtesy: gentlemen from the town and country, patients eager for medicine, and neighbors who seemed never weary of dropping in to watch and listen to all that was going on.

All that was necessary had been accomplished. The curiosity of the neighborhood was satisfied, visitors had for the most part carried away favorable impressions, the house was whitewashed and sufficiently set in order, forms were ready for "the chapel," and best of all, the conviction had gone abroad that the young missionary had come to Tsungming not for pleasure and comfort merely, but to do good, to relieve suffering, and to tell them something everybody ought to know.

After that, things settled down to a regular routine. Patients were seen and daily meetings held, and to the thankfulness of the missionary and his helpers, a few inquirers began to gather about them. One of these was a blacksmith named Chang and another was an assistant in a grocery store, men of good standing in the town, "whose heart[s] the Lord opened" (Acts 16:14). And all about them stretched the populous island: a parish of a million, each one of whom he longed to reach. The town itself contained only twenty to thirty thousand, but villages were numerous in every direction, and the medical work was making friends. Wherever Mr. Taylor and his helpers went, they found somebody ready to welcome them, and as frequently as possible, they spent a day in the country preaching the Gospel.

This good work went on. Six weeks was a long time to have been enabled to reside in one place, preaching the Gospel daily, forty miles from the nearest treaty port. The young missionary was more than ever earnest in making the most of his opportunities. To see the inquirers growing in grace and in the knowledge of the Lord was a joy no words could express. One of these, the blacksmith, Chang, now closed his shop on Sundays, and both he and another, Sung, openly declared themselves Christians. The change that had come over them awakened not a little interest among their fellow townsmen, several of whom were attending the services regularly. Therefore, the blow, when it fell, was all the more painful for being unexpected, and it came from an unforeseen quarter. Certain doctors and druggists in the area saw Hudson Taylor as their rival, even though he did not charge for his services, and plotted to have him removed. When he had to go over to Shanghai to obtain money, send off letters, and obtain supplies, to his surprise, an important-looking document from the British consul was awaiting him at the South Gate.

Of course he went at once and explained the true facts of the case, which were listened to with interest. But his plea to be allowed to remain on the island, where all now seemed peaceful and friendly, was in vain. The consul reminded him that the British Treaty only provided for residence in the five ports and that if he attempted to settle elsewhere he rendered himself liable to a fine of five hundred dollars. But there was a supplementary treaty, as the young missionary well knew, in which it was stipulated that all immunities and privileges granted to other nations should apply to British subjects also. Roman Catholic priests and Frenchmen were living on the island supported by the authority of their governments, and why should he be forbidden the same consideration?

Yes, replied the consul, that was undoubtedly a point, and if he wished to appeal for a higher decision, Her Majesty's representative would be arriving in Shanghai before long. But as far as his own jurisdiction went, the matter was at an end. Mr. Taylor must return to Tsungming at once, give up his house, remove his belongings to Shanghai, and understand that he was liable to a fine of five hundred dollars if he again attempted residence in the interior.

Well was it that the next day was Sunday, and he had time to lay it all before the Lord. Little by little as it came over him, and he began to realize that all the happy, encouraging work on the island must be suddenly abandoned, it seemed almost more than he could bear. Those young inquirers, Chang, Sung, and the others, what was to become of them? Were they not his own children in the faith? How could he leave them with no help and so little knowledge in the things of God? And yet the Lord had permitted it. The work was His. He would not fail nor forsake them. But for himself, the sorrow and disappointment were overwhelming.

The last days on Tsungming, however, were not wholly sad. It was hard to pack up and send everything to the boat, hard to answer the interrogations of neighbors and bid farewell to the old landlord and many friends. But the very parting brought with it elements of comfort.

Could he ever forget, for example, that last evening spent with the inquirers?

"My heart will be truly sorrowful," said the blacksmith, "when I can no longer join you in the daily meetings."

"But you will worship in your own family," replied his friend. "Still shut your shop on Sunday, for God is here whether I am or not. Get someone to read for you, and gather your neighbors in to hear the Gospel."

"I know but very little," put in Sung, "and when I read I by no means understand all the characters. My heart is grieved because you have to leave us, but I do thank God He ever sent you to this place. My sins, once so heavy, are all laid on Jesus, and He daily gives me joy and peace."

"Come again, come again," the neighbors called the following morning. "The sooner you return, the better! We will miss the good doctor and the heavenly Words."

As Rivers of Water in a Dry Place

"And a man shall be as an hiding place from the wind, and a covert from the tempest; as rivers of water in a dry place, as the shadow of a great rock in a weary land" (Isa. 32:2). Spoken primarily of the Lord and wholly true of Him alone, yet how often these words find a limited and human, but very blessed, fulfillment in an earthly friendship, through which He comes to us in time of need. Thus it was for Hudson Taylor in the friendship of William Burns. Alone, perplexed, and disappointed, he had indeed come to a time of need. The restrictions imposed upon him as a Protestant missionary, compared with the liberty granted to priests of the Roman Catholic Church, opened up a difficulty he had not anticipated in his evangelistic work.

Beloved all over Scotland by those to whom he had been made a blessing, the name of William Burns was in the best sense a household word. For where in town or country was there a Christian household that did not recall with thankfulness the Revival of 1839? The young evangelist of those days, who had moved in Pentecostal power from place to place, everywhere accompanied by marvelous tokens of the divine presence and blessing, had become the toil-worn missionary: his hair already tinged with gray, his spirit more mellow, though no less fervent, his sympathies enlarged through experience and deeper fellowship with the sufferings of Christ.

Nanking was on his heart, as well as the unknown leaders of the Taiping movement, in whose hands the future of China still seemed to lie. No missionary had until this time succeeded in reaching them, though the rebel king had earnestly pleaded for Christian teachers to aid in the great work of national regeneration upon which he thought himself to have embarked. Certainly, if anyone in China could have strengthened him for this hopeless task, it would have been William Burns with his easy mastery of the language, intense force of character, and deeply prayerful spirit. But as events had already proved, this was not the purpose for which he had been brought to central China.

Unsuccessful in his attempt to reach Nanking, Mr. Burns had returned to Shanghai by the southern reaches of the Grand Canal, much impressed with the need and accessibility of that part of the country. With the acceptance of the local missionaries, who were all too few to meet the overwhelming needs, he had devoted himself for several months to its evangelization: living on boats in a very simple style and traveling up and down the endless waterways spread like a network over the vast alluvial plain. Thus it was that, in the providence of God, he was still in that locality when Hudson Taylor returned from Tsungming and engaged in the very work so dear to the younger missionary's heart.

Where and how they met is not clear, but one can readily believe that they were drawn together by sympathies of no ordinary kind. The grave, keen-eyed Scotsman soon detected in the English missionary a kindred spirit, and one sorely in need of help that he might give. The attraction was mutual. Each was without a companion, and before long they had arranged to join forces in the work to which both felt specially called.

In the little house at the South Gate or on Mr. Burns's boat, almost the first subject they would discuss would be the difficulty about Tsungming, with its bearing on the future, and it was not long before the spiritual point of view of the older man seemed to change the whole situation. It was not a question really of standing on one's rights or claiming what it might be justifiable to claim. Why deal with second causes? Nothing would have been easier for the Master to whom "all power is given" (Matt. 28:18) than to have established His servant permanently on the island, had He so desired it. And of what use was it, if He had other plans, to attempt to carry the thing through on the strength of government help? No, "the servant of the Lord must not strive" (2 Tim. 2:24) but must be willing to be led by just such indications of the divine will, relying not on the help of man to accomplish a work of his own choosing, but on the unfailing guidance, resources, and purposes of God.

And so, very thankfully, Hudson Taylor came to realize that all was well. A measure of trial had been allowed, over which perhaps he had felt unduly discouraged. But all was in wise and loving Hands. Nothing the Lord permitted could lastingly hinder His own work. And all the while, had He not been preparing for His servant this unexpected blessing, by far the most helpful companionship he had ever known?

It was the middle of December 1855 when Hudson Taylor left Shanghai once more, setting out on his tenth evangelistic journey, the first with Mr. Burns. Traveling in two boats, each with their Chinese helpers and a good supply of literature, they were at the same time independent and a comfort to one another. Practical and methodical in all his ways, Mr. Burns had a line of his own in such work that his companion was glad to follow.

Choosing an important center, in this case the town of Nan-zin, just south of the Great Lake, in Cheh-kiang, they remained there eighteen days, including Christmas and New Year's Day. Every morning they set out early with a definite plan, sometimes working together and sometimes separating to visit different parts of the town. Mr. Burns believed in beginning quietly on the outskirts of a place in which foreigners had rarely if ever been seen and working his way by degrees to the more crowded quarters. Accordingly, they gave some days to the suburban streets, preaching whenever a number of people collected, and giving away Gospels and tracts. They repeated this in all the quieter parts of the town, gradually approaching its center, until at length they could pass along the busiest streets without endangering the shopkeepers' tempers as well as their wares.

Then they visited temples, schools, and tea shops, returning regularly to the most suitable places for preaching. These were usually tea shops on quiet thoroughfares, on open spaces left by demolished buildings. Announcing after each meeting when they would come again, they had the satisfaction of seeing the same faces frequently, and interested hearers could be invited to the boats for private conversation.

It was hinted to Mr. Burns that he change to Chinese dress as Hudson Taylor had. This hint was not without effect, though other more important considerations caused Mr. Burns to decide upon this step. Ever since leaving Shanghai, he had not failed to notice the benefit derived by his companion from wearing Chinese dress. Although so much younger and in every way less experienced, Mr. Taylor had the more attentive hearers and was occasionally asked into private houses; he himself was requested to wait outside, as the disturbance occasioned by his presence would make attention impossible. The riffraff of the crowd always seemed to gather round the preacher in foreign dress, while those who wished to hear what was being said followed his less noticeable friend.

This change into Chinese dress was found to have so many advantages that Mr. Burns never again resumed European clothing. Among the people of Nan-zin it was received with cordial favor. Returning from the tea shop a few days later, both the missionaries were invited by one who had been present to go with him to his home and repeat there the wonderful Story. It was evening and they had already been preaching for a couple of hours, but such invitations were none too frequent and they gladly accompanied him. Of this event, Hudson Taylor wrote:

> It was very interesting to see all the family collected...that we might speak to them of Him who died to atone for the sins of the world. Close to me was a bright little girl about ten years of age, her arms crossed upon the table and her head resting on them. Beside her was her brother, an intelligent boy of fourteen. Next came Mr. Burns and on his other side a young man of twenty, and so on. The men sat round the table, while the mother, two older daughters, and another woman kept in the background, half out of sight. While I was speaking, as I did on their account, of the prayers of my mother and sister before my conversion, I noticed that they were attending closely. Oh, may God give China *Christian mothers and sisters* before long! Returning to our boats, I could not help tears of joy and thankfulness that we had been induced to adopt this costume, without which we could never have such access to the people.

Of the comfort of the dress there could be no doubt, according to Mr. Taylor:

> It is real winter now, and the north wind is very cutting. But instead of being almost "starved to death" as I was last year, I am now, thanks to the Chinese costume, thoroughly comfortable and as warm as toast.
>
> Indeed, we have many mercies to be thankful for. A good boat, costing about two shillings a

day, gives me a nice little room to myself; one in front for my servant to sleep in, used in the daytime for receiving guests; and a cabin behind for my teacher, as well as a place for cooking, storing books, etc. My tiny room has an oyster-shell window that gives light while it prevents people from peeping in...a table at which I write and take meals...a locker on which my bed is spread at night...and a seat round the remaining space, so that two visitors, or even three, can be accommodated. For family worship we open the doors in front and behind my cabin, and then the boat people, teachers, servant, and Mr. Burns can all join in the service....

How very differently our Master was lodged! "[No]where to lay his head" (Matt. 8:20). And this for my sins—amazing thought!...Then I am no longer my own. Bought with His precious blood....Oh, may I be enabled to glorify *Him* with my whole spirit, soul, and body, which are His.

Deep as his longing had ever been for likeness to and fellowship with the Lord, Hudson Taylor was increasingly conscious of this heart hunger in his companionship with William Burns. Mr. Burns, too, had found how sadly possible it is to be professedly a witness for Christ amid the darkness of a heathen land and yet breathe little of the love of God or the grace of the Gospel. Nothing was more real to him than the fact that a low-level missionary life can, and too often does, make even "the cross of Christ...of none effect" (1 Cor. 1:17). But great and many though the dangers may be, and the pressures brought to bear on every missionary to lower his spiritual standards and draw him away from living contact with the Lord, Mr. Burns had proved the faithfulness of that divine

Master in coming to the help of His own. He wrote:

> I was preaching last Sabbath day from Matthew 24:12, "Because iniquity shall abound, the love of many shall wax cold"; and alas! I felt they were solemnly applicable to my own state of heart. Unless the Lord the Spirit continually uphold and quicken, oh how benumbing is daily contact with heathenism! But the Lord is faithful, and has promised to be "as rivers of water in a dry place, as the shadow of a great rock in a weary land" (Isa. 32:2). May you and all God's professing people in a land more favored, but alas! more guilty also, experience much of the Lord's own presence, power, and blessing; and when the enemy comes in as a flood, may the Spirit of the Lord—nay, it is said, "the Spirit of the LORD *shall* lift up a standard against him" (Isa. 59:19, italics added).

Upon such promises he counted, and he had not found them to fail. The presence of the Lord was the one thing as real to him in China as it had been at home. "He did not consider that he had a warrant to proceed in any sacred duty," his biographer, the Rev. Islay Burns, D.D., tells us, "without a consciousness of that divine presence. Without it, he could not speak even to a handful of little children in a Sunday School; with it, he could stand unabashed before the mightiest and wisest in the land."

Ruled by such a master principle, it was no wonder there was something about his life that impressed and attracted others even while it inspired a sense of awe. The brightest lamp will burn dim in an impure or rarefied atmosphere, but William Burns was enabled so to keep himself "in the love of God" (Jude 1:21) that he was but little affected by his surroundings. Prayer was as natural to him as breathing, and the Word of God, his God, was as necessary as daily food. He was always cheerful, always happy, witnessing to the truth of his own memorable words:

> I think I can say, through grace, that God's presence or absence alone distinguishes places to me.

Cultured, genial, and overflowing with mother wit, he was a delightful companion, and the contrast—for those who knew him in China—was very marked between the mind and thoughts so trained to higher things and the heart so content with that which was lowly. A wonderful fund of varied anecdotes gave charm to his society, and he was generous in recalling his experiences for the benefit of others. Sacred music was his delight, greatly to the satisfaction of his young companion. Many were the hymns they sang together both in English and Chinese, Hudson Taylor, no doubt, appreciating Mr. Burns's rendering of these into colloquial words and phrases for the use of the illiterate. Their communication with one another was carried on almost entirely in the language of their native helpers. Mr. Burns lived habitually and by choice in a Chinese element, and with this line of things and the courtesy it indicated toward those around them, Hudson Taylor was in fullest sympathy. The fact that they did not belong to the same missionary society, the same denomination, the same country even, made no difference in their relations. Mr. Burns was far too large-hearted to be narrowed by circumstances or creeds. He was at home with all Protestant Christians and cooperated with missionaries of many societies, German, English, and American, with the greatest goodwill and the most universal spirit, aiming at the advancement of the kingdom of God rather than of his own particular cause.

And this man, the friendship of this man with all he was and had been, was the gift and blessing of God at this particular juncture to Hudson Taylor. Week after week, month after month, they lived and traveled together, the exigencies of their work bringing out resources of mind and heart that otherwise might have remained hidden. Such a friendship is one of the crowning blessings of life. Money cannot buy it; influence cannot command it. It comes as love unsought, and only to the equal soul. Young and immature as he was, Hudson Taylor had the capacity to appreciate, after long years of loneliness, the preciousness of this gift. Under its influence he grew and expanded and came to an understanding of himself and his providential position that left its impression on everything in his life that followed. William Burns was better to him than a college course with all its advantages, because he lived out before him right there in China the reality of all he most needed to be and know.

On Whom the Mantle Fell

Six months of close cooperation with William Burns had now gone by, and little as either of them expected it, they were nearing the close of their helpful, happy fellowship. To them it seemed on the contrary, that their work together was only just beginning. The needs around them were so great and the help they were to one another so evident that they could not but look forward to doing something really adequate together, by the blessing of God, for the important region to which He had called them. They were now in Swatow, but it was only one needy field out of the vast whole of unreached China. For that wider work to be done the Lord was making preparation, as well as for widespread blessing in the region He had specially laid upon their hearts. William Burns for Swatow and other strategic points in the great seaboard provinces, and Hudson Taylor, by and by, for far-reaching inland China: such was the purpose of Him who sees the end from the beginning. So the days of their pilgrimage together drew to a close, filled, as all that went before had been, with helpful fellowship in the Lord.

Mr. Burns and Mr. Taylor had almost decided to begin hospital work, or at any rate to open a dispensary in Swatow. They were still praying about it, wondering whether the latter should take the long journey to Shanghai to fetch his instruments and medicines, when the chief mandarin of the place was taken ill and the native doctors were unable to relieve him. Hearing from a friend that one of the foreigners in native dress was a skillful physician, he sent for Hudson Taylor and put the case into his hands. The treatment proved beneficial, and no sooner was he well himself than he strongly advised his benefactor to commence medical work in Swatow for the assistance of other sufferers. This seemed very like the guidance they were seeking, especially when the mandarin, in the grateful spirit so characteristic of his people, undertook to help them about premises. Backed by his approval, they were soon enabled to rent the entire house in which they had hitherto occupied a single room, which gave them the advantage of beginning in a neighborhood in which they were already known and respected.

As though the shadow of a longer parting lay upon his heart, Hudson Taylor was very reluctant, even then, to leave his loved and honored friend. But when just at this juncture a free passage was offered him all the way to Shanghai by an English captain, the matter seemed taken out of his hands. Mr. Burns would not be left alone or without fellow workers. One of the native Christians would assist him in Swatow, and another in the country districts. It really seemed, at last, as though the way were opening before them, and all they needed was the medical outfit waiting in Shanghai to enable them to enter upon fruitful labors.

And so, early in July, the parting came, and full of thankfulness for the past and hope for greater blessing in the days to come, they committed one another to the care and keeping that had never failed them hitherto. Hudson Taylor wrote long after about his experiences with Mr. Burns:

> Those happy months were an unspeakable joy and comfort to me. His love for the Word was delightful, and his holy, reverential life and constant communings with God made fellowship with him satisfying to the deep cravings of my heart....His views, especially about evangelism as the great work of the church, and the order of lay evangelists as a lost order that Scripture required to be restored, were seed thoughts which were to prove fruitful in the subsequent organization of the China Inland Mission.

For, in the providence of God, they never met again. All unexpectedly Hudson Taylor found his path diverging from that of his friend. Dark clouds were gathering over southern China, soon to lead to war. On a boat near Swatow Mr. Burns was taken prisoner and sent under escort, by river and canal, a journey of thirty-one days to Canton and the nearest British authorities. Returning to Swatow some months later, he was enabled to take advantage of the growing feeling in his favor to establish a permanent work. Known as "The Man of the Book," he was allowed to go in and out freely, the trusted friend of the people, when all other Europeans were confined to their houses and in considerable danger on account of the evils of the coolie traffic, and the Swatow Mission of the English Presbyterian Church flourishes today as an outcome of those early labors.

Chapter 5

Settled Work

A brief absence was all that Hudson Taylor anticipated when he parted from Mr. Burns in Swatow. He was badly needing change while the hot season lasted, and this journey to fetch his medicines fit in very well with the plans they had in view. It was to his surprise and distress, therefore, to learn upon reaching Shanghai that the premises of the London Mission had been visited by fire and that his medical outfit left there for safety was entirely destroyed.

What could it mean? Why had it been permitted? Never had he needed these belongings more. Everything in Swatow seemed to depend upon the medical work they were now in a position to undertake, and Mr. Burns was alone, waiting for him.

But what was the use of returning without medicines? And where was a new supply to come from, or the means to obtain them? Purchase in Shanghai he could not, on account of the extravagantly high prices of imported articles, and six or eight months might be required before they would reach him from home. It was a difficult position, and the young missionary, as he tells us, was more disposed to say with Jacob, "All these things are against me" (Gen. 42:36), than to recognize with cheerful faith that "all things work together for good to them that love God" (Rom. 8:28):

> I had not then learned to think of God as the Great Circumstance in whom "we live, and

move, and have our being" (Acts 17:28), and of all lesser circumstances as necessarily the kindest, wisest, best, because either ordered or permitted by Him. Hence my disappointment and trial were very great.

The only thing was to write and tell Mr. Burns what had happened, and to put off his return until he could go to Ningpo and see what Dr. Parker could do to help them. If he could spare a small supply of medicines to go on with, they might still be able to begin work as soon as the great heat was over. So in the hope of retrieving his losses, Hudson Taylor set out for the neighboring city.

And then a whole set of new difficulties began. Three or four days, under ordinary circumstances, would have taken him to Dr. Parker, but on this occasion he found himself three weeks after he first started no nearer his destination than at the beginning. True, he had made the trip as much of an evangelistic journey as possible, preaching and distributing literature along the first part of the way. But this was not the reason that he ended up where he began, penniless and destitute, without having reached Ningpo at all or having communicated with Dr. Parker. Of this, he wrote long after:

> It is interesting to notice the various events which united in the providence of God in preventing my return to Swatow, and ultimately led to my settling in Ningpo and making that the center for the development of future labors.

But during this trying summer and the many unsettled months that followed, the young missionary was sorely perplexed to understand the way divine providence was taking in the ordering of his affairs. Life turns at times on a small pivot, and in looking back, one is startled to realize the importance of what seemed a very little thing.

How could Hudson Taylor have imagined, for example, that a robbery that left him in such distress upon this journey was to result in the deliverance of the entire mission he was yet to found during a period of financial danger? How could he suppose that the upset of all his plans, and the severance of a partnership in service more precious than any he had ever known, was to prove the crowning blessing of his life on the human side, bringing him into association and at last union with the one of all others most suited both to him and his work?

But so it is that God leads. His hand is on the helm. We are being guided, even when we feel it least. The closed door is as much His providence as the open, and is equally for our good and the accomplishment of His own great ends. And one learns at last that it is not what we set ourselves to do that really tells in blessing, so much as what He is doing through us, when we least expect it, if only we are in abiding fellowship with Him.

Who Shuts and No Man Opens

So Hudson Taylor finally found himself in Ningpo in August 1856, and he was able to throw himself heartily into all that was going on, prepared by his experiences to appreciate fully both the missionaries already there and their work. Never before had he realized the comfort and advantage of laboring among comparatively friendly people, who were not embittered against the missionary simply on account of his being a foreigner. Although there was of course the usual ignorance and superstition in Ningpo, and at times much antiforeign feeling, there was also a large element of interest and even inquiry about the Gospel. And then the missionaries themselves—how delightful to be in the midst of so united and efficient a community!

The two American missions had the priority, due to the fact that they were the first to arrive, and because of their strength of numbers, and an interesting feature, both in connection with them and with the Church Missionary Society, was that the pioneers were all still on the field, men rich in experience and devotion.

Across the river from this group lived Dr. Parker and his friendly neighbors, the American Presbyterians. Within the city itself, enclosed by the five-mile circuit of its ancient wall, lived the pioneers of the Church Missionary Society and Miss Aldersey with her young companions. They, the only unmarried ladies in that missionary circle, had established themselves in the affections of the people. In a large native house in the southern part of the city, they were carrying on the first girls' school ever established by Protestant missionaries in China.

Miss Aldersey's fellow workers, the young sisters Burella and Maria Dyer, so ably filled their place as self-supporting workers in the school. Born under the tropical sun of the Straits Settlements and brought up in a missionary home, theirs had been an inheritance of no ordinary kind. Their father, one of the earliest agents of the London Missionary Society, came from a family in government service and was educated at Cambridge for the English bar. Burning with love for Christ, he had left all to go as a missionary to China, "The Gibraltar of Heathenism," almost as unknown in those days as it was inaccessible. Unable to effect a landing upon its shores, he had devoted himself for sixteen years to work among the Chinese in and near Singapore, and especially to the perfecting of a process by which the Word of God might go where the missionary could not and the printed page might be produced with a facility impossible before. In this task he had been prospered, and though cut off by fatal illness just after the opening of the treaty ports—when he with many another was rejoicing in the freedom to enter the land for which they had so long prayed and labored—Samuel Dyer possesses more than a missionary grave upon its shores, the first to mark that great advance. When his work was done and he was laid to rest in a little lonely churchyard at Macao, that spirit still lived on—both in the son, whose life was subsequently given to China, and in the daughters who had already been with Miss Aldersey several years. With an exceptionally good knowledge of the Ningpo vernacular, these young missionaries were as efficient as they were beloved, and added not a little to the brightness of the foreign community.

Such then was the circle into which Hudson Taylor was introduced by this visit, and greatly must he have rejoiced to see the value set upon his former colleague by its members. Welcomed in a most generous spirit, Dr. Parker had been successful in building up a practice among the foreign residents, the proceeds of which he devoted entirely to his medical mission. Rapidly acquiring the local dialect, in spite of every hindrance to study, he had made the spiritual care of the patients his first work. In this he was assisted by both English and American missionaries, who took in turn to preach in the dispensary (in which nine thousand patients received treatment within the first twelve months) and to visit the temporary hospital.

When, as was not infrequently the case, these labors resulted in blessing, the converts were free to join any of the churches. Dr. Parker declined to influence them and made it very clear that his sympathies were with all. At the time of Mr. Taylor's visit he was rejoicing in the conversion of a man whose baptism in connection with the C.M.S. had taken place the week before, and was full of thankfulness also for a forward step in the interests of his projected buildings.

With money contributed in Ningpo, he had been enabled to purchase a site on the city side of the river. And such a site: open, central, commanding, on the brink of the great waterway and close to the Salt Gate with its constant stream of traffic! A better position could hardly have been found for the permanent hospital, and already the energetic doctor was having the ground leveled for building operations.

All this, of course, was deeply interesting to the visitor from Swatow, who was expecting to return to such very different scenes. He worked with all his usual energy in spite of summer heat. Careful attention to the peculiarities of local speech soon enabled him to make himself understood even by Ningpo people, and there were so many strangers settled there from other places that he found all the dialects he knew to be of service.

The place where the need was greatest, however, had for him the strongest claim, and before the month was over he was ready to return to Mr. Burns at Swatow. Dr. Parker had fitted him out with medicines, and much benefited by his change of work and surroundings, Mr. Taylor was just setting out for Shanghai when a delay arose. Mr. and Mrs. Way of the Presbyterian Mission had to take the journey too. They would have little children with them, and traveling is always so precarious: if Mr. Taylor could wait a day or two, they would hurry their preparations for the sake of joining his party. He was already escorting Mr. Jones and his little son, newly arrived members of his own mission, and it would mean a great deal to the Ways to travel in their company.

Regretting the delay, but having no reason against it, Hudson Taylor waited, and almost a week went by before the final start could be made. And when they did get away, the journey proved especially trying. For the winds were against them, which made the actual traveling tedious, and serious illness in the party caused Mr. Taylor much anxiety. His colleague, Mr. Jones, to whom he had become sincerely attached during the weeks spent together at Dr. Parker's, developed a painful malady, and as the child was ill too, it meant constant nursing.

Early in October they reached their destination, and thankfully exchanged the drafty boat for a missionary home in which they were received as paying guests. And then, having discharged his commissions and handed over the patients to the care of Dr. Lockhart, it only remained for Hudson Taylor to put his things on board the vessel that was taking him to Swatow.

Recent letters from that port made him feel afresh how much he was needed. Though not expecting him back until the great heat was over, Mr. Burns had been sorely missing him and was now daily awaiting news of his return to take up the work they had planned for the winter. Providentially, as it seemed, a captain Hudson Taylor knew, Captain Bowers, was in Shanghai on the eve of sailing and cordially welcomed the young missionary as his passenger. So with as little delay as possible, Hudson Taylor sent his belongings on board the *Geelong* and prepared to leave Shanghai, perhaps forever.

And then the unexpected happened. A letter from the south coming to one of the members of the London Mission made him go hurriedly in search of Hudson Taylor. Mr. Burns had written:

> If he has not started, please inform him at once of this communication.

It was to the effect that all they had looked forward to in Swatow was at an end for the time being, Mr. Burns having been arrested in the interior and sent to Canton. Happily, he had escaped summary punishment at the hands of the Chinese, but in all probability it would be long before he could return to the district from which he had been ejected.

* * * * *

It was Thursday morning, October 9. The *Geelong* was sailing in a few hours for Swatow, and all his things were on board. What could be the meaning of these tidings? Mr. Burns imprisoned and sent to Canton? The mission premises empty? The British authorities unwilling that they should return?

Almost dazed, it all came over him. First one check and then another: medicines destroyed, robbery and all it had entailed, visit to Ningpo, delay in getting away, tedious return journey, and now at the last moment a closed door—nothing but a closed door—and a dear, sick brother waiting to be taken back to the city from which they had come.

Yes, there was no question but to go. But what about Mr. Burns? Could it be that all they had looked forward to was not of the Lord?

"Thine ears shall hear a word behind thee, saying, This is the way, walk ye in it" (Isa. 30:21).

But for the moment the path that had seemed so clear before them was lost in strange uncertainty.

By a Way That They Knew Not

It still stands, that little house on the Wu-Family Bridge Street in which Hudson Taylor made his Ningpo home. To reach this somewhat retired spot, one crosses the broad river from the settlement and enters the city by the Salt Gate on the east. Then a walk of rather over a mile through the principal streets leads to the neighborhood of the Lakes, between the ancient pagoda and the southwest corner of the city wall. Here a small stone bridge over one of the many canals gives access to a narrow thoroughfare, at the end of which another bridge spans the junction of two large sheets of water, the Sun and Moon Lakes, respectively. From the slightly elevated arch of either of these bridges, one can look down the little street and watch the tide of life that eddies in and out of its temple, shops, and homes.

And there on the left, after crossing the canal, stood and still stands the low two-storied building—just an ordinary shop in front and a little yard behind—destined to become the first home and preaching station of the China Inland Mission. Dr. Parker was using the premises that winter for a boys' school and a dispensary, and was glad to let his former colleague do what he could with the spacious attic above, of which Hudson Taylor said years later:

> I have a distinct remembrance of tracing my initials on the snow which during the night had collected on my coverlet in the large barnlike upper room, now divided into four or five smaller ones, each of which is comfortably ceiled. The tiling of a Chinese house may keep off the rain, if it happens to be sound, but does not afford so good a protection against snow, which will beat up through crannies and crevices and find its way within. But however unfinished may have been its fittings, the little house was well adapted for work among the people, and there I thankfully settled, finding ample scope for service, morning, noon, and night.

The only other foreigners in the southern part of the city were Miss Aldersey with her helpers and Mr. and Mrs. Jones of his own mission. The latter had rented an unoccupied house, semi-foreign in style, belonging to the American Presbyterians, and were doing their best to acquire the language and adapt themselves to the life of the people.

Busy as he was in his own corner, almost a mile away, Hudson Taylor made time to go over frequently to the help of his friends, and the more he saw of them, the more he was impressed by their devotion and sweetness of spirit. With his assistance, Mr. Jones was soon able to begin regular meetings, and many were the preaching excursions they made both in and around the city.

Meanwhile, Mrs. Jones, too, had found a helper in the younger of the sisters associated with Miss Aldersey. When the new family came to settle near them, this bright, attractive girl laid herself out to be useful to the busy mother. As often as possible they went visiting together, Miss Dyer's perfect fluency in the language enabling her to make the most of such time as they could give to this work. Young as she was, not yet twenty, and much occupied with her school classes, she could not be satisfied with anything less than soulwinning. With her, missionary work was not teaching the people merely, it was definitely leading them to Christ.

"That was what drew out my interest," said Hudson Taylor long after. "She was spiritually-minded, as her work proved. Even then she was a true missionary."

For it could not but be that the young Englishman living alone on Bridge Street should meet Miss Dyer from time to time at the house of his friends, and it could not but be also that he should be attracted. She was so frank and natural that they were soon on terms of good acquaintance, and then she proved so like-minded in all important ways that, unconsciously almost to himself, she began to fill a place in his heart never filled before.

Vainly he strove against the longing to see more of her and did his utmost to banish her image from his mind. He was deeply conscious of his call to labor in the interior and felt that for such work he should be free from claims of wife and home. Besides, all was uncertain before him. In a few weeks or months the way might open for his return to Swatow. Was he not waiting daily upon the Lord for guidance, with the needs of that region still in view?

And if it were not to be southern China, it was his hope and purpose to undertake pioneering work nearer at hand, work that might at any time cost his life. No, it was not for him to cherish thoughts such as would rise unbidden as he looked into the face he loved. And yet he could not but look, strange to say, and long to look again.

And then arguments were not wanting along other lines that would array themselves before him. What right had he to think of marriage without a home, income, or prospect of any that he could ask her to share. Accredited agent of the C.E.S. though he was, it did not at all follow that they were to be depended upon for financial supplies. For months he had not drawn upon his letter of credit, knowing the society to be in debt. Chiefly through the ministry of Mr. Berger, who financially supported Hudson Taylor at times and became a lifelong helper to him, the Lord had supplied his needs. But this might not continue. It could not at any rate be counted on. And what would she say, and those responsible for her, to a life of faith in China, faith even for daily bread?

Yes, it was perfectly clear; he was in no position to think of marriage and must subdue the heart hunger that threatened at times to overwhelm him. And to a certain extent he was helped in turning his thoughts to other matters by events transpiring in the south.

For like a bolt out of the blue had come the sudden tidings that England was involved again in war with China. On the spot and on the spur of the moment, the British had fanned a tiny spark into a blaze, and the Chinese, all unconscious of results, had dared to disapprove and even resent our high-handed conduct. But this meant war, if war it could be called between combatants so unequal, and within forty-eight hours British guns were thundering at the gates of Canton.

All this had taken place earlier in the autumn, but it was only in the middle of November that the news began to reach the northern ports. When he first heard of it and saw from the revengeful spirit of the Cantonese in Ningpo how they regarded the attack upon their native city, Hudson Taylor's first thought was for Mr. Burns. What a comfort that he was no longer at Swatow, exposed to the rage of that hotheaded southern people. Now at last a reason was manifest, not only for the removal of his friend, but also for his own detention on the very eve of returning.

But following on feelings of thankfulness for the escape of his friend would come sadder reflections as to the motive and the meaning of the war. He could not but know that for fourteen uneasy years England had been pressing China by every argument that could be devised to legalize the importation of opium; that in spite of the refusal of the Emperor Tao-kwang to admit at any price "the flowing poison," the smuggling trade had gone on growing in defiance of treaty rights; that one war having failed to bring the Chinese to our point of view, there had long been an inclination in certain quarters to bring on a second; and that although for the moment the British admiral had suspended hostilities, the inevitable outcome of so one-sided a conflict must be the humiliation of China and the triumph of England's opium policy.

As to immediate results, they appeared for the moment to be in the other direction. The Cantonese, in the elation of their supposed victory over the British fleet, were trying high-handed measures against the hated foreigner. They could not know that although Admiral Seymour had withdrawn from Canton, evacuating the dismantled forts along the river, Sir John Bowring had sent home for reinforcements, and that in spite of the condemning voice of a large majority in the British Parliament, the war would be adopted by the nation. They only saw their chance of retaliation and very naturally made the most of it. Thus, the British factories were set on fire at Canton, and a price was put on the head of every foreigner.

All this, of course, raised a serious question: To what lengths would the revengeful spirit run? How about other ports and settlements, and especially Ningpo with its large proportion of Cantonese? Previously, they had contented themselves merely with threatenings, but would it, could it, continue so much longer?

The wildest rumors were now everywhere afloat, and in the event of a general war with China, Shanghai might be the only port held by foreigners. It seemed desirable to secure accommodation there at once. And as it was accessible by regular steamer service, the removal could be accomplished without difficulty, and the return in the spring or summer would be equally simple.

Thus it was that Hudson Taylor, three months after settling in Ningpo, found himself called to move again. No one else seemed so free to escort the party, and his knowledge of the Shanghai dialect made it easy for him to do so. He could be just as useful in Shanghai as in Ningpo, an important consideration when the stay might be a long one.

Personally, he would have given a good deal to have remained in Ningpo just then, if only to watch over the safety of the one he loved. For Miss Aldersey would not leave, and her young helpers decided to stay with her. She was just handing over her school, from the superintendence of which she felt it wise to retire, to the American Presbyterian Mission. A connection of the Misses Dyer had come over from Penang, and into her hands the sixty girls with all the school affairs had to be committed. It was no time for unnecessary changes, and, taking what precautions she could for her own safety and that of her charges, Miss Aldersey stayed to complete her work.

But to leave them then and in such a situation was no easy matter to Hudson Taylor. The elder of the sisters had recently become engaged to his friend Mr. Burdon and seemed in consequence to have a special protector, but the younger was left all the more lonely and claimed for that very reason a deeper love and sympathy from his heart. Of course, he dared not show it. He had no reason to think that it would be any comfort to her, and—was he not trying to forget? So he suffered keenly as he left his little home on Bridge Street, not knowing if he would ever see it or her again.

During this absence, the young missionary was specially cast upon God, through his deep and growing love for the one who he still felt could never be his. He had thought, he had in a sense hoped, that absence would enable him to forget, that his love for her would be more under control when she was out of sight. And now quite the reverse was the case. Silently but steadily, it gained a stronger hold upon his inmost being. He had loved before in a more or less boyish way, but this was different. A light beyond the brightness of the sun had risen upon him. It flooded all his being.

Everything he thought, felt, and did seemed permeated with the sense of that other life—so much a part of his own. He could not separate himself in thought from her, and when he was most consciously near to God, he felt the communion of her spirit, the longing for her presence most.

In everything she satisfied his mind and heart, not only embodying his ideal of womanly sweetness, but being herself devoted to the work to which his life was given. As one who, having put his hand to the plow, dared not look back, he could rest in the assurance that she would help and not hinder him in his special service. And yet the old question remained: How could he marry with such prospects, such a future? And, if anything, more serious still, what would she say to it all?

Of her thoughts and feelings about him, if she had any, he knew nothing. She had always been kind and pleasant, but that she was to everyone, with a sweetness of spirit that was unfailing. Apparently she did not wish to marry. Far more eligible men than he had failed to win her! What chance then could there be for one so poor and insignificant?

If anyone had known, if there had been anyone with whom he could have shared the hopes and fears within him, those first months in Shanghai would have been easier to bear, but it was not until the end of March (1857), and through most unexpected circumstances, that the friends with whom he was living began to perceive the trouble of his heart. They had loved him from the first, and had been drawn very closely to him through their Shanghai experiences, but it was not until Mrs. Jones contracted smallpox among the people she was seeking to relieve, and had to hand over the care of household and children to their young fellow worker, that they fully realized what he was. Devoted in his care of the little ones, he earned the parents' deepest gratitude, and in the weeks of convalescence that followed they were so united in prayer and sympathy that—how, he could not tell—the love he had meant to hide was a secret no longer from his nearest friends.

And then he was even more surprised at the satisfaction they expressed. Far from discouraging him, they were full of thankfulness to God. Never had they seen two people more suited to each other! As to the outcome, his duty was perfectly clear, the rest must be left with Him to whom both their lives were given.

So the question that had been burning in his heart for months was committed to writing. Mr. Gough was just returning to Ningpo and kindly undertook to place the letter in the right hands. And then Hudson Taylor could only wait—a week, ten days, two weeks, how long it seemed!—until the answer came.

But little was he prepared, in spite of all the prayer there had been about it, for the tone and purport of this communication. It was her writing surely, the clear, pretty hand he knew so well. But could it, could it be her spirit? Brief and unsympathetic, the note simply said that what he desired was wholly impossible and requested him, if he had any gentlemanly feeling, to refrain from ever troubling the writer again upon the subject.

Could he have known the anguish with which those words had been penned, his own trouble would have been considerably lessened. But the one he loved was far away. He could not see her, dared not write again after such a request, and had no clue to the painful situation. Then it was that the tender, unspoken sympathy of his friends, Mr. and Mrs. Jones, became so great a solace. He could hardly have borne it without them, and yet the sight of their mutual happiness reminded him constantly of the blessing he had lost.

Meanwhile, far away in Ningpo, that other heart was even more desolate and perplexed. For the love that had come to Hudson Taylor was no mistaken infatuation; it was the real thing, given by God. Impossible as he would have felt it, it was a love wholeheartedly returned on the part of the one who had always seemed so far above him. Maria Dyer's was a deep and tender nature. Lonely from her childhood, she had grown up longing for a real heart friend. Her father she could hardly remember, and from the mother whom she devotedly loved, she was parted by death at ten years of age. After this, the doubly orphaned Maria and her brother and sister had been brought up under the care of an uncle in London, most of their time being spent at school.

Then came the call to China, through Miss Aldersey's need of a helper in her Ningpo school. In offering for this post, the sisters were influenced not so much by a desire to take up missionary work as by the knowledge that it was what their parents would have desired. Young as they were, they had had some training as teachers, and as they were self-supporting and did not wish to be separated, Miss Aldersey invited both to join her instead of only one.

To the younger sister, the voyage to China was memorable as the time of her definite entrance into peace with God. Previously, she had striven to be a Christian in her own strength, feeling all the while that she lacked the "one thing...needful" (Luke 10:42) and seeking vainly to obtain it. Now her thoughts were turned to Christ and His atoning work as the only ground of pardon and acceptance, the all-sufficient ground to which our prayers and efforts can add nothing at all. Gradually it dawned upon her that she was redeemed, pardoned, cleansed from sin, because He had suffered in her stead. God had accepted Christ as her substitute and Savior, and she could not do less. Simply and trustfully as a little child, she turned away from everything and everyone else, content to take God at His word. "There is therefore now no condemnation to them which are in Christ Jesus" (Rom. 8:1), and to prove that, "the Spirit itself beareth witness with our spirit, that we are" here and now "children of God" (Rom. 8:16).

This true conversion, with all that flowed from it, made her entrance upon missionary work very different from what it would otherwise have been. No longer a philanthropic undertaking to which she devoted herself out of regard for her parents' wishes, it had become the natural and even necessary expression of her great and growing love to Him who was her Savior, Lord, and King. He had changed everything for her, for time and for eternity, and the least she could do was to give herself entirely to His service. So with a peace and joy unknown before, she took up her busy and often difficult life in Miss Aldersey's school.

It was a lonely post for a girl in her teens, and especially one of so thoughtful and loving a spirit. Her sister's companionship no doubt was precious, and the missionary circle in Ningpo gave her several attached friends. But her heart had never found its mate in the things that mattered most.

And then he came—the young missionary who impressed her from the first as having the same longings after holiness, usefulness, and nearness to God. He was different from everybody else, not more gifted or attractive, though he was bright and pleasing and full of quiet fun, but there was something that made her feel at rest and understood. He seemed to live in such a real world and to have such a real, great God. Though she saw little of him, it was a comfort to know that he was near, and she was startled to find how much she missed him when, after only seven weeks, he went away.

Very real was her joy, therefore, as well as surprise, when from Shanghai he had to turn back again. Perhaps it was this that opened her eyes to the feeling with which she was beginning to regard him. At any rate, she soon knew, and with her sweet, true nature did not try to hide it from her own heart and God. There was no one else to whom she cared to speak about him, for others did not see in him, always, just what she saw. They disliked his wearing Chinese dress and did not approve of his making himself so entirely one with the people. His Chinese dress, how she loved it or what it represented, rather, of his spirit. His poverty and generous giving to the poor, how well she understood, how much she sympathized! Did others think him visionary in his longing to reach the great beyond of untouched need? Why, that was just the burden on her heart, the life she too would live, only for a woman it seemed if anything more impossible. So she prayed much about her friend, though to him she showed but little. For the love of her life had come to her, and nobody knew but God.

And then he went again, went in the interests of others, and she did not know it cost him anything to leave her. But all the while he was away she prayed to be more like him, more worthy of his love, if that should ever be hers.

Month after month went by and then at last a letter! Sudden as was the joy, the great and wonderful joy, it was no surprise, only a quiet outshining of what had long shone within. So she was not mistaken after all. They *were* for one another, two whom God has chosen to walk together before Him.

When she could break away from her first glad thanksgiving, she went to find her sister who was most sympathetic. The next thing was to tell Miss Aldersey, then living on the north side of the city with her former ward and fellow worker, Mrs. Russell. Eagerly the sisters told their tidings, hoping she would approve this engagement as she had Burella's. But great was the indignation with which she heard the story.

"Mr. Taylor! That young, poor, unconnected nobody. How dare he presume to think of such a thing? Of course the proposal must be refused at once, and that finally."

In vain Maria tried to explain how much he was to her. That only made matters worse. She must be saved without delay from such folly. And her kind friend proceeded, with the best intentions, to take the matter entirely into her own hands. The result was a letter written almost at Miss Aldersey's dictation, not only closing the whole affair but requesting most decidedly that it might never be reopened.

Bewildered and heartbroken, the poor girl had no choice. She was too young and inexperienced, and far too shy in such matters, to withstand the decision of Miss Aldersey, strongly reinforced by the friends with whom she was staying. Stung to the quick with grief and shame, she could only leave it in the hands of her heavenly Father. He knew; He understood. And in the long, lonely days that followed, when even her sister was won over to Miss Aldersey's position, she took refuge in the certainty that nothing, *nothing*, was too hard for the Lord. "If He has to slay my Isaac," she assured herself again and again, "I know He can restore."

To Hudson Taylor in his sorrow, sympathizing hearts were open, but for her there were none. And she did not know that he would ever cross her path again. After such a refusal, if he really cared, he would surely stay away from Ningpo, especially in view of the recommencement of work at Swatow which she knew he longed to share. Nothing was more probable now than that he would return to his friend Mr. Burns. And this, no doubt, he would have done had he been acting on impulse and not holding steadfastly to the guidance of God. As it was, though he knew nothing of her feelings and had little if any hope of a more favorable issue, he was winning in the depths of his sorrow just the blessing it was meant to bring. He wrote of this situation to his sister:

> We have need of patience, and our faithful God brings us into experiences which, improved by His blessing, may cultivate in us this grace. Though we seem to be tried at times almost beyond endurance, we never find Him unable or unwilling to help and sustain us; and were our hearts *entirely* submissive to His will, desiring it and it only to be done, how much fewer and lighter would our afflictions seem.

> I have been in much sorrow of late, but the principal cause I find to be want of willing submission to, and trustful repose in, God, my Strength. Oh, to desire His will to be done with my *whole* heart...to seek His glory with a single eye! Oh, to realize more of the fullness of our precious Jesus...to live more in the light of His countenance, to be satisfied with what He bestows...ever looking to Him, following in His footsteps and awaiting His glorious coming! Why do we love Him so little? It is not that He is not lovely. "Fairer than the children of men" (Ps. 45:2)! It is not that He does not love us...that was forever proved on Calvary. Oh, to be sick out of love for Jesus, to be daily, hourly longing, hungering, thirsting for His presence!...May you find your love to Him ever increasing, and His likeness in you be apparent to all. Continue to pray for me...that God will supply all my need, Jesus be all my delight, His service all my desire, rest with Him all my hope.

It is perhaps not surprising that one book in the Bible that had never meant much to him before should have opened up at this time in undreamed-of beauty. His deep understanding of the Song of Solomon seems to have begun in these days when the love that welled up so irresistibly within him could only be given to God. Never had he understood before what the Lord can be to His people and what He longs to find in His people toward Himself. It was a wonderful discovery and one that only grew with all the glad fruition that lay beyond this pain. To those who knew Hudson Taylor best in later years, nothing was more characteristic than his love for the Song of Solomon and the way in which it expressed his personal relationship to the Lord.

Winter was over, summer was drawing on, and with the first hot days came a change in the conditions that had detained Hudson Taylor and his colleagues in Shanghai. For one thing, the famine refugees began to disappear. Spring harvests drew them back to country villages all over the plain, and for the few who could not leave, a local missionary undertook to care.

Then, a lull in the war with England made aggressive work in Ningpo and the neighborhood more possible, and though the house Mr. and Mrs. Jones had previously occupied was no longer available, other and even better premises were. The retirement of one of the senior workers, for health reasons, had left one of the C.M.S. buildings vacant, and this Mr. Jones was able to rent for a moderate sum. Dr. Parker also was glad to hand over the entire premises on Bridge Street, part of which Hudson Taylor had formerly occupied. Thus, without any effort on their part, they were provided with a dwelling house and a street chapel in the busiest parts of the city.

With growing experience, Hudson Taylor was increasingly drawn, it should be said, to the more settled forms of missionary work. The war with England made it out of the question to attempt to live at any distance from the treaty ports. Itinerations were still possible, but speaking generally, the interior was more inaccessible than ever. Believing, however, that the time was near for a change in this respect, Mr. Taylor and his colleague realized the importance of laboring in some one, settled spot until a native church could be raised up that should afford them, by the blessing of God, pastors and evangelists for the wider opportunity of coming days.

With this hope in view, therefore, they turned their faces to Ningpo again, but not before they had taken a step of great importance in its bearing on the future. For it was in the month of May, three years and three months after his arrival in China, that Hudson Taylor felt the time had come to resign his connection with the Chinese Evangelization Society. Not all the difficulties under which he had labored would have led him to this step. He loved the secretaries and many members of the committee known to him personally, and valued their sympathy and prayers. But the society, as we have seen, took a very different position from his own in the matter of debt, a position in which he felt he could no longer participate. In recalling the circumstances he wrote:

> Personally, I had always avoided debt, and kept within my salary, though at times only by very careful economy. Now there was no difficulty in doing this, for my income was larger, and the country being in a more peaceful state, things were not so dear. But the society itself was in debt. The quarterly bills which I and others were instructed to draw were often met with borrowed money, and a correspondence commenced which terminated in the following year by my resigning from conscientious motives.
>
> To me it seemed that the teaching of God's Word was unmistakably clear: "Owe no man any thing" (Rom. 13:8). To borrow money implied, to my mind, a contradiction of Scripture—a confession that God had withheld some good thing and a determination to get for ourselves what He had

not given. Could that which was wrong for one Christian to do be right for an association of Christians? Or could any amount of precedents make a wrong course justifiable? If the Word taught me anything, it taught me to have no connection with debt. I could not think that God was poor, that He was short of resources, or unwilling to supply any want of whatever work was really His. It seemed to me that if there were lack of funds to carry on work, then to that degree, in that special development, or at that time, it could not be the work of God. To satisfy my conscience I was therefore compelled to resign my connection with the society....It was a great satisfaction to me that my friend and colleague, Mr. Jones...was led to take the same step, and we were both profoundly thankful that the separation took place without the least breach of friendly feeling on either side. Indeed, we had the joy of knowing that the step we took commended itself to several members of the committee, although the society as a whole could not come to our position. Depending on God alone for supplies, we were enabled to continue a measure of connection with our former supporters, sending home journals, etc., for publication as before, so long as the society continued to exist.

The step we had taken was not a little trying to faith. I was not at all sure what God would have me do, or whether He would so meet my need as to enable me to continue working as before....I was willing to give up all my time to the service of evangelization among the heathen if, by any means, He would supply the smallest amount on which I could live, and if He were not pleased to do this, I was prepared to undertake whatever work might be necessary to support myself, giving all the time that could be spared from such a calling to more distinctly missionary efforts.

But God blessed and prospered me, and how glad and thankful I felt when the separation was really effected! I could look right up into my Father's face with a satisfied heart, ready by His grace to do the next thing as He might teach me, and feeling very sure of His loving care.

And how blessedly He did lead me I can never, never tell. It was like a continuation of some of my earlier experiences at home. My faith was not untried; it often, often failed, and I was so sorry and ashamed of the failure to trust such a Father. But oh! I was learning to know Him. I would not even then have missed the trial. He became so near, so real, so intimate. The occasional difficulty about funds never came from an insufficient supply for personal needs, but in consequence of ministering to the wants of scores of the hungry and dying around us. And trials far more searching in other ways quite eclipsed these difficulties and, being deeper, brought forth in consequence richer fruits. How glad one is now not only to know, with dear Miss Havergal, that

> They who trust Him wholly
>   Find Him wholly true,

but also that when we fail to trust fully, He still remains unchangingly faithful. He is wholly true whether we trust or not. "If we believe not, yet he abideth faithful: he cannot deny himself" (2 Tim. 2:13). But oh, how we dishonor our Lord whenever we fail to trust Him, and what peace, blessing, and triumph we lose in thus sinning against the Faithful One! May we never again presume in anything to doubt Him.

What the more searching trials were that brought forth richer blessing it is not difficult at this point to divine. Twice daily in his walks to and from Bridge Street, Hudson Taylor had to pass very near Miss Aldersey's school. Carried on now by Mrs. Bausum and her young relatives, it was still the home of the being dearest to him on earth. He had seen her again since returning to Ningpo in June, but a barrier had been raised between them that was hard to pass. Kind and gentle as she still was, he could not forget that she had charged him never again to trouble her upon a certain subject, and Miss Aldersey had so spoken her mind to the friends with whom he lived that the position was doubly trying.

Soon after their return from Shanghai, Mrs. Jones had invited Miss Dyer to go out visiting with her as before. There was no one else to whom Mrs. Jones could look for help, and the need was very pressing. Besides, it was the best, the only way in which the young people could see more of each other. To the girl herself she said nothing, nor did Maria allude to the matter of which their hearts were full. But Miss Aldersey knew no such reticence, and seeking Mrs. Jones after the ladies' prayer meeting, in another part of the city, poured out the vials of her wrath. She had good reason, she felt, to be indignant. Miss Dyer belonged to a different social circle from that of Mr. Taylor and had a small but reliable income of her own. She was educated, gifted, attractive, and had no lack of suitors far more eligible in Miss Aldersey's eyes. It was unpardonable that this person should presume upon her youth and inexperience, and still more so that he should return to Ningpo after it had been made plain that he was not wanted.

In the course of such a conversation many things come out, and before it ended Mrs. Jones could see pretty clearly how the land lay. Miss Aldersey's object was to obtain from her a promise that she would do nothing to forward Mr. Taylor's suit and that the latter would never see or speak to Miss Dyer in their house. While not committing herself as far as this, Mrs. Jones felt it desirable to state that she would refrain from throwing the young people together and that Mr. Taylor would not take advantage of Miss Dyer's visits to attempt to see her alone. At the same time, she earnestly put before Miss Aldersey the other side of the matter, trying to make her feel how serious a thing it is to tamper with such affections. But the older lady would hear no good of Hudson Taylor, and deeply pained by her criticisms, Mrs. Jones came away.

After this, of course, Hudson Taylor felt himself bound by Mrs. Jones's promise. He could not write to Miss Dyer or seek an interview in the house of his friends, and yet as the days went by he found it impossible to let matters drift indefinitely. Having learned that Miss Aldersey was not related to the Dyers and was not even their guardian, he determined to call on the sisters both together and ask whether he might write to their uncle in London for permission to cultivate a closer acquaintance. More than this he dared not venture at present, nor was it necessary after his Shanghai letter.

* * * * *

Hudson Taylor was wonderfully sustained. The matter had been left entirely in the hands of

God, and though he had no means of communicating with the one he loved, it was not difficult for the Lord to bring them together. He who can use ravens, if need be, or angels to do His bidding, was answering His children's prayers, and on this occasion He seems to have employed a waterspout!

It was a sultry afternoon in July when, in regular rotation, the ladies' prayer meeting came to be hosted by Mrs. Jones. The usual number gathered, representing all the societies, but as the following episode proves, it was easier to come to the meeting that day than to get away. For with scarcely any warning a waterspout, sweeping up the tidal river, broke over Ningpo in a perfect deluge, followed by torrents of rain. Mr. Jones and Mr. Taylor were over at Bridge Street as usual, and on account of the flooded streets were late in reaching home. Most of the ladies had left before they returned, but a servant from the school was there who said that Mrs. Bausum and Miss Maria Dyer were still waiting for sedan chairs.

"Go into my study," said Mr. Jones to his companion, "and I will see if an interview can be arranged."

It was not long before he returned saying that the ladies were alone with Mrs. Jones and that they would be glad of a little conversation.

Hardly knowing what he did, Hudson Taylor went upstairs and found himself in the presence of the one being he supremely loved. True, others were there too, but he hardly saw them, hardly saw anything but her face, as he told much more than he would have ever thought possible in public. He had only meant to ask if he might write to her guardian for permission, but now it all came out; he could not help it! And she? Well, there was no one present but friends who loved them and understood, and it might be so long before they could meet again! Yes, she consented, and did much more than that. With her true woman's heart she relieved all his fears, as far as they could be relieved by knowing that he was just as dear to her as she to him. And if the others heard, were there not angels too? And presently Hudson Taylor relieved the situation by saying: "Let us take it all to the Lord in prayer."

So the letter was written upon which so much depended, and they had to look forward to four long months of prayer and patience before the answer could be received. Under the circumstances, they did not feel free to see one another or even communicate in writing, for they had, as far as possible, to mitigate Miss Aldersey's displeasure. Maria of course informed her that Mr. Taylor had written to her uncle asking permission for a definite engagement. That matters should have come to such a pass in spite of all her precautions seemed incredible to the older lady. But they should proceed no further. She would at once communicate with Mr. Tarn herself, and he of course would see the impropriety of the request. So with the keenest desire for her young friend's happiness, she set to work to bring the distant relatives to her own point of view.

This, of course, made it very hard for the lovers, especially as Miss Aldersey observed no reticence on the subject. Impressions she had gained about Hudson Taylor, happily as unfounded as they were unfavorable, were soon made known to the rest of the community. Her object was to alienate the affections of Miss Dyer from one whom she considered unworthy of her, and she did not hesitate to encourage the attentions of other suitors with the same end in view. The Chinese dress worn by Hudson Taylor was one strong point against him and seemingly awakened not aversion only but contempt. His position also as an independent worker, upon the uncertain basis of faith, was severely criticized, and he was represented as "called by no one, connected with no one, and recognized by no one as a minister of the Gospel." Had this been all it would have been bad enough, but other insinuations followed. He was "fanatical, undependable, diseased in body and mind," and in a word, "totally worthless!" And the two most concerned could not tell how far all this would influence Mr. Tarn in London, to whom Miss Aldersey had written in a similar strain.

As month after month went by and these strange misrepresentations came to be believed in certain sections of the community, Hudson Taylor had to learn in a new way what it was to take refuge in God. It was a fiery furnace seven times heated, for he knew how his loved one must be suffering, and he could not explain anything or reassure her even of his devotion. And what was to be the outcome? What if her guardian in London were influenced by Miss Aldersey's statements? What if he refused his consent to the marriage? If there was one thing of which Hudson Taylor had no doubt, it was that the blessing of God rested upon obedience to parents or those in parental authority. Nothing would have induced him to act contrary to a command from his own parents, nor could he encourage the one he loved to disregard her guardian's wishes. Years after, when experience had confirmed these convictions, he wrote upon this important subject:

> I have never known disobedience to the definite command of a parent, even if that parent were mistaken [in regard to a call to missionary work], that was not followed by retribution. Conquer through the Lord. He can open any door. The responsibility is with the parent in such a case, and it is a great one. When son or daughter can say in all sincerity, "I am waiting for you, Lord, to open the door," the matter is in His hands, and He will take it up.

But at this time it was theory more than experience, his conviction of what must be rather than his knowledge of what was, and the test was all the more severe.

No wonder he needed to be very still in those days before the Lord. Never before had he had to walk so carefully, or so felt his helplessness apart from sustaining grace. This can be seen in a letter to his sister:

> It is not sufficient to have the every road pointed out merely, to be prevented from straying to the right hand or to the left, though this is no little blessing....We need Him to direct our *steps*...step after step. Nay more, we need to pass through this wilderness *leaning*, always leaning on our Beloved. May we in reality do this, and *all* will be well.

Meanwhile, in another part of the city, another lonely, suffering heart was learning the same lessons. Deeply she too felt the sacredness of parental authority and that the divine blessing could not rest upon a step taken in defiance of its control. She would have waited, if need be, for years had her guardian disapproved the marriage, and as the slow months went by, times of desolation could not but come over her in view of all he was likely to hear.

She was visiting Mr. and Mrs. Gough of the C.M.S. on one such occasion, who entertained a warm regard for Hudson Taylor. He may have been spoken of with appreciation; at any rate, the longing for him that was always there filled and overflowed her heart. It was a summer evening, and going to her room alone, the poor child knelt long in silent grief. But her Bible was at hand, and as she turned its pages the precious words shone out: "Trust in him at all times; ye people, pour out your heart before him: God is a refuge for us" (Ps. 62:8). And that just met her need.

"I marked it at the time," she wrote to her loved one seven years later, "and the light-colored ink still remains to remind me of that night."

"My soul, wait thou only upon God; for my expectation is from him" (Ps. 62:5). He only, He alone; always El Shaddai—"The God that is Enough."

Joy Comes in the Morning

Passing the open door of the mission house one evening soon after Mr. Jones and his colleague had settled there, a businessman in the city, Mr. Nyi, observed that something was going on. A big bell was ringing, and a number of people were passing in as if for a meeting. Hearing that it was a "Jesus Hall," or place where foreign teachers discoursed upon religious matters, he too turned in, for, as a devout Buddhist, there was nothing about which he felt more concern than the pains and penalties due to sin, and the transmigration of the soul on its long journey he knew not where.

A young foreigner in Chinese dress was preaching from his Sacred Classics, and this was the passage he read:

> *As Moses lifted up the serpent in the wilderness, even so must the Son of man be lifted up: that whosoever believeth in him should not perish, but have eternal life. For God so loved the world, that he gave his only begotten Son, that whosoever believeth in him should not perish, but have everlasting life. For God sent not his Son into the world to condemn the world; but that the world through him might be saved. (John 3:14–17)*

It is scarcely possible to imagine, much less describe, the effect upon such a man of such a message, heard for the first time. To say that Nyi was interested scarcely begins to express all that went on in his mind. For he was a seeker after truth, one of the leaders of a reformed sect of Buddhists devoted to religious observances. The story of the brazen serpent in the wilderness, illustrating the divine remedy for sin and all its deadly consequences; the facts of the life, death, and resurrection of the Lord Jesus; and the bearing of all this upon his own need, brought home to him the power of the Holy Spirit—well, it is the miracle of the ages, and thank God we see it still! "I, if I be lifted up...will draw all men unto me" (John 12:32).

Nyi came into the hall that evening one of the vast, the incredibly vast multitude "who through fear of death were all their lifetime subject to bondage" (Heb. 2:15), and as he sat there listening, hope dawned in his heart, old things forever passed away, and he was conscious of the sunrise that makes all things new.

But the meeting was drawing to a close; the "foreign teacher" had ceased speaking. Looking round upon the audience with the instinct of one accustomed to leading in such matters, Nyi rose in his place and said with simple directness:

"I have long sought the Truth, as did my father before me, but without finding it. I have traveled far and near but have never searched it out. In Confucianism, Buddhism, Taoism, I have found no rest, but I do find rest in what we have heard tonight. Henceforward I am a believer in Jesus."

The effect of this declaration was profound, for Nyi was well-known and respected. But no one present was more moved than the young missionary to whom he especially addressed himself. Many interviews followed, and Hudson Taylor experienced the joy no words can express as he saw the Lord working with him and claiming this soul for His own.

Shortly after his conversion, a meeting was held of the society over which Mr. Nyi had formerly presided, and though he had resigned from its membership, he obtained permission to be present and to explain the reasons for his change of faith. Mr. Taylor, who had the pleasure of accompanying him, was deeply impressed by the clearness and power with which he set forth the Gospel. One of his former coreligionists was led to Christ through his instrumentality, and with Nyi himself, became of great value to the church. Nyi, as a dealer in cotton, frequently had time at his disposal, which he now devoted to helping his missionary friends. With Mr. Jones he went out almost daily, taking no payment for his services, and everywhere winning an entrance for the message he was so keen to bring.

He it was who, talking with Mr. Taylor, unexpectedly raised a question, the pain of which was not easily forgotten.

"How long have you had the Glad Tidings in England?" he asked all unsuspectingly.

The young missionary was ashamed to tell him and vaguely replied that it was several hundreds of years.

"What," exclaimed Nyi in astonishment, "several hundreds of years! Is it possible that you have known about Jesus so long, and only now have come to tell us?"

"My father sought the truth for more than twenty years," he continued sadly, "and died without finding it. *Oh, why did you not come sooner?"*

* * * * *

Turning back to the concern most deeply on Hudson Taylor's heart, the start to his relationship with Miss Dyer was not becoming any easier. For as time went on, Miss Aldersey seemed, if anything, to have increased her opposition to Maria's engagement. Not content with having written fully to Mr. Tarn in London, she continued to bring accusations of a serious nature against Hudson Taylor. It came to such a pass at length that Maria herself almost wondered that her confidence did not waver in the one of whom she knew so little. But their love was too deep, too God-given.

It was rare that the young people could meet even in public at this time, for the school in which the Misses Dyer were teaching had been moved across the river to the compound of the Presbyterian

Mission. Living with Mrs. Bausum in the brown, gable-roofed house adjoining the school building, they were near neighbors of the Ways, whose love and admiration for Hudson Taylor must have been a comfort to the younger sister. He would be frequently spoken of with gratitude as one who had risked his life in ministering to their brother.

For the reason that he might avoid causes of offense, he refrained from visiting Mr. and Mrs. Way on the Presbyterian compound and waited as patiently as he might without communication of any kind with the one who was in all his thoughts, until the letter should arrive on which so much depended.

Toward the end of November the long-looked-for letters came—and were favorable! After careful inquiry in London, Mr. Tarn had satisfied himself that Hudson Taylor was a young missionary of unusual promise. The secretaries of the Chinese Evangelization Society had nothing but good to say of him, and from other sources also he had the highest references. Taking therefore any disquieting rumors he may have heard for no more than they were worth, he cordially consented to his niece's engagement, requesting only that the marriage should be delayed until she came of age. And that would be in little more than two months' time!

Oh, China, China! How the said young missionary longed, after that, to see what someone else would say, and how distractingly difficult it was to arrange an interview! To cross the river forthwith and present himself at Mrs. Bausum's would have outraged all proprieties. Anywhere on the compound where she lived, indeed, they could not have met under the circumstances, and his own home was still more out of the question. But news of this sort flies fast, and in some way Mrs. Knowlton of the American Baptist Mission heard of the situation. She was in favor of the engagement and lived in a quiet place outside the city wall and close to the river. She would send a note to the school. Miss Dyer could come to see her at any time, and if somebody else were there—well, such things will happen, even in China!

So it was in Mrs. Knowlton's drawing room he waited while the messenger went slowly, slowly across the river and seemed as if he never would return. Let us hope that the windows overlooked the ferry and that Hudson Taylor did not have to keep up the form of conversation. At last, at last! The slender figure, quick step, bright young voice in the passage—then the door opened, and for the first time they were together alone.

Fifty years later the joy of that moment had not left him: "We sat side by side on the sofa," he said, "her hand clasped in mine. It never cooled—my love for her. It has not cooled now."

Perfect in One

After this they were openly engaged and could meet from time to time in the company of friends; how those happy winter days made up for all that had gone before! Of these days, Hudson Taylor wrote:

> I never felt in better health or spirits in my life. To God who alone doeth wondrous things, who raiseth up those that are bowed down and has caused every effort to injure me to work only for good...to Him be praise and glory.

The engagement was not to be a long one, for in January 1858 Miss Dyer would be twenty-one years of age and free to follow the dictates of her heart. So the closing weeks of the year were full of joyous anticipation.

It is good to know that in a life so serious as regards its outward surroundings, there were still times when they could be young and gay. One refreshing glimpse into this side of things is afforded by an intimate friend of those days:

> To those who only knew Mr. Taylor in later life it may be a surprise to learn that when he "fell in love" it was a headlong plunge and by no means a slight or evanescent passion. And his fiancée, with her strong, emotional nature, was in this respect not unlike him.
>
> One evening the young people were seated round a table playing a game that required their hands to be hidden beneath it. To his surprise, Mr. Nevius received an unexpected squeeze. Guessing at once that it was a case of mistaken identity, and enjoying the situation, he returned the pressure with interest. In a moment Maria, his next neighbor, discovered her mistake, but when she would have withdrawn her hand it was held fast by its captor's strong fingers. Not until flushed cheeks and almost tearful eyes warned him that the joke had gone far enough did he release her. Those were days when to laugh was easy, and not such very funny things were sufficient to evoke much merriment.

The preparations for the wedding went on, outwardly with the kind help of many friends, and inwardly with the blessing of God. Some of the lessons he was learning at this time may be gathered from the last letters Hudson Taylor penned before the happy event:

> I can scarcely realize, dear Mother, what has happened, that after all the agony and suspense we have suffered we are not only at liberty to meet and be much with each other, but that within a few days, we are to be married! God *has* been good to us. He has indeed answered our prayer and taken our part against the mighty. Oh, may we walk more closely with Him and serve Him more faithfully. I wish you knew my Precious One. She is such a treasure! She is all that I desire.

Yet the first place in his heart was truly given to Him "whose love exceeds all human affection," as he wrote in another letter, "and who can fill the soul with gladness to which all other joy is unworthy to be compared."

> Now I know what it is to have my name written on His heart...and why He never ceases to intercede for me...His love is so great that He *cannot.* It is overwhelming, is it not? Such depths of love, and for me!

The wedding day, January 20, 1858, was perfect, setting a crown on all that had gone before. Very sweet and fair she looked in more than Hudson Taylor's eyes that day in her simple gray silk gown and wedding veil. He was wearing ordinary Chinese dress, and to some the contrast between them must have seemed remarkable. But to those who could see below the surface, the noteworthy thing about this wedding was the way in which bride and bridegroom were already "perfect in one" (John 17:23). Of his union, Hudson Taylor wrote:

> Oh, to be married to the one you *do* love, and love most tenderly and devotedly...that is bliss

beyond the power of words to express or imagination conceive! There is no disappointment *there.* And every day as it shows more of the mind of your Beloved—when you have such a treasure as mine—makes you only more proud, more happy, more humbly thankful to the Giver of all good for this best of earthly gifts.

Our Joy and Crown of Rejoicing

A new home, especially if it is to receive a bride, is just as interesting in China as elsewhere, and Hudson Taylor found himself quite popular on Bridge Street when in the early spring he remodeled the barn-like attic in which he had formerly lived alone. Not only was he married, a change that in itself entitled him to consideration, but he had married the well-known Miss Dyer, who for five years had lived and worked in that part of the city. In addition to being a bride, she was the trusted friend of many a woman and girl throughout the neighborhood, so that visitors were numerous when the young couple came into residence.

It was there over the chapel, between the narrow street in front and the canal behind, in the little rooms that were to form the cradle of the China Inland Mission and are now its oldest home, that the young missionaries began their settled work. Downstairs everything remained as before, but a few small chambers were fashioned above with inexpensive partitions. Chinese furniture was easily to be had, and housekeeping was a simple matter to one so familiar with the language and ways of the people.

Then it was that Hudson Taylor discovered fresh meaning in the inspired Word, "Whoso findeth a wife findeth a good thing, and obtaineth favour of the LORD" (Prov. 18:22). Missionary life was no longer a one-sided bachelor affair but rounded out and complete in all its relations. He began to feel in touch with the people in a new way and was able to understand and serve them better at every point. And the gentle presence that made the sunshine of his home was loved and welcomed by the neighbors all about them. Quite freely she went in and out of their courtyards, seeking pupils for her little school, chatting with the children, delighting the women with her understanding of their everyday affairs, and cheering the old people with ready sympathy. There was something about her bright face and pleasant ways that made them want to know the secret of the peace she possessed, and many came to the meetings in the mission house to hear more from her lips of the Savior who made her life so different from their own. Thus a light began to shine from the new home on Bridge Street that brightened many a heart in that great heathen city, and both husband and wife discovered how much marriage may help the missionary in his work when it is not only in the Lord, but "of him, and through him, and to him" (Rom. 11:36).

Special faith and devotion were needed to enable the missionaries to do so much themselves. And in their insufficiency, God worked, bringing them in contact with hearts ready to receive the Gospel, and giving them as their children in the faith men and women who should become soul-winners and in the fullest sense their "joy, or crown of rejoicing" (1 Thess. 2:19).

One of the first of these after their marriage was the basket maker, Fang Neng-kuei. Introduced at Bridge Street by his friend Mr. Nyi, there was something about the Christians that greatly attracted him. Long had he been seeking peace of heart, but neither in the ceremonies of Buddhism nor the philosophy of Confucius had he found any help. He had even attended for a time the services of the Roman Catholics, but not until he joined the little circle at Bridge Street did he begin to understand the rest of faith. Then nothing would satisfy him but to be there every night as soon as his work permitted, following eagerly all that was said and done.

It was about this time that Mr. Taylor, finding his audiences diminishing, thought of a plan to arouse fresh interest. He had at hand a set of colored pictures illustrating the Gospel stories and put up a notice to the effect that these would be on view at the evening services, when they would also be fully explained. The result was all he had hoped, for the Chinese dearly love pictures and stories.

One night the subject was the Prodigal Son, and the young missionary preached with more than ordinary freedom. With the crowded room before him and eager faces peering in from the street, one can well imagine how he would speak on the experiences of the wanderer and all the father's love. The thought of God as such a Father was strangely new to most of his hearers, and when at the close Mr. Taylor invited any who wished to hear more to stay behind for conversation, almost the whole audience remained. Among the most interested were Neng-kuei and two friends whom he had brought to the meeting. Others drifted out by degrees, but these three stayed on and seemed much in earnest when they said they wished to become followers of Jesus.

Mr. Taylor had recently started a night school in which inquirers might learn to read the New Testament by means of roman letters. This exactly suited Neng-kuei and his friends, and for some time they were regular in their attendance. Then it began to be rumored abroad that the basket makers were becoming Christians, and they had a good deal of persecution to put up with. This of course tested the reality of their faith, and to the sorrow of the missionaries, first one and then another ceased to come. Would Neng-kuei also drift away? But in his case the work proved deep and real. Persecution only brought him out more boldly as a "good soldier of Jesus Christ" (2 Tim. 2:3), and ridicule taught him to defend his newfound faith in such a way that he became a most effective preacher of the Gospel.

But Neng-kuei's earnestness in making known the truth as it is in Jesus was due to something deeper than external opposition. He was a man called of God to a special service and placed by divine providence in a special school. In spite of more than one fall like Peter's, whom he closely resembled in character, Neng-kuei was to be widely used in winning souls to Christ. Wherever he went in later years, he was enabled to raise up little churches that continued to thrive and grow under the care of others. Neng-kuei was not one who could long minister to them himself, but he realized this and was always ready to pass on to new fields when his special work was done. And the zeal and devotion that characterized him must be attributed, under God, to the influences by which his Christian life was formed and nurtured.

Few though they were in number, Hudson Taylor gave himself to the young converts at this time as if the evangelization of China depended upon their future efforts. In addition to all his other work, he devoted several hours daily to their instruction. Mr. Jones was the recognized pastor of the church, and Sunday services were held in his house. The older Christians, several of whom were already baptized, were just as eager to attend the Bridge Street classes as were the most recent inquirers.

First came the public meeting every evening, when the little hall would be filled with more or less regular attendants, and when that was over and outsiders had for the most part withdrawn, three periods were given to regular and carefully considered study.

To begin with, a lesson was taken from the Old Testament, the young missionary delighting to dwell upon the spiritual meaning of its matchless stories; then a chapter was read from some important book, frequently *Pilgrim's Progress;* and finally a passage from the New Testament was talked over, the version used being the romanized colloquial.

Nor was this all. Sunday, with its special meetings, morning, afternoon, and evening, was made the very most of for the inner circle. It cost the Christians a great deal to leave their regular employment, sacrificing the practical possibilities of one day in seven. It was perhaps the hardest thing their Christian faith required of them. Yet the command was plain, "Remember the sabbath day, to keep it holy" (Exod. 20:8), and Mr. Taylor and his fellow missionaries were convinced that no strong, self-propagating church could be built on any other basis. So they constantly enjoined upon the native Christians, by teaching and example, the requirements of Scripture in this connection.

And as due compensation, if it may be so expressed, they felt it incumbent upon them to make the sacrifice worthwhile, as far as in their power lay, by filling the hours thus given to God with profitable occupation. In addition, therefore, to the regular meetings, they had two periods of teaching after the fashion of the American Sunday school, when old and young—Christians, inquirers, patients, schoolchildren, and servants—were divided into classes and taught in a helpful, personal way. This made Sunday a heavy day for the missionaries, of whom there were only four, but if it cost some toil and weariness they were the better able to appreciate the sacrifices made by the converts.

Some had to walk long distances and go without food for the greater part of the day, and others had to face persecution and financial loss. Nengkuei, for example, found that it cost him a full third of his weekly wages to attend the meetings on Sunday. He was a skilled workman, and his master was quite willing that he should get through all there was to be done in six days, provided he went without pay on the seventh. If it gave him satisfaction to waste four days in every month he was at liberty to do so, only he must of course provide his food on those occasions and draw wages only for the time in which work was done. It was a clever arrangement as far as the master was concerned, but one that took a heavy toll on the poor basket maker. Two pence a day and his food had been little enough before, but now, out of only twelve pence a week (instead of fourteen), he had to spend two or three on provisions for Sunday, which meant a total lessening of his hard-earned income by a third. But he was willing, quite willing for this, if only he could have the Lord's Day for worship, and there could be no doubt that he was richly repaid in the strength and blessing it brought him all through the week.

Another element of great importance in the training of these young converts was the emphasis placed on reading for themselves the Word of God. This it was that brought out the exceeding value for the uneducated among them of the romanized version of the Ningpo New Testament. For the local dialect differed greatly from the written language, and hence the more literary versions were unintelligible to the majority. But there was no one who could not understand the romanized version. It was a very fair translation, direct from the original language, into the vernacular in everyday use, and as such had a special charm for the women, who could soon read it easily and found that what they read was understood by others.

Mrs. Taylor was fully one with her husband as regards the importance of teaching every inquirer to read, including women and children, and she gave a good deal of time to preparing and even printing on her own printing press suitable literature in the romanized colloquial. She found that by the use of this system a child of ordinary intelligence could read the New Testament in a month. Older people with less time at their disposal might take longer, but even for busy women it was no difficult task. Experience proved that those who accomplished it rarely if ever failed to become Christians.

When people were able to read the New Testament, leading them to faith in the one true God, it was a great encouragement to the missionaries and quickened their zeal for the instruction of all over whom they had any influence. The burden on their hearts increasingly was that of raising up, as workers together with God, a band of native evangelists for the as-yet-unreached interior of China. To go themselves seemed for the time being out of the question, and yet the country was accessible as never before. The Treaty of Tientsin signed during the summer had opened the way at last to all the inland provinces. Foreigners had now the right to travel freely, under the protection of passports, and it only remained to make use of the facilities for which they had prayed so long.

Nothing would have kept Hudson Taylor and his young wife from proceeding at once to the interior. But the claims of that little band of believers could not be set aside because these Christians, Nyi, Neng-kuei, and the rest, were men whom the Lord could use. Poor and unlearned like most of the first disciples, they too were to become "fishers of men" (Matt. 4:19). No less than six or seven, indeed, of the converts gathered about Mr. and Mrs. Taylor that winter were to come to their help in later years as fellow workers in the China Inland Mission. Had it not been for them, the planting of that little seed amid so many difficulties would have been almost impossible, and much of its promise might never have come to fruition.

Already, there were signs that allowed the missionaries to rejoice in the midst of much to try both faith and love. But, even so, they little realized the importance of the influence they were exercising, directly and indirectly. What they were themselves, in the deepest things, this to a large extent their children in the faith became, and there is no better, surer way of passing on spiritual blessing.

A Wealthy Place

It was February 9, 1859, and in a darkened room Hudson Taylor knelt beside the bedside of his dying wife. Only a few weeks had elapsed since the New Year dawned upon their perfect happiness, and now—was she to be taken from him and his life shadowed with irreparable loss? Internal inflammation, the result apparently of chill, had brought her so low that life seemed ebbing fast away, and every remedy the physicians could suggest had proved unavailing.

Elsewhere in the city the united prayer meeting was going on, and the knowledge that others were praying with him upheld the lonely watcher as nothing else could have done. Noting with anguish the hollow temples, sunken eyes, and pinched features, all indicating the near approach of death, Hudson Taylor was indeed shipwrecked upon God. Faith was the only spar he had to cling to, faith in the Will that even then was perfect wisdom, perfect love.

Kneeling there in the silence—how was it that new hope began to possess his heart? A remedy! They had not tried it. He must consult Dr. Parker as quickly as possible. But would she, could she hold out until he came back again?

When he got back from Dr. Parker's with the necessary remedy, he found that, as he wrote, "the desired change had taken place in the absence of this or any other remedy." The Great Physician had been there. His presence had rebuked the approach of death. His touch had once again brought healing.

This experience of what the Lord could and would do for His people in answer to believing prayer was one of the most wonderful Hudson Taylor ever had and strengthened him for many an emergency, including those of the summer near at hand. Never could he forget those days and hours in which it seemed as though the Lord were saying, "Son of man, behold, I take away from thee the desire of thine eyes with a stroke" (Ezek. 24:16). But it was not on his home the sore affliction fell.

Spared thus in the mercy of God the loss of his own loved one, Hudson Taylor felt the more deeply for Dr. Parker when the angel of death visited his home. With scarcely any warning, Mrs. Parker was stricken with dangerous illness and passed away, leaving four little ones motherless. The young missionaries at Bridge Street did what they could to come to the help of their friend, and others were ready with practical sympathy, but the shock proved too much for the bereaved husband. One of the children was seriously ill, and amid the difficulties of his changed position, the doctor began to realize how much his own health was impaired by five years spent in China. He had neither heart nor strength for added burdens and decided before long to take his family home to the care of relatives in Scotland.

But what about the medical mission, outcome of so much prayer and labor? The hospital was full of patients, and the dispensary crowded day by day with a constant stream of people, all of whom needed help. No other doctor was free to take his place, and yet to stop the work seemed out of the question with the winter coming on. How would it be, in default of better arrangements, to ask his former colleague, Hudson Taylor, to continue the dispensary at any rate? He was quite competent for this, and with the hospital closed he would not have much financial responsibility.

The suggestion, it need hardly be said, came as a great surprise to Mr. and Mrs. Taylor and sent them to their knees in earnest prayer. All they wanted was to know the Lord's will in the matter, and as they waited upon Him for guidance it was clearly given, but in a direction they little anticipated.

Yes, the dispensary must be kept open, and more than that, the hospital must not be closed. The Lord had given them helpers just suited for such an emergency: a band of native Christians who would rally round them and make the most of the opportunities which the hospital especially afforded. And as to funds, or lack of funds—for Dr. Parker had very little to leave—the work was not theirs but the Lord's. To close it on account of the small balance in hand would practically mean that prayer had lost its power, and if so they might as well retire from the field. No, for the good of the native Christians, the strengthening of their own faith, and the comfort and blessing of many, they must go forward, and above all for the glory of God. Of this, Hudson Taylor wrote:

> After waiting upon the Lord for guidance, I felt constrained to undertake not only the dispensary but the hospital as well, relying solely on the faithfulness of a prayer-hearing God to furnish means for its support. At times there were no fewer than fifty inpatients, besides a large number who daily attended the dispensary. Thirty beds were ordinarily allotted to free patients and their attendants, and about as many more to opium smokers who paid for their board while being cured of the habit. As all the wants

of the sick in the wards were supplied gratuitously, as well as the medical appliances needed for the outpatient department, the daily expenses were considerable. A number of native attendants also were required, involving their support. The funds for the maintenance of all this had hitherto been supplied by the proceeds of the doctor's foreign practice, and with his departure this source of income ceased. But had not God said that whatever we ask in the name of the Lord Jesus shall be done? And are we not told to seek first the kingdom of God—not means to advance it—and that "all these things" (Matt. 6:33) shall be added to us? Such promises were surely sufficient.

Strong therefore in the Lord and in the inward assurance of His call to this enlarged service, Mr. and Mrs. Taylor prepared to move over to Dr. Parker's. The care of the Bridge Street Christians remained in the hands of their beloved colleague, Mr. Jones, who from the first had been pastor of the little church, and cordial indeed was the prayer and sympathy with which all its members endorsed the action of their missionaries.

To Mrs. Taylor, as she thought over it all, it must have seemed very wonderful, this sudden change that brought her husband into a position of usefulness he was so well qualified to fill. They had sought nothing for themselves, but in going about their work they had quietly lived down misunderstandings, leaving their reputation in the hands of God. And now He had led them out into "a wealthy place" (Ps. 66:12), putting them in charge of a work second to none in Ningpo in its importance, and the common meeting ground of all the other missions.

Looking across the river to the Presbyterian compound, Mrs. Taylor could not but recall a conversation of the previous summer, to which she alludes in the following letter:

> You will no doubt be surprised at my speaking of patients in this way, but perhaps still more so when I mention that Dr. Parker is leaving his hospital in dear Hudson's care. A few months ago I was walking with a friend, Mrs. McCartee, in one of the gardens of the Presbyterian Mission, when she said,
>
> "Do you know what I prophesy? That in a few years Dr. Parker will be taking his family home, and that you and Mr. Taylor will come to live in his large house and carry on the work."
>
> I reminded her that Hudson was not a qualified medical man, and said I did not think we should ever live outside of the city. Little could we have imagined that in a few short months Dr. Parker would be on his way home with his motherless children and that we should be in his house and Hudson taking charge of his work.

She herself, far though she was from supposing it, was one of the most important elements in his success at this time. For God works through human means, and but for his wife and Chinese helpers, this winter could never have been what it was in Hudson Taylor's experience and in the annals of the Ningpo hospital. Thoroughly competent to undertake the direction of their enlarged establishment, Mrs. Taylor relieved him of account keeping, correspondence, and all household cares, managing the servants and to a certain extent the staff so admirably that his strength was conserved for the medical and spiritual part of the work. She even found time to do a good deal in the wards herself, especially among the women patients, and spent many an hour caring both for body and soul in the dispensary. Of his wife, Hudson Taylor wrote, "She was accustomed, too, to seek His counsel in all things and would not write a note, pay a call, or make a purchase without raising her heart to God."

In the same way, he too drew upon divine resources. Outwardly he was carrying on a great work; inwardly he was conscious of a great cry to Him without whom it could not be sustained for a moment. Had he been depending upon man for help, he would have waited until the need could be made known before assuming such heavy responsibilities. But it had come about so suddenly that no one at any distance was aware of the position or could be more prepared than he himself.

But the Lord had anticipated it, and already His provision was on the way, as events were happily to prove.

The first step taken by the young missionary upon assuming independent charge of the hospital was to call together the assistants and explain the real state of affairs. Dr. Parker, as he told them, had left funds in hand for the expenses of the current month, but little more. After this provision was used up they must look to the Lord directly for supplies, and it would not be possible to guarantee stated salaries because whatever happened he would not go into debt. Under these circumstances, any who wished to do so were at liberty to seek other employment, though he would be glad of their continued service if they were prepared to trust the simple promises of God.

This condition of things, as Mr. Taylor had expected, led all who were not decided Christians to withdraw and opened the way for other workers. It was a change Dr. Parker had long desired to make, only he had not known how to obtain helpers of a different sort. But Mr. Taylor did, and with a greatly lightened heart he turned to the little circle that at this critical juncture did not fail him. For to the Bridge Street Christians it seemed quite as natural to trust the Lord for temporal as well as for spiritual blessings. Did not the greater include the less? And was He not, as their "teachers" so often reminded them, a *real* Father who never could forget His children's needs? So to the hospital they came, glad not only to strengthen the hands of their missionary friends but to prove afresh both to themselves and all concerned the loving-kindness of God.

Some worked in one way and some in another: some giving freely what time they could spare, and others giving their whole time without promise of wages, though receiving their support. And all took the hospital and its concerns upon their hearts in prayer.

No wonder a new atmosphere began to permeate dispensary and wards! Account for it the patients could not—at any rate at first—but they enjoyed nonetheless the happy, homelike feeling and the zest with which everything was carried on. The days were full of a new interest. For these attendants—Wang the grass cutter and Wang the painter, Nyi, Neng-kuei, and others—seemed to possess the secret of perpetual happiness and had so much to impart! Not only were they kind and considerate in the work of the wards, but all their spare time was given to telling of One who had transformed life for them and who they said was ready to receive all who came to Him for rest.

Then there were books, pictures, and singing. Everything indeed seemed set to song! And the daily meetings in the chapel only made one long for more.

There are few secrets in China, and the financial basis upon which the hospital was now run was not one of them. Soon the patients knew all about it and were watching eagerly for the outcome. This too was something to think and talk about, and as the money left by Dr. Parker was used up and Hudson Taylor's own supplies ran low, many were the conjectures as to what would happen next. Needless to say that Hudson Taylor, alone and with his little band of helpers, was much in prayer at this time. It was perhaps a more open, and in that sense crucial, test than any that had come to him, and he realized that the faith of not a few was at stake, as well as the continuance of the hospital work. But day after day went by without bringing the expected answer.

At length, one morning Kuei-hua the cook appeared with serious news for his master. The very last bag of rice had been opened and was disappearing rapidly.

"Then," replied Hudson Taylor, "the Lord's time for helping us must be close at hand."

And so it proved. For before that bag of rice was finished a letter reached the young missionary that was among the most remarkable he ever received.

It was from Mr. Berger and contained a check for fifty pounds, like others that had come before. Only in this case the letter went on to say that a heavy burden had come upon the writer, the burden of wealth to use for God. Mr. Berger's father had recently passed away, leaving him a considerable increase of fortune. The son did not wish to enlarge his personal expenditure. He had had enough before and was now praying to be guided as to the Lord's purpose to what had taken place. Could his friends in China help him? The bill enclosed was for immediate needs, and would they write fully, after praying over the matter, if there were ways in which they could profitably use more?

Fifty pounds! There it lay on the table, and his far-off friend, knowing nothing about that last bag of rice or the many needs of the hospital, actually asked if he might send them more. No wonder Hudson Taylor was overwhelmed with thankfulness and awe. Suppose he had held back from taking charge of the hospital on account of lack of means, or lack of faith rather? Lack of faith—with such promises and such a God!

There was no Salvation Army in those days, but the praise meeting held in the chapel fairly anticipated it in its songs and shouts of joy. But unlike some Army meetings it had to be a short one, for were there not the patients in the wards? And how they listened—these men and women who had known nothing all their lives but blank, empty heathenism!

"Where is the idol that can do anything like that?" was the question upon many lips and hearts. "Have they ever delivered us in our troubles or answered prayer after this sort?"

Chapter 6

A Time of Rest

Nothing is more contagious than spiritual joy when it is the real thing, and of this there was abundance in the Ningpo hospital the winter that Hudson Taylor took it over. For answers to prayer were many in connection with other than financial needs. There were critical cases of illness in which life was given back when every hope seemed gone, there were operations successfully performed under unfavorable conditions, and patients restored from long and hopeless suffering. And best of all, there were dead souls brought to life in Christ Jesus and slaves of sin set free so that within nine months sixteen patients had already been baptized, and more than thirty others were enrolled as candidates for admission to one or another of the Ningpo churches.

This did not come all at once, it need hardly be said, but only as the result of unremitting prayer and labor. One man from the hospital was desiring baptism by the end of October. In November there were four new candidates for church membership. More than six hundred outpatients were treated before the end of the year, and sixty inpatients had been, for longer or shorter periods, under the influence of the Gospel. A new glow of spiritual life and love pervaded everything. All felt it, and Mr. Taylor was able to write: "Truly the Lord is with us and is blessing us abundantly."

But it all took its toll, this blessed work, upon those whose hearts were in it. "Nothing without the cross" is true above all in spiritual things, and for Hudson Taylor the price that had to be paid was that of health, almost of life itself. Six years in China, six such years, had left their mark, and now, under the strain of day and night work in the hospital, entailing much exposure to wintry weather, strength was failing fast.

But in a sense his work was completed, or the preparation, rather, for which he had been sent to China. "Whosoever will be great among you, shall be your minister: and whosoever of you will be the chiefest, shall be servant of all" (Mark 10:43). "He that is faithful in that which is least is faithful also in much" (Luke 16:10). "Faithful over a few things, I will make thee ruler over many" (Matt. 25:21, 23).

Not that any thought of large developments was in Hudson Taylor's mind as he faced the probability that he must return to England before long. He was conscious only of two things: great and growing opportunities on the one hand and rapidly failing health on the other; so while longing to multiply himself into a hundred missionaries, he was increasingly unequal to the work of one.

It is deeply interesting to notice, at this juncture, the means the Lord was using to bring about purposes of His own in connection with this little Ningpo Mission, of which those most interested in it never dreamed. Poor, uninfluential, and without what would ordinarily be regarded as training or talent for leadership, how unlikely that Hudson Taylor should ever become the founder and director of a worldwide organization embracing missionaries from all evangelical denominations and every Protestant land. Yet this was indeed to be the case, for He who is the great, the only Worker, still delights to use what has been well called "God's five-rank army of weakness."

> *Not many wise after the flesh, not many mighty, not many noble, have part therein: but God hath chosen the foolish things of the world to confound the wise; and God hath chosen the weak things of the world to confound the things which are mighty; and base things of the world, and things which are despised, hath God chosen, yea, and things which are not, to bring to nought things that are: that no flesh should glory in his presence...according as it is written, He that glorieth, let him glory in the Lord.*
>
> *(1 Cor. 1:26 RV margin; 27–29, 31)*

A beginning was to be made even now along the lines of that future development, and how were Hudson Taylor and his colleague, Mr. Jones, to be launched upon it but by a constraining sense of the greatness of the need and their own insufficiency to meet it. Fellow workers they must have to enter doors of opportunity that never before had seemed so open. Had he gone on living quietly at Bridge Street, it might have been long before the young missionary would have been driven to such a step in asking for fellow workers to come and labor in China. There, he and Mr. Jones were able to overtake the work, and with the help of the native Christians might have carried it on for years. But removed suddenly from that position and entrusted with larger, more fruitful labors, the result was very different. Here was something too great for him, and as the Lord wrought with them, confirming His own Word "with signs following"

(Mark 16:20), the outlook and possibilities were overwhelming.

If souls had not been saved in the hospital and the Christians had not developed in usefulness and promise, the situation would still have been other than it was. But with a growing family manifesting no little gift for spiritual ministry, Hudson Taylor was impressed as never before by the need of watchfulness in utilizing the resources of the native church. This it was that brought him to the point of appealing for fellow missionaries. The converts must have supervision; as yet they could not stand alone. The fall, through pride and even dishonesty, of the basket maker, their most devoted worker, had burned this upon his heart. Prayer and loving personal influence alone could restore him and safeguard others, and all needed, as he had learned from experience, the most painstaking instruction in spiritual things.

And besides all this, the care of the hospital was proving too much for his strength. With sixteen members in fellowship and a dozen or more awaiting baptism; with work opening up in the villages round about, and native Christians fitted to undertake it if only they could have supervision; with no difficulty as to funds, for the Lord was abundantly supplying their need, both he and Mr. Jones were so run down that it was with difficulty they could get through present duties. Had any of these elements been lacking, the effect produced might have been less definite, but taken all together, one conclusion only was possible. Help they must have, the help of fellow missionaries willing for their own simple line of things. So the appeal went home that was to result in the coming out, to begin with, of just the workers prayed for, two of whom are still laboring in China as the senior members of the Inland Mission. But there was no thought in Hudson Taylor's mind that he would have to be their leader, indeed there was no immediate thought at all, save that he must seek in one way or another to meet the claims of the ever-growing work.

Into the prepared soil at home a little seed was to fall that would take root and grow all the more surely because the time was so opportune. Hudson Taylor's life, past, present, and to come, was needed in the province of God to foster that little seed. He must be taken home, and that before long. So the trial of failing health continued until it was evident that a voyage to England was the only hope of saving his life.

Closing the hospital with great reluctance, the Hudson Taylors set out for Shanghai toward the end of June. Many arrangements had to be made in Shanghai, and they were thankful for the two weeks that elapsed before they could sail for home. It was providential that they were able to secure passages at all, for the *Jubilee,* bound for London, was the only vessel by which they could have traveled for a long time to come.

It was daybreak on that summer morning, and as the brown waters of the Yangtze were left behind them, how the travelers' hearts went up to God! With what thankfulness they looked back over long years of "goodness and mercy" (Ps. 23:6) in China; with what confidence they looked forward to "goodness and mercy" still through all the untried way.

The voyage, though not prolonged beyond four months, was an unusually trying one, on account of illness and the awful temper of the captain, and the little party had no comfort but in one another. Often they prayed together in Chinese and talked over Ningpo days the way in which the Lord had led them. Often too, they thought of the future and dwelled on the time when with restored health and fellow workers given in answer to prayer they might be returning to China by the blessing of God. But never on quiet nights in the prow, never under the shining stars, never in moments of most earnest prayer or appropriating faith did they imagine what really was to be.

No, they only prayed and trusted, the future veiled from their eyes. All that Hudson Taylor saw was the great need and the unutterable privilege of giving oneself, one's all, to meet it, in fellowship with Christ. Going home, invalided though he was, few if any expecting to see him return, one longing only filled his heart, one prayer: with his remaining strength to do something more for China, whether by life or by death:

> Oh, there is such a boundless sphere of usefulness, but the laborers are few, weak, worn and weary. Oh that the church at home were awake to its duties, its privileges! How many would then come and labor here.

And as they followed faithfully, living out the spirit of their prayers, the reality of their consecration, God in His infinite faithfulness did the rest.

Hidden Years

In the heart of the East End of London, among the toilers of Whitechapel, Hudson Taylor had made his home. Invalided from China in 1860, it had been like a death sentence to be told that he must never think of returning unless he wished to throw his life away. Six and a half years of strenuous work in Shanghai, Ningpo, and elsewhere had taken heavy toll of a constitution none too strong at the outset, and with a delicate wife and child it looked for a time as though he would never see China again.

His one consolation in leaving the converts in Ningpo had been that he could serve them in England. A hymnbook and other simple works in their local dialect were much needed, and above all a more correct translation of the New Testament with marginal references. Immediately on landing, the young missionary had thrown himself into the task of getting the Bible Society and the Religious Tract Society to undertake these publications, and so engrossed was he with meetings, interviews, and correspondence, that almost three weeks elapsed before he could visit his beloved parents in Barnsley.

Then came the question as to where to settle. If he should be detained at home but a year or two, Mr. Taylor was anxious to make the most of the time. No thought of a holiday seems to have entered his mind. Furlough to him simply meant an opportunity for finding fellow laborers and fitting himself and them for future usefulness. His colleagues in Ningpo, Mr. and Mrs. J. Jones, whose work had been the means of much blessing, were no longer equal to the burdens pressing upon them. Even before Mr. Taylor left, five additional helpers had been appealed for, and much prayer was being made in the faith that they would be given. Meanwhile, tidings were none too good from the little mission, as shown in a letter from Hudson Taylor to his parents:

> You know what it is to have a sick child at a distance, and we are feeling separation from children in the Lord who are spiritually sick. But what can we do? We can scarcely go back at once. I know how we are needed, but the object sought in our coming home does not yet seem gained. It is true that our friends (Mr. and Mrs. Jones) are apt to look on the dark side of things, so we must hope for the best, and join our prayers with yours for God to work in the hearts of the dear but feeble lambs of His flock, redeemed with His own precious blood. Oh, yes! He will bear the lambs in His bosom. He loves them more than we do.

Curbing his eagerness to be back in China, Mr. Taylor had decided to complete his medical studies and take his diplomas. Facing the broad thoroughfare of Whitechapel stood his old alma mater, the London Hospital. Its doors were open to him, and turning resolutely from an easier line of things, he brought his wife and children to East London, renting a house on a side street near the hospital, that no time might be lost in going to and from to attend his lectures, etc.

Here, then, began the discipline that was to lengthen out, little as Hudson Taylor expected it, until he was ready for the wider vision that was yet to dawn upon him. Four years were to elapse—quiet, hidden years—in which little apparently was to be accomplished, while God was doing the real, the inner work which was to bear fruit not only in Ningpo but in every part of China.

Well was it that the young missionaries could not foresee all that lay before them. At twenty-nine and twenty-four, long patience is not easy. They were in England truly, but with every thought, every breath, loving China, living for China! In addition to his medical studies, they had undertaken the important task of revising the Ningpo Testament, the Bible Society having agreed to publish a new edition. They were in correspondence also with candidates for the mission, and as health improved their hope brightened that a couple of years might set them free—medical degrees obtained, romanized publications in hand, and the fellow workers given about whom they were waiting upon God. And it was to be four years before the pillar of the cloud moved for them even a little, four years that were to bring them but one missionary, and in which, though Mr. Taylor's medical studies were completed, the revision was to prove a task that grew upon their hands. Yet it was right, all right, and the one way to answer their deepest prayers.

Of these hidden years of work and waiting little would have been known in detail but for the preservation of a number of brief journals whose very existence was unsuspected. Providentially brought to light while these pages were being written, they fill a gap until this time passed over in silence. Here they lie upon the table, twelve thin paper-covered notebooks, worn with years, but not one of them missing. Beginning soon after Mr. Taylor's medical degrees were taken, they cover a period of three years. Daily entries in his small, clear writing fill the pages, which breathe a spirit words are poor to express.

Scarcely a day is recorded in which he did not have correspondence, visitors, meetings, lessons in Chinese to give to intending missionaries, medical visits to pay to friends or suffering neighbors, attendance at committees, or other public or private engagements in addition to the revision of the Ningpo Testament. That the latter was his chief occupation, and one to which he devoted himself with characteristic thoroughness, is evident from the journals. Every day he noted the number of hours spent in this work alone, and one frequently comes across such entries as the following:

> April 13, 1863: Commenced with Mr. Gough at 10 A.M. and worked together about eight hours. Revision, total nine hours.
> April 14: Revision nine hours.
> April 15: Revision ten and a half hours.
> April 16: Revision eight hours.
> April 17: Revision eleven and a half hours.
> April 18: Revision eleven hours.
> April 19, Sunday: Morning, wrote to James Meadows...had service with Lae-djün. Afternoon, took tea with Mr. John Howard, having walked to Tottenham to inquire after Miss Stacey's health. Evening, heard Mr. Howard preach. Proposed to Miss Howard, as subjects for prayer, that we should be helped in revision—to do it well and as quickly as is consistent with so doing. Walked home.

Thus the record runs on, putting to shame our easygoing service by its intensity and devotion. And this was a returned missionary, detained at home on account of seriously impaired health through equally strenuous labors in China!

But it was not work only, it was faith and endurance under searching trial that made these years so fruitful in their after results. The testing permitted was chiefly along two lines, those of the Ningpo Testament and the supply of personal needs. Mr. Taylor, it should be recorded, never at any time received financial help from the funds of the mission. Even in these early days he felt it important to be entirely independent, in this sense, of the work. He had long been looking to the Lord in temporal matters as in spiritual, proving in many wonderful ways the truth of the promise, "No good thing will he withhold from them that walk uprightly" (Ps. 84:11). These years in East London, however, were marked by very special exercise of mind in this connection, and some periods of extremity never afterwards repeated.

Meanwhile, what of the bright hopes with which Mr. Taylor had entered upon the work entrusted to him by the Bible Society? To obtain a correct version of the New Testament, not in Chinese character but in roman letters, representing the sounds of the local dialect, and thus comparatively easy both to read and understand, was an object worthy of considerable sacrifice. With the help of Wang Lae-djün and Mrs. Taylor, who was as much at home in the Ningpo dialect as in English, he hoped to accomplish it in reasonable time. After a beginning had been made, he was joined also by the Rev. F. F. Gough of the C.M.S., whose knowledge of Greek as well as Chinese enabled him to translate with confidence from the original. They were thus well qualified for the work, and progress was not hindered by lack of diligence. But the task itself proved far more laborious than they had anticipated, extended as it was to include the preparation of marginal references.

Moreover it met, strange to say, with the strongest opposition. People whose position gave them weight criticized the undertaking at the Bible house to such an extent that, once and again, it seemed as if it must be abandoned, and this not at the beginning, but after months and years of toil, during which Mr. Taylor's friends and the mission circle had become interested in the matter. To fail after having sacrificed so much, delaying even his return to China, was a possibility that cost him keen distress. Yet he had to face it, especially when Mr. Gough seemed on the point of giving way. For two or three months the situation was painful in the extreme. But the difficulties only increased until Mr. Gough could go on no longer. Of these difficulties, Mr. Taylor wrote the following to his mother:

> Humanly speaking, there is little hope of the continued aid of either the C.M.S. or the Bible Society. For this I care but little, as the Lord can easily provide the funds we need. But the help of Mr. Gough in the remainder of the work is very desirable, and under these circumstances it is improbable that we should have it. I would ask special prayer then.
>
> I. That the C.M.S. and the Bible Society may be brought to that conclusion which will be most for the glory of God and the real (not apparent) good of the work.
>
> II. That, if, as is almost certain, they throw up the revision, and if it be most for the good of the dear converts of Ningpo, Mr. Gough may be induced to continue his share in it.
>
> III. That if he should not do this, we may be guided aright as to our path—whether simply to reprint the Epistles and Revelation, or in some measure to revise them, correcting where we can any glaring errors; or whether to give up the work altogether.
>
> My present full conviction, not a little confirmed by the character of the opposition to our work, is that it is of the Lord, and that He is saying to us, "Be strong and of good courage, and

do it: fear not, nor be dismayed: for the LORD God...will be with thee;...until thou hast finished all the work for the service of the house of the LORD" (1 Chron. 28:20). If this is really His will, by His grace I will go forward. May He teach me if it be not so.

"Whatsoever ye shall ask in my name, that will I do, that the Father may be glorified in the Son" (John 14:13). Plead this promise, dear Mother, in behalf of our work. And may He, whose we are and whom we serve, guide us aright.

Nothing is more striking in the records of the period than Mr. Taylor's dependence upon prayer, real dependence for every detail, every need. He leaned his whole weight on God, pleading the promises. Was it Lae-djün's affairs, the wife and child who needed him, or the difficulties of their long task; was it a question of health, their own or the children's, of house moving, money for daily bread, or guidance as to their return to China? All, all was brought to their Heavenly Father with the directness of little children, and the conviction that He could and would undertake, direct, and provide. It was all so real, so practical!

Equally characteristic was the faithfulness with which he followed when the Lord's way was made plain. Barely two weeks after the above letter was written, the Bible Society reached a decision which bound him more than ever to the revision, and his friend, Mr. Pearse, wrote to him about it, forestalling the letter of the committee: "There is no intention of taking it out of your hands. They are evidently satisfied with what you are doing and the way you are doing it."

This meant that the romanized Testament would be completed, and Mr. Taylor greatly rejoiced in it as a definite answer to prayer. It also meant that he was pledged more than ever to his part of the work, and the years were passing on. With returning strength, the longing grew upon him to be back in China, especially when the death of Mr. Jones left the Bridge Street converts almost without pastoral care. Great changes had swept over Ningpo with the devastation of the Taiping Rebellion. After indescribable sufferings, the population had largely lost faith in idols which could not protect even themselves, and many were ready as never before for the consolations of the Gospel. Everything pointed, humanly speaking, to Mr. Taylor's return and increased his longing to be in direct missionary work once more. Important as the revision was, he was young and craved activity and the joy of winning souls to Christ. Yet did not the very answers to prayer that had been so marked bind him to continue the work that was detaining him and carry it to completion?

But all the while another longing was taking possession of his soul, looming large and ever larger with strange persistence. Do what he would, he could not escape the call of inland China, the appeal of those Christless millions for whom no man seemed to care. On his study wall hung the map of the whole vast empire; on the table before him lay the ever-open Bible; and between the two how close and heart-searching the connection! Feeding, feasting, upon the Word of God, his eye would fall upon the map—and oh, the thought of those for whom nothing was prepared! Of this, he wrote:

> While on the field, the pressure of claims immediately around me was so great that I could not think much of the still greater need farther

> inland, and could do nothing to meet it. But detained for some years in England, daily viewing the whole country on the large map in my study, I was as near the vast regions of the interior as the smaller districts in which I had personally labored—and prayer was the only resource by which the burdened heart could obtain any relief.

Laying aside their work, for Mr. Gough in measure shared this experience, they would call Mrs. Taylor and Lae-djün, and unitedly pour out their hearts in prayer that God would send the Gospel to every part of China. And they did more than pray. Alone, or together, they interviewed the representatives of the larger missionary societies, pleading the cause of those unevangelized millions. Everywhere they were met with sympathy, for the facts were their own argument, but everywhere also it was evident that nothing could, or rather would, be done. The objections raised were twofold. In the first place, financially, any aggressive effort was impossible. Neither the men nor the means were forthcoming. And were it otherwise, those remote provinces were practically inaccessible to foreigners. True, the treaty of 1860 provided for journeys and even residence inland, but that was merely on paper, and everywhere the conclusion was the same: "We must wait until God's providence opens the door; at present we can do nothing."

These objections, however, did not lessen the need or bring any lightening of the burden. Returning to the East End and his quiet study, Hudson Taylor found himself still challenged by the open Bible, the ever-accusing map. The Master had said nothing about politics or finance in His

Great Commission. "Go ye...lo, I am with you" (Matt. 28:19–20)—so read command and promise. Was He not worthy of trust and utmost allegiance?

And there were others who thought as he did, friends and candidates of the mission who gathered weekly for prayer at Beaumont Street. Few though they were in number, the spirit of prayer was so outpoured that for a couple of hours at a time those fervent hearts went up in continued supplication. Thus, as the silent years drew to a close, with their restraining providence and all their deepening and development, to the man upon his knees came at length some apprehension of that for which also he was apprehended of God.

There Wrestled a Man with Him

Mr. Taylor had been drawn into a new undertaking which was absorbing time and thought. Early in the year the pastor of the church to which he belonged (who was also editor of the *Baptist Magazine*) had asked for a series of articles on China, with a view to awakening interest in the Ningpo Mission. These Mr. Taylor had begun to prepare, and one had even been published, when Mr. Lewis returned the manuscript of the next. The articles, he felt, were weighty and should have a wider circulation than his paper could afford.

"Add to them," he said earnestly; "let them cover the whole field and be published as an appeal for inland China."

The study necessary for these papers was bringing to a crisis the exercise of mind through which Mr. Taylor had been passing. Compiling facts as to the size and population of every province in China, and making diagrams to show their neglected condition, stirred him to a desperate sense of the sin and shame of allowing such a state of things to continue. Yet what was to be done? The number of Protestant missionaries, as he had discovered, was diminishing rather than increasing. Despite the fact that half the heathen population of the world was to be found in China, the missionaries engaged in its evangelization had actually been reduced, during the previous winter, from a hundred and fifteen to only ninety-one. This had come to light through his study of the latest statistics, and naturally added fuel to the fire that was consuming him. But he had done all that was possible. No one would move in the matter. He must leave it now, until the Lord....But somehow that was not the final word.

Leave it, when he knew that he, small, weak, and nothing as he was, might pray in faith for laborers and they would be given? Leave it, when there stood plainly in his Bible that solemn word:

> *When I say unto the wicked, Thou shalt surely die; and thou givest him not warning, nor speakest to warn the wicked from his wicked way, to save his life; the same wicked man shall die in his iniquity; but his blood will I require at thine hand.* *(Ezek. 3:18)*

Of this critical time, Hudson Taylor wrote:

> I knew God was speaking. I knew that in answer to prayer evangelists would be given and their support secured, because the name of Jesus is worthy. But there unbelief came in.
>
> Suppose the workers are given and go to China: trials will come; their faith may fail; would they not reproach you for bringing them

into such a plight? Have you ability to cope with so painful a situation?

And the answer was, of course, a decided negative.

It was just a bringing in of *self,* through unbelief, the Devil getting one to feel that while prayer and faith would bring one into the fix, one would have to get out of it as best one might. And I did not see that the Power that would give the men and the means would be sufficient to keep them also, even in the far interior of China.

Meanwhile, a *million a month* were dying in that land, dying without God. This was burned into my very soul. For two or three months the conflict was intense. I scarcely slept night or day more than an hour at a time and feared I should lose my reason. Yet I did not give in. To no one could I speak freely, not even to my dear wife. She saw, doubtless, that something was going on, but I felt I must refrain as long as possible from laying upon her a burden so crushing—these souls, and what eternity must mean for every one of them, and what the Gospel might do, would do, for all who believed, if we would take it to them.

The break in the journal at this point is surely significant. Faithfully the record had gone on for two and a quarter years, but now—silence. For seven weeks, from the middle of April, lovely weeks of spring, there was no entry. First and only blank in those revealing pages, how much the very silence has to tell us! Yes, he was face to face with the purpose of God at last. Accept it, he dare not; escape it, he could not. And so, as long ago, "there wrestled a man with him until the breaking of the day" (Gen. 32:24).

* * * * *

It was Sunday, June 25, 1865, a quiet summer morning by the sea. Worn out and really ill, Hudson Taylor had gone to friends at Brighton, and, unable to bear the sight of rejoicing multitudes in the house of God, had wandered out alone upon the sands left by the receding tide. It was a peaceful scene about him, but inwardly he was in agony of spirit. A decision had to be made and he knew it, for the conflict could no longer be endured.

"Well," the thought came at last, "if God gives us a band of men for inland China, and they go, and all die of starvation even, they will only be taken straight to heaven; and if one heathen soul is saved, would it not be well worthwhile?"

It was a strange way round to faith—that if the worst came to the worst it would still be worthwhile. But something in the service of that morning seems to have come to mind. God-consciousness began to take the place of unbelief, and a new thought possessed him as dawn displaces night:

"Why, if we are obeying the Lord, the responsibility rests with Him, not with us!"

This, brought home to his heart in the power of the Spirit, wrought the change once and for all.

"You, Lord," he cried with relief that was unutterable, "You will have all the burden! At Your bidding, as Your servant I go forward, leaving results with You."

For some time the conviction had been growing that he ought to ask for, at any rate, two evangelists for each of the eleven unoccupied provinces, and two for Chinese Tartary and Tibet. Pencil in hand, he now opened his Bible, and with the boundless ocean breaking at his feet wrote the simple memorable words: "Prayed for twenty-four willing, skillful laborers at Brighton, June 25, 1865."

Recalling the deliverance of that hour, he wrote:

> How restfully I turned away from the sands. The conflict ended, all was joy and peace. I felt as if I could fly up the hill to Mr. Pearse's house. And how I did sleep that night! My dear wife thought Brighton had done wonders for me, and so it had.

Chapter 7

The Origin of a Mission That Had to Be

New life, evidently, had come to Hudson Taylor with the decision taken that June Sunday on the sands at Brighton, for he was up with the lark next morning and off to London at 6:30 A.M. No record remains of that day, save that Mrs. Taylor was cheered to see him better and that he went to have special prayer with one who was wishing to join the mission, whose way was beset with difficulties. But next day brought just the practical step that might have been expected:

> June 27: Went with Mr. Pearse to the London & County Bank, and opened an account for the China Inland Mission. Paid in £10.

It is the first appearance of the new name.

And then came days of activity in striking contrast with the silence of preceding weeks. Complete surrender to the will of God not only set the joy bells ringing, it gave the clue to much that before had seemed perplexing and started the suspended energies on a clear course. Delays and difficulties explained themselves, and how thankful Mr. Taylor felt for the restraining Hand that had kept him from leaving England previously, and had returned that unpublished manuscript for a purpose he little anticipated. Now he had something to write about, something definite to lay before the Lord's people, new power in pleading the cause of inland China, and an object worthy of highest endeavor. He had found himself at last, found life's best and deepest, not in the way of his own choosing, but in the "good works, which God hath before ordained that [he] should walk in them" (Eph. 2:10).

Now that his mission was decided, Mr. Taylor began to plan for his next journey to China. Through this decision, the branches were spreading out, and the roots were striking deeper in quiet hours of thought and prayer. Many consultations were held with Mr. Berger about practical questions, and as responsibilities increased it was an untold comfort to have his help in bearing them. Mr. Taylor said the following of this summer:

> When I decided to go forward, Mr. Berger undertook to represent us at home. The thing grew up gradually. We were much drawn together. The mission received its name in his drawing room. Neither of us asked or appointed the other: it just *was so.*

And what will be said of the still more intimate help of the life nearest of all to his own—the tender love, the spiritual inspiration and practical wisdom of the one who shared his every experience? To Mrs. Taylor, necessarily, the new departure meant more than to any other, for, young as she was, not yet thirty, she had to mother the mission as well as care for a growing family. To take four little children out to China was no light matter, and when the object in view is remembered—nothing less than to plant messengers of the Gospel in every one of the unopened provinces—a mother's heart alone can realize what hers must often have felt. It was not her husband's faith however, upon which she leaned, great as were her joy and confidence in him. From girlhood, orphaned of both parents, she had put to the test for herself the heavenly Father's faithfulness. Family burdens and the pressure of need might come, and this immense responsibility be added as well, but her resources did not fail, for she drew moment by moment upon "all the fulness of God" (Eph. 3:19).

The chief work that claimed Mr. and Mrs. Taylor after the decision at Brighton was that of completing the manuscript returned by Mr. Lewis. It may have been easy to say, "Add to it; let it cover the whole field and be published as an appeal for inland China," but to carry out the suggestion was another matter. Little information was to be had about that great closed land, and to make its needs real and appealing needed a touch other than they could give. The writing meant much study, thought, and prayer. Too busy during the week to obtain quiet, they gave what time they could on Sunday, without neglecting public worship, to this important task. Together in their little sitting room they prayed and wrote, wrote and prayed. *China's Spiritual Need and Claims* was the outcome.

"Every sentence was steeped in prayer," Mr. Taylor recalled. "It grew up while we were writing—I walking up and down the room and Maria seated at the table."

As one reads this book, the mind almost reels before such a situation. No wonder this man is burdened! No wonder he cannot get away from the awful sense of responsibility. And he looks upon it all, makes the reader look upon it all, with God. That is where the deep solemnity comes in. One is standing in the light of eternity, in the presence of the crucified, risen Lord of Glory. His unconditional command, "Go...I am with you alway" (Matt. 28:19–20) is sounding on and on, while with it mingles the low wail of thousands, passing hour by hour into Christless graves. It is profoundly, unutterably real. "A million a month in China are dying without God," and we who have received in trust the Word of Life, we are responsible. It was not China's need alone that called the Inland Mission into being; it was China's claim.

The overwhelming greatness of the task before the mission is felt rather than dwelt upon, for yet another Reality shines out from these pages, preoccupying mind and heart. One thing only is greater than the greatness of the need—the fact of God: His resources, purposes, faithfulness; His commands and promises. "All power is given unto me....Go ye therefore" (Matt. 28:18–19). That is enough; that alone could be enough. The need is great, immensely great, but God is greater, infinitely greater. And this God the writer knows, has proved, trusts.

Hence it follows that the principles of the new mission are simply an adjustment of these two considerations—the need to be met and God. He stands behind the work He has called into being. The writer has no other resources, absolutely none, and he desires no other. Every problem resolves itself into a fresh appeal to God, for there can be no need unmet in Him. In his manuscript, Mr. Taylor wrote:

> We have to do with One who is Lord of all power and might, whose arm is not shortened that it cannot save, nor His ear heavy that it cannot hear; with One whose unchanging Word directs us to ask and receive that our joy may be full, to open

our mouths wide that He may fill them; and we do well to remember that this gracious God, who has condescended to place His almighty power at the command of believing prayer, looks not lightly on the bloodguiltiness of those who neglect to avail themselves of it for the benefit of the perishing.

Feeling, on the one hand, the solemn responsibility that rests upon us, and on the other the gracious encouragements that everywhere meet us in the Word of God, we do not hesitate to ask the great Lord of the Harvest to call forth, to thrust forth twenty-four European and twenty-four native evangelists, to plant the standard of the Cross in the eleven unevangelized provinces of China proper and in Chinese Tartary. To those who have never been called to prove the faithfulness of the covenant-keeping God in supplying, in answer to prayer alone, the every need of His servants, it might seem a hazardous experiment to send twenty-four European evangelists to a distant heathen land, "with *only God to look to*"; but in one whose privilege it has been through many years to put that God to the test in varied circumstances, at home and abroad, by land and sea, in sickness and health, in dangers, in necessities, and at the gates of death, such apprehensions would be wholly inexcusable.

Instance after instance is given from Mr. Taylor's experience of direct, unmistakable answers to prayer, and the deduction drawn is that with such a God it is safe and wise to go forward in the pathway of obedience—it is indeed the only safe and wise thing to do. When he comes to touch upon the practical working of the mission, the application of Scriptural principles is just as direct. Not much is said, for the organization is of the simplest, but Bible precedents cast light on every problem. The writer is dealing with an unchanging God and confidently expects Him to work in the same way still. The very greatness of the need, considered in the light of divine, not human, resources, called for methods as new and distinctive as the proposed sphere of the mission itself.

How could the work be limited, for example, to any one section of the church of Christ? No denomination, however generous its support, could be equal to it, just as no one class in society could provide the laborers needed. The mission must be free to accept "willing, skillful workers," no matter what their church connection or previous training, provided they were wise to win souls, men and women who knew their God and could sink lesser differences in the one great bond of union.

Then, as to funds: how could the mission, possessing nothing, promise stated salaries to its members? How could Mr. Taylor let them look to him for support? All that was sent in answer to prayer he would gladly use or distribute among his fellow workers, but more than that he could not promise, except that under no circumstances would he go into debt for the mission any more than for himself. Each individual member must know that he or she was sent by God, and must be able to trust Him for supplies—strength, grace, protection, enablement for every emergency, as well as daily bread. No other basis would be possible. If the mission were to be fruitful, were to continue at all amid the perils that must be faced, it could only be as each one connected with it contributed his quota of faith in the living God. Mr. Taylor said of this period:

> We had to consider whether it would not be possible for members of various denominations to work together on simple, evangelistic lines

without friction as to conscientious differences of opinion? Prayerfully concluding that it would, we decided to invite the cooperation of fellow believers irrespective of denominational views, who fully held the inspiration of God's Word, and were willing to prove their faith by going to inland China with only the guarantee they carried within the covers of their pocket Bibles.

That Word had said, "Seek...first the kingdom of God, and his righteousness; and all these things [food and raiment] shall be added unto you" (Matt. 6:33). If anyone did not believe that God spoke the truth, it would be better for him not to go to China to propagate the faith. If he did believe it, surely the promise sufficed. Again, "No good thing will he withhold from them that walk uprightly" (Ps. 84:11). If anyone did not mean to walk uprightly, he had better stay at home; if he did mean to walk uprightly, he had all he needed in the shape of a guarantee fund. God owns all the gold and silver in the world, and the cattle on a thousand hills. We need not be vegetarians.

We might indeed have had a guarantee fund if we had wished it, but we felt it was unneeded and would do harm. Money wrongly placed and money given from wrong motives are both to be greatly dreaded. We can afford to have as little as the Lord chooses to give, but we cannot afford to have unconsecrated money, or to have money placed in the wrong position. Far better have no money at all, even to buy food with, for there are plenty of ravens in China, and the Lord could send them again with bread and flesh. (See 1 Kings 17:6.)

Our Father is a very experienced One. He knows very well that His children wake up with a good appetite every morning, and He always provides breakfast for them, and does not send them supperless to bed at night. "[Thy] bread shall be given him; [and thy] waters shall be sure" (Isa. 33:16). He sustained three million Israelites in the wilderness for forty years. We do not expect He will send three million missionaries to China, but if He did, He would have ample means to sustain them all. Let us see that we keep God before our eyes, that we walk in His ways and seek to please and glorify Him in everything, great and small. Depend upon it, God's work done in God's way will never lack God's supplies.

It was men and women of faith, therefore, who were needed for the Inland Mission, prepared to depend on God alone, satisfied with poverty should He deem it best, and confident that His Word cannot be broken.

Much else comes out in these earnest pages, and much that is not said is significant by its absence. There is no mention even of a committee, no reliance upon organization or great names. The entire direction of the mission was to be in the hands of its founder, himself the most experienced of its members, who, like a general on active service, would be with his forces in the field. So natural does this arrangement seem that one hardly recognizes the greatness of the innovation, or that in this as in other new departures, Hudson Taylor was making a contribution of exceeding value to the high politics of missions. He had simply learned from painful experience how much a missionary may have to suffer, and the work be hampered, if not imperiled, by being under the control of those who, however well-intentioned, have no firsthand knowledge of its conditions, and are, moreover, at the other side of the world.

Another striking absence is that of any pleading for financial help. It is mentioned that an annual expenditure of five thousand pounds might be anticipated when the outgoing party of ten or twelve should be added to those already on the field. Mr. Berger's address is given as Mr. Taylor's representative in England, to whom gifts might be sent by any desiring to have fellowship with the work. And for the rest, the quiet words express a sense of wealth rather than need: "Although the wants are large, they will not exhaust the resources of our Father."

Finally, there is not a word about government protection or dependence upon treaty rights. Many instances are given of divine protection in the dangers inseparable from pioneering work such as the mission looked forward to. Unarmed, in native dress, and claiming no aid from consular authorities, the writer had found times of peril to be always times of proving the watchful care of One who is a refuge better than foreign flag or gunboat. It is God who looms large, not man.

Many were the letters that reached Mr. Taylor during the weeks that followed, showing that the book was doing its quiet work, and that in widely differing circles the C.I.M. was hailed with thankfulness as a mission that had to be. Offers of service came from the students' hall, the business counter, and the mechanic's shop. Invitations for meetings were numerous, and so great was the demand for literature that *China's Spiritual Need and Claims* had to be reprinted within three weeks.

Meanwhile, preparations for a party of ten or twelve were going forward, and in the midst of other engagements they proved almost more than

Mr. Taylor could manage. As he was reviewing the progress made since that memorable Sunday at Brighton, with all that it had brought—besides the eight fellow workers already in China, twenty or thirty others were desiring to join the mission—he wrote to the wider circle of his prayer helpers:

> How much we need guidance both for them and for ourselves. We have undertaken to work in the interior of China, looking to the Lord for help of all kinds. This we can only do in His strength. And if we are to be much used of Him, we must live very near to Him.

The last day of December was set apart, therefore, as a day of fasting and prayer, fitly closing the year that had witnessed the inauguration of a mission so completely dependent upon God.

According to His Working

It might have been, as Mr. Taylor felt from the first, quite possible to rob Peter to pay Paul, or in other words to deflect interest and gifts from previously existing channels. Every effort on behalf of China and other heathen lands was more than needed, and he longed that the new work should, by the blessing of God, be helpful to all and a hindrance to none. But how to avoid trespassing, in this sense, on the preserves of others was a problem not easy to solve.

To cut at the root of the difficulty, he and Mr. Berger, his chief adviser, saw that the faith principles of the mission must be carried to the point of making no appeals for money or even taking a collection. If the mission could be sustained by the faithful care of God in answer to prayer and prayer alone, without subscription lists or solicitation of any kind for funds, then it might grow up among the older societies without the danger of diverting gifts from their accustomed channels. It might even be helpful to other agencies by directing attention to the Great Worker, and affording a practical illustration of its underlying principle that "God Himself, God *alone,* is sufficient for God's own work."

Was money after all the chief thing, or was it really true that a walk that pleases God and ensures spiritual blessing is of more importance in His service? Except for the quiet years in Beaumont Street in which, like Paul in Arabia or Moses at the backside of the desert, Hudson Taylor had been shut in with God, he might have given a different answer to this and many other questions. He wrote of that period in which he was largely occupied with work on the Ningpo Testament:

> In my shortsightedness, I had seen nothing beyond the use that the book with its marginal references would be to the native Christians. But I have often realized since that without those months of feeding and feasting on the Word of God, I should have been quite unprepared to form, on its present basis, a mission like the China Inland Mission. In the study of that divine Word I learned that to obtain successful laborers, not elaborate appeals for help, but first, earnest prayer to God "to thrust forth laborers," and second, the deepening of the spiritual life of the church, so that men should be unable to stay at home, were what was needed. I saw that the apostolic plan was not to raise ways and means, but to go and do the work, trusting in His sure promise who has said, "Seek ye first the kingdom

of God, and his righteousness; and all these things shall be added unto you" (Matt. 6:33).

The chief need, as he saw it, was faith in God for such an increase of spiritual life among His people as to produce the missionary spirit. Not money, not the collection was to him the object of a meeting, but to get people under the power of the Word and into fellowship with God. He often said:

> If our hearts are right, we may count upon the Holy Spirit's working through us to bring others into deeper fellowship with God—the way the work began at Pentecost. We do not need to say much about the C.I.M. Let people see God working, let God be glorified, let believers be made holier, happier, brought nearer to Him, and they will not need to be asked to help.

And the satisfaction of that way of working was that people would be sure to help their own missions first, the church work for which they were responsible. They would probably increase their gifts, indeed, to those objects, for there is no heart as generous as one that is "satisfied with favour, and full with the blessing of the LORD" (Deut. 33:23). And if they wanted, over and above, to help the China Inland Mission, such gifts would be given with prayer and followed by prayer that would immeasurably increase their value. It was no figure of speech with Mr. Taylor when he said, as he often did, that he would rather have a consecrated shilling, representing real spiritual fellowship, than an unconsecrated pound; and gifts given spontaneously, apart from solicitation or the pressure even of a collection, were more likely to have that quality. It was a strange sort of deputation work, perhaps, but it left the speaker free in spirit, occupied with God rather than man, and more eager to give than to get.

Then there were other problems, many of them—such as how to test and train candidates, how to organize the mission in China and carry on the work at home. But though these were duly considered among the friends who met at Saint Hill, the Bergers' home, Mr. Berger's illustration of the tree was manifestly in point:

> You must wait for it to grow before there can be much in the way of branches. First you have only a slender stem with a few leaves or shoots. Then little twigs appear. Ultimately these may become great limbs, all but separate trees, but it takes time and patience. If there is life, it will develop after its own order.

Thus they were content with little to begin with in the way of organization. Essential, spiritual principles were talked over with the candidates and clearly understood as the basis of the mission. A few simple arrangements were agreed to in Mr. Berger's presence, that was all. Mr. Taylor summed up the matter as follows:

> We came out as God's children at God's command to do God's work, depending on Him for supplies, to wear native dress and go inland. I was to be the leader in China, and my direction implicitly followed. There was no question as to who was to determine points at issue.

In the same way, Mr. Berger was responsible at home. He would correspond with candidates, receive and forward contributions, publish an *Occasional Paper* with audited accounts, send out suitable workers as funds permitted, and keep clear of debt. This last was a cardinal principle with all concerned.

But upon the many conferences on these and kindred subjects at Saint Hill, we must not linger. Time was getting short. It was hoped that Mr. Taylor and his party would sail in May, and much had to be gotten through in the way of preparation. In answer to all inquiries as to how many would be going with him, the leader of the mission could only reply:

> If the Lord sends money for three or four, three or four will go, but if He provides for sixteen, we shall take it as His indication that sixteen are to sail at this time.

Not that this meant uncertainty in his own mind. He had little doubt that the larger number would be provided for, and though no solicitation was made for money, the matter was not left to drift. He believed that to deal with God is at least as real as to deal with man, that when we get to prayer we get to work, and work of the most practical kind. Two thousand pounds, as nearly as he could tell, would be needed if the whole party were to be sent out, and in preparing the first *Occasional Paper* of the mission, early in the New Year (1866), Mr. Taylor mentioned this sum. The manuscript went to press on February 6, and that very day a noon prayer meeting for funds was begun. Faith did not mean inaction. From twelve o'clock to one o'clock the households gathered for daily united waiting upon God, the would-be missionaries realizing that their first work was to obtain—from Him who was so ready to give—whatever would be necessary for as many of their number as He was sending forth.

After a journey to deepen interest in China, Mr. Taylor, back in London, took the opportunity of going over the mission cash book to see how far the daily prayer for funds had been answered. In the first five weeks of the year, up to February 6, when the noon meeting was begun, a hundred and seventy pounds had been received. Another five weeks had now elapsed, and eagerly he made the reckoning necessary to compare the periods. Only the day before he had received from Liverpool, as a result of his recent visit, a gift of no less than six hundred and fifty pounds from a gentleman who, upon reading Mr. Taylor's pamphlet, was impressed with the importance of making sacrifices that the Gospel might be preached to the Christless millions of inland China. Deeply interested, Mr. Taylor was anxious to see how far other hearts had been moved in the same direction, and what was the surprise and thankfulness with which he discovered that all they were praying for—not the smaller but the larger sum—was actually in hand! Not only was prayer answered, it was manifest also that all the praying band were to go forward without delay to China. Of this, some years later, Mr. Taylor wrote:

> We were reminded of the difficulty of Moses, and of the proclamation he had to send throughout the camp to prepare no more for the building of the tabernacle, as the gifts in hand were more than sufficient. We are convinced that if there were *less* solicitation for money and *more* dependence upon the power of the Holy Ghost and the deepening of spiritual life, the experience would be a common one in every branch of Christian work.

But all this time, strange to say, they had no ship in view to take them to China. Avoiding the expensive "overland" route, via Suez, Mr. Taylor wished to travel round the Cape and was seeking a sailing vessel of which they might engage the entire accommodation. As the party was to consist of eighteen adults and four children, the cabin space of an ordinary three-master would be none too much, and there were decided advantages for so long a voyage in being the only passengers. But here was already the beginning of May, and a suitable ship had not been found. Daily the matter was remembered in the noon prayer meeting, the outgoing missionaries not only asking for a Christian captain, but for a crew every one of whom might find blessing through the voyage. Mr. Taylor was not anxious; he was sure the Lord would meet the need in good time, through he would have been glad to have it settled.

Just then, on May 2, he was due in Herfordshire for an important meeting; Colonel Puget was his host and chairman. To this new friend it seemed a peculiar arrangement to have a missionary meeting without a collection, but understanding it to be Mr. Taylor's wish, the announcement had been made accordingly. When the time came, however, and the speaker proved unusually interesting, Colonel Puget realized that people would give generously if they only had the opportunity.

Rising therefore at the close of the address, he said that interpreting the feelings of the audience by his own, he took it upon himself to alter the decision about the collection. Many present were moved by the condition of things Mr. Taylor had represented and would go away burdened unless they could express practical sympathy. Contrary, therefore, to previous announcements, an opportunity would now be given....But at that point Mr.

Taylor interposed, asking to be allowed to add a few words.

It was his earnest desire, he said, that his hearers should go away burdened. Money was not the chief thing in the Lord's work, especially money easily given under the influence of emotion. Much as he appreciated their kind intention, he would far rather have each one go home to ask the Lord very definitely what He would have them do. If it were to give of their substance, they could send a contribution to their own or any other society. But in view of the appalling facts of heathenism, it might be much more costly gifts the Lord was seeking: perhaps the life service of one's own son or daughter. No amount of money could save a single soul. What was wanted was that men and women filled with the Holy Spirit should give themselves to the work in China and to the work of prayer at home. For the support of God-sent missionaries, funds would never be lacking.

"You made a great mistake, if I may say so," remarked his host at supper. "The people were really interested. We might have had a good collection."

In vain Mr. Taylor explained the financial basis of the mission and his desire to avoid even the appearance of conflicting with other societies. Colonel Puget, though sympathetic, was unconvinced.

Next morning, however, he appeared somewhat late at breakfast, explaining that he had not had a good night. In the study, after handing Mr. Taylor several contributions given for the mission, he went on to say:

"I felt last evening that you were wrong about the collection, but now I see things differently.

Lying awake in the night, as I thought of that stream of souls in China, a thousand every hour going out into the dark, I could only cry, 'Lord, what will You have me to do?' (See Acts 9:6.) I think I have His answer."

And he handed Mr. Taylor a check for five hundred pounds.

"If there had been a collection I should have given a five-pound note," he added. "This check is the result of no small part of the night spent in prayer."

It was Thursday morning, May 3, and at the breakfast table a letter had reached Mr. Taylor from his shipping agents offering the entire accommodation of the *Lammermuir,* about to sail for China. Bidding farewell to his now deeply interested host, he returned to London, went straight to the docks, and finding the ship in every way suitable, paid over the check just received on account. This done, with what joy he hastened home with the tidings!

So the time came at length for the quiet, unostentatious start. To see God working—to look up to Him moment by moment, conscious of His arm to enfold, His right hand to protect and guide, and the light of His countenance—was more to that little band than thousands of gold and silver. Before setting out, Mr. Taylor wrote:

> Utter weakness in ourselves, we should be overwhelmed at the immensity of the work before us, were it not that our very insufficiency gives us a special claim to the fulfillment of His promise, "My grace is sufficient for thee: for my strength is made perfect in weakness" (2 Cor. 12:9).

Chapter 8

Back to China

Human nothingness, divine sufficiency—the one just as real as the other—was the atmosphere of those last days in England. None could come and go without feeling it. Among packing cases and bundles the Saturday prayer meetings were held, friends from far and near crowding the room, sitting on the staircase and on anything that came to hand. Upon the wall still hung the great map; on the table lay the open Bible; and all else was lost sight of.

"A foolhardy business!" said those who saw only the difficulties.

"A superhuman task!" sighed others who wished them well. And many even of their friends could not but be anxious.

"You will be forgotten," was the chief concern of some. "With no committee to represent you at home you will be lost sight of in that distant land. Claims are many nowadays. Before long you may find yourselves without even the necessaries of life!"

"I am taking my children with me," was Mr. Taylor's reply, "and I notice that it is not difficult for me to remember that the little ones need breakfast in the morning, dinner at midday, and something before they go to bed at night. Indeed, I could not forget it. And I find it impossible to suppose that our heavenly Father is less tender or mindful than I."

Little wonder that the quietness and simplicity of it all, combined with such aims, such faith, drew out the sympathy of many hearts.

* * * * *

Never surely were travelers more prayed for, as the long months of the voyage wore on, and none could have more needed such aid. Sailing from London on May 26, 1866, it was the end of September before they reached Shanghai, and very determined were the attacks of the Enemy, first to wreck the unity and spiritual power of the missionary party, and then to wreck the ship on which they traveled, sending them all to the bottom. But from the hour of parting, when they were commended to God in the stern cabin of the *Lammermuir* by Mr. Berger and a company of those nearest to them, they were daily sustained in this most important way.

And prayer was wonderfully answered on board that little sailing ship tossed on the mighty deep. Most of Trinity Sunday, their first whole day at sea, they were anchored awaiting a favorable breeze. Freedom from much motion gave opportunity for morning and evening services and for rest which was greatly needed. Next day was occupied with putting things in order and steadying the heavy baggage, piled up in the corners of the saloon upon which the cabins opened. On Tuesday, regular studies were begun, Mr. Taylor taking a class in Chinese every morning and Mrs. Taylor another in the afternoon.

After that came rougher weather, when many were down with seasickness and Mr. and Mrs. Taylor, in the absence of a stewardess, had their hands full. By the time Madeira was reached, almost all had their sea legs, and great advance had been made in getting into touch with the crew. From that time on, all across the Atlantic (for their course took them westward almost to Brazil), round the Cape of Good Hope, and up to the East Indian Islands, the weather was wonderfully fine—few gales and no distressing heat. Eleven and a half weeks were occupied in this part of the voyage, weeks chiefly memorable for the change they brought to many a life on board.

For the sailors had been watching these unusual passengers, whose company they had looked forward to with anything but satisfaction. One missionary would have been bad enough, but a whole ship's load of them! For the *Lammermuir* carried a godless crew, though the captain was a Christian. This was a great help, as he gave permission for Sunday services and put no hindrance in the way of discourse with the men. But the latter held aloof for some time, and the missionaries were wise enough to give them plenty of line.

There are some things, however, that cannot be hid, chiefest of which is the fragrance of Christ in a spirit made loving and helpful by His presence. This was not lacking on board the *Lammermuir,* and before long it began to be strangely attractive. Hardly knowing what it was that drew them, the men found their hearts open to spiritual influences as never before. The missionaries, after all, were not such a bad lot. When a difficult piece of forging had to be done, Nicol, the Scotch blacksmith, was better at it than any of themselves. Jackson and Williamson, the carpenters, were always ready to lend a hand. In the absence of a ship's doctor, Mr. Taylor's surgical skill, gladly placed at their disposal, was invaluable. Then he gave capital lectures—talks on the eye, the circulation of the blood, first aid to the injured, etc.—which helped to pass the time. And there was more than that. Seen at close quarters, these people were downright happy: always busy, always kind, and given to singing.

It was curious, that part of it! For what could there be in the life they had chosen to make them want to sing? Yet morning, noon, and night, in the stern cabin with their harmonium or out on deck, whether two or three alone or the whole company together, they seemed never to tire. True, it was only hymns they sang, but what could touch deeper chords? "Yes, we part, but not forever," "Jesu, Lover of my soul," "Rock of Ages, cleft for me"—to them it all seemed so real!

Yes, it was plain enough: religion meant something to these people. And little by little, not a few on board, instead of wishing themselves out of it, began to wish they were in it in a real sense.

Before ever they had seen the *Lammermuir*, or the crew had been engaged for the voyage, much prayer had been made for those with whom they were to travel all the way to China. Very definitely they had asked for a ship's company to whom the Lord would bless His Word. That prayer was still going up, both on board and at home, and they were eagerly looking for the answer. "A voyage across the ocean will not make anyone a soulwinner," as Mr. Taylor often said, but these fellow workers, whatever they may have lacked in some directions, possessed that personal knowledge of God which makes men keen about bringing others to know Him too.

And Mr. Taylor's example helped them not a little. Soulwinning was to him, as it had always been, the very object of his existence as a Christian. For this he lived, prayed, labored; and amid the many responsibilities that had come upon him he was still, in this sense, the true missionary. He encouraged his fellow workers also in putting prayer, definite, believing prayer, before any other means to bring about conversion, and in seeking to live the life that makes such prayer possible. Well he knew how easy it is on board ship to drift into an unhelpful spirit and lose all influence for good over others. Novel reading, waste of time, and self-indulgence at table were carefully watched against, and the daily prayer meeting kept up, which registered unerringly the spiritual temperature of the little company. Chinese study and useful reading occupied a good part of the day, Mr. Taylor himself having a Greek grammar on hand, and Wordsworth's commentary on Leviticus. But the eternal welfare of those with whom they traveled was sought directly, as well as in these indirect but potent ways.

The conversion of the second officer, twenty-five days out from Plymouth, was a welcome answer to prayer, and was quickly followed by that of two of the midshipmen. This was the beginning of an awakening among the crew which continued for some time. Concern about spiritual things began to lay hold of them, and there was great joy among the missionaries as one after another came out into the light.

High-water mark was reached early in August when the first mate, who had been a savage bully among the men, experienced a real change of heart. For a month or more his wretchedness had been pitiable, but though under deep conviction of sin, it was not without a desperate struggle he was able to break with the old life and enter into peace in believing.

To Search Out a Resting Place

Through storm and near shipwreck, through times of discord within the missionary group, and through coming back to spiritual usefulness, the *Lammermuir* at length came to anchor off the foreign settlement of Shanghai. Her broken, dismantled condition made her an object of general curiosity among the gaily-painted junks and foreign ships; but when it became known that she only carried missionaries, albeit the largest party that had yet come to China, interest soon subsided, and beyond a few facetious remarks in the papers, little notice was taken of the new arrivals.

To them, that quiet Sunday was specially grateful. They did not go ashore, and out on the river they were protected from many visitors. Their hearts were full of thankfulness for recent deliverances—more wonderful, even, than they realized at the time. A vessel coming in soon after their own proved to have lost sixteen out of a ship's company of twenty-two, while on the *Lammermuir* none were missing or seriously injured, and no sooner had they reached a place of safety than terrific gales again swept the coast, which in their disabled condition they could not possibly have weathered.

The voyage over, Mr. Taylor's difficulties were in a sense begun. Looking out on that familiar scene—the crowded river, the European houses along the Bund, and the wall of the Chinese city beyond—he realized in a very practical way the responsibilities that had come to him. Where was he to find accommodation for so large a party that would afford the facilities required? Boxes from the hold, more or less soaked with sea water, and all the baggage from the cabins had to be unpacked, dried, and rearranged. Much must be left in Shanghai for a time, as in addition to personal belongings, they had with them household goods, a considerable quantity of stores, printing and lithographic presses, and a large supply of drugs and medical apparatus. All these, after careful examination, needed safe, dry storage; and the washing machines, mangle, and ironing-stove must be unpacked and set to work, for there was the clothing of more than twenty people to be laundered after a four months' voyage. Little wonder he was tempted to feel anxious, remembering the difficulty of obtaining even temporary accommodation in the settlement.

For those were not the days of missionary homes and agencies. Foreign hotels were few and very costly; Chinese inns were out of the question for such a party; and the native boats to which they might have been transferred would not have met the case. Furnished houses were rarely to be had, even if expense were no consideration, and the hospitality of European residents could not reasonably be counted on. The missionary community in Shanghai at the time consisted of only nine married and three single men, and who among them would be able, however willing, to receive so many visitors? Then again, if the party had to be divided, some in one home and some in another, how was the work to be attended to? Altogether the situation was complicated and would have given rise to anxiety, had it not been that, both from the *Lammermuir* and from friends at home, prayer had been going up for months past that the Lord would Himself see and provide.

Meanwhile, unknown to Mr. Taylor, a friend of Ningpo days had moved up to Shanghai, bringing with him the printing press of the American Presbyterian Mission. In a semi-foreign house he was living near the Chinese city (East Gate), and with a view to future needs he had purchased a disused building intended for a theater, which formed a convenient warehouse connected with his premises. Large and empty, this building immediately suggested itself when the *Lammermuir* appeared in the river and he learned that it carried Mr. Taylor's party. How they must need the cheer of a friendly welcome and some place in which to dispose their belongings! If nothing better was offered, his home was open to them, such as it was. So taking a sampan that very afternoon, William Gamble sought out his friends to put at their disposal a bachelor's hospitality.

Almost too good to be true must it have seemed when, three days later, Mr. Taylor returned from a trip to Ningpo to remove his family and fellow workers to the quarters thus provided. Captain Bell had insisted on their remaining on the *Lammermuir* meanwhile, and though absent so short a time, Mr. Taylor had been greatly prospered. He had been enabled to come into touch with all the senior members of the C.I.M., save Mr. and Mrs. Stevenson, who were some distance inland. The church at Bridge Street, amid their rejoicing, had come to his help in a practical way, for which he was most thankful—sending back with him the evangelist Tsiu, one of the fruits of his own early labors, and a Christian woman as well as two men to help in caring for the new arrivals.

In the midst of many occupations, Hudson Taylor had little time for writing, and little thought to give to the criticisms that buzzed about the foreign community. That ladies should be brought out to wear Chinese dress and live in the interior roused indignation in certain quarters. It was freely hinted that Mr. Taylor must be a madman or worse, and that Bedlam would have been a safer destination for himself and his companions than Shanghai. "But he went quietly on," as Mr. Rudland, one of the Inland Mission's original missionaries, remembered, "saying little or nothing about it; always letting discourtesies drop out of sight so graciously, without affecting his own friendliness."

The next stage of their journey was to be a leisurely one, via the Grand Canal to Hangchow, the far-famed capital of the neighboring province. Here it was hoped they might be enabled to commence operations and, with Mr. Stevenson between them and Ningpo, complete a chain of C.I.M. stations a hundred miles into the interior. At one or other of the cities en route, Mr. Taylor expected to leave some of the young men with the evangelist. They were to travel by native houseboats, giving regular hours to study and waiting on God as to their ultimate location.

To take so large a party inland at all was a step of faith, especially as it included an English nurse and four little children, besides six unmarried ladies. In the whole of China at that time, there was not one unmarried lady missionary to be found away from the treaty ports, and the entire staff of such workers, including these new arrivals, numbered only seventeen. Seventeen missionary women free to devote their time to schools, hospitals, and evangelization—it was a mere nothing, even for the ports! And away from those few, coastal cities, scarcely a voice was raised to tell of redeeming love to the women and children of half the heathen world. "The Lord giveth the word: the women that publish the tidings are a great host." To add to their number in China and facilitate their all-important work was one of Mr. Taylor's chief objects in the formation of the Inland Mission, and he was prepared to let devoted women make the sacrifices necessary and to take upon himself the responsibility of helping them in every way possible.

For their protection as well as to lessen difficulties he considered the wearing of native dress essential, with a large measure of conformity to Chinese manners and customs. Mr. Taylor's companions of the *Lammermuir* party being one with him in these convictions, the change into native dress was effected without delay. They did not remain long enough in Shanghai to complete the ladies' outfits, but the young men submitted to the somewhat trying process of shaving the front part of the head and donning the *queue* and loose-fitting garb of the country, Mr. Taylor doing the same. Mrs. Taylor also appeared in Chinese costume at Mr. Gamble's table. To her it meant no little sacrifice. She had not worn it during her previous residence in China, and experience enabled her to realize something of the restrictions it must involve. Of this, she wrote to Mrs. Berger:

> Things which are tolerated in us as foreigners, wearing foreign dress, could not be allowed for a moment in native ladies. I do not at all mean to imply a doubt as to the desirability of the change, but the nearer we come to the Chinese in outward appearance, the more severely

will any breach of propriety according to their standards be criticized. Henceforth I must never be guilty, for example, of taking my husband's arm out of doors! And in fifty or a hundred other ways we may, without great watchfulness, shock the Chinese by what would seem to them grossly immodest and unfeminine conduct....Pray much for us in respect to this matter.

Four weeks later it was a company thoroughly Chinese as to outward appearances that drew near the famous city of Hangchow. The gypsy life so romantic at first had become wearisome enough in their slow-going boats. Happily, the days were fine with the crisp freshness of autumn; but the nights were bitterly cold, and it had become an urgent matter to find more adequate shelter. Nowhere on the way, however, had it been possible to rent premises. Again and again, just when it seemed they had succeeded, negotiations had fallen through, and from place to place they had been obliged to move on, an unbroken party.

Bravely they had kept up their studies and used every opportunity, with the help of their Chinese companions, for making known the Way of Life. But crowded quarters, repeated disappointments, and growing concern with regard to the reception that might be expected at their destination made the journey a trying one, bringing out both the strength and weakness of individual characters. All were suffering from the cold; several, including the children, were more or less ill; and the Ningpo servants began to talk about going home for the winter. The boat people, needless to say, were full of complaints. Far from their accustomed waters, in a district dangerously unsettled through the rebellion, they too were feeling the stress of anxiety and were clamoring to be set free to return to Shanghai. Altogether the situation was a critical one, and prayer was the only resource of much-tried hearts.

It was upon Mr. Taylor the burden pressed most heavily, as he left the boats in an unfrequented place near the city and set out with the evangelist to seek the home it was so necessary to find. When he was gone and they were left in a good deal of suspense, Mrs. Taylor gathered all the party for united prayer. The circumstances affected her in quite a special way, for before long she was to lay in little Gracie's arms the baby sister for whom the child, the Taylors' eldest, was daily asking in her prayers. Yet that mother heart, so tender in its solicitude, was perfectly at rest. "Who will bring me into the strong city?" had come in her psalm for that morning, "Who will lead me into Edom? Wilt not thou, O God...? Give us help from trouble: for vain is the help of man. Through God we shall do valiantly" (Ps. 60:9–12). Quietly she read the passage now, and none who were present could ever forget the prayer that followed. It changed an hour of painful suspense into one of soul outpouring, preparing the young missionaries as nothing else could have done for whatever news Mr. Taylor might bring.

And very soon he came. Before they could have expected it, his voice was heard near the boats, and with radiant face he was among them. Yes, all was well. The Lord had indeed gone before. Just as in Shanghai, a home was ready, waiting!

Knowing that a friend of Ningpo days, belonging to the same mission as Mr. Gamble, had recently moved to Hangchow, Mr. Taylor called on him first of all to acquaint him with their arrival.

"We have been expecting you," was Mr. Green's kindly welcome, "and I have a message you may be glad to receive."

A young American missionary, it appeared, had just left the city to bring his wife and child from Ningpo to the home he had prepared for them. His house, furnished and ready, would be empty for a week at least, and he had thought of Mr. Taylor's party.

"Tell them," he had said to Mr. Green, "to go straight to my place when they come. It is at their disposal for the time being."

The house was on a quiet street and could be reached in boats without observation. Mr. Kreyer was not expected back for several days, and all they had to do was to take possession. Well can one imagine the praise meeting that was held then and there, before the boats moved on!

"Who will bring me into the strong city? Who will lead me into Edom? Wilt not thou O God?"

"Oh That Thou Wouldest Bless Me Indeed"

It was no time for resting on their oars, however. Under cover of darkness the whole party had entered Hangchow without causing any excitement, and had taken up their abode in Mr. Kreyer's premises. But the latter was returning shortly, and the question of a home of their own was urgent. Where in the great city, still suffering from the ravages of the Taiping Rebellion, they were to find quarters large enough for themselves and the work they hoped to do was indeed a problem. But in this again the Lord had gone before them.

Nothing could have been more suitable, as Mr. Taylor soon discovered, than the very first house to which he was directed. Large and well built, it had been a mandarin's residence, but was sadly dilapidated now, and a regular rabbit warren occupied by a number of families. The situation was excellent, in a quiet corner, near the city wall and busy streets. The upper story offered sleeping accommodation for the whole party, a second staircase making it possible to shut off a separate wing for the young men. This was so manifest an advantage that it made Mr. Taylor decide to obtain the premises if possible—the downstairs rooms being adaptable for guest halls, chapel and dispensary, printing press, dining room, servants' quarters, etc.

Almost with fear and trembling, after hearing the rent demanded, he made an offer which was not accepted. The landlord, perceiving that the matter was urgent, hoped by prolonged negotiations to drive a better bargain. Sunday, however, intervened—putting a stop, as far as the missionaries were concerned, to business transactions—and to the surprise of the landlord he saw no more of his would-be tenants. But though they had nothing to say to him apparently, they had much to lay before the Lord. The day was given to prayer, and when on Monday morning his decision was asked it was much more favorable.

"They must have other houses in view," he said to himself. "If I am not careful I shall lose good tenants."

With surprising alacrity, after this, he came to terms, so that by Tuesday evening the necessary documents were signed and sealed. Some of the occupants had already moved out to liberate the upper story. Five families remained, but there was plenty of room, the landlord urged, for Mr. Taylor's household. Let them only move in, and before long they should have the entire premises. On Wednesday morning, accordingly, November 28—the very day Mr. Kreyer was to return—so early that the sleeping city knew nothing of what was happening, the *Lammermuir* party made their way through the silent streets and entered upon a home of their own after six months of traveling and unsettlement.

It is interesting to notice that Hudson Taylor had not been in Hangchow three weeks before he was informing Mr. Berger about postal and banking communication with the inland provinces:

> You will be glad to learn that facilities for sending letters by native post and transmitting money through native banks to various points in the interior are very good. I do not think there will be any difficulty in remitting money to any province in the empire which will not be easily overcome. In the same way letters from the most distant places can be sent to the ports. Such communication is slow and may prove rather expensive, but is tolerably sure. Thus we see the way opening before us for work in the interior.

Meanwhile, there was no lack of work immediately around him. Happily, a spell of milder weather favored the process of getting their premises somewhat into order. To the uninitiated, the latter looked more like a collection of outhouses and barns, in deplorable condition, than the handsome residence Mr. Taylor assured them it once had been. In any case, the work of settling in involved scraping thick dirt from the floors of the upper rooms—and they were clean compared with the downstairs quarters. Mr. Taylor wrote, concerning these living quarters:

> It is pretty cold weather to be living in a house without any ceilings and with very few walls and windows. There is a deficiency in the wall of my own bedroom six feet by nine, closed in with a sheet, so that ventilation is decidedly free. But we heed these things very little. Around us are poor, dark heathen—large cities without any missionary, populous towns without any missionary, villages without number, all destitute of the means of grace. I do not envy the state of mind that would forget these, or leave them to perish, for fear of a little discomfort. May God make us faithful to Him and to our work.

Well was it that the party were in Chinese dress, for they lived at close quarters for a month or more with the families who shared their rambling abode. Although the house took on by degrees a measure of cleanliness, it had little acquaintance with "foreign" things and ways that could prove disquieting. Knives and forks, together with English crockery and cooking, had been left behind in Shanghai, and the simplest of Chinese furniture was found to meet all requirements. There were the regulation chairs and tables in the guest hall, for the proper reception of visitors, but for the rest, boards and trestles, wooden benches, and beds consisting of a wooden frame strung with coconut fibers sufficed. At mealtimes a Chinese company, to all appearances, gathered round the table minus a cloth, set with basins and chopsticks, and the food served was equally familiar to the neighbors who were looking on. Perhaps it was this that disarmed prejudice and made a way for friendly intercourse. There was nothing to be afraid of.

"These people are like ourselves," was the conclusion soon come to. "They eat our rice and wear our dress, and their words we understand."

So from the first, one and another began to drop in to Chinese prayers, attracted by the singing, and before the new arrivals had been a week in the house one woman was openly interested in the Gospel. Miss Faulding, who had made good progress with the language and was welcomed by the native tenants, wrote:

> We have been getting the house a little more comfortable, though there is plenty still to be done. Mr. Taylor and the young men have contrived paper ceilings fixed on wooden frames, which keep out some of the cold air, for the upstairs rooms have roofs such as you find in chapels at home. They also have papered some of the walls or wooden partitions between the rooms. Of course we are as yet in confusion, but we are getting on and I hope shall be settled some day.
>
> The lodgers are to leave next week; they occupy principally the ground floor....I am so glad for them to have been here, for many come to Chinese prayers and listen attentively. We could not have visited out-of-doors just yet...but I read and talk with these women every day, and they seem to like it. One woman I have great hope of. She has given up burning incense and says that since we came she has begun to pray to God. They are all employed in making imitation money out of silver paper, to be burnt for the use of dead relatives—a great trade here. While I am reading to them, they often take out their pipes and have a few whiffs, almost choking me with

smoke. Of course I don't say anything, for every woman seems to smoke. They ask plenty of questions about ourselves, and sometimes such things as, "Where must we go to worship God?"...Yesterday we had a congregation of ten neighbors, gathered in by the woman who is so interested, besides our lodgers and servants.

Thus the good work began, and with what interest the young missionaries watched these developments, and how fervently in their noon prayer meetings they sought the life-giving touch of the Holy Spirit for one and another who seemed impressed! Among these a soldier, for example, reading for the first time a Gospel and a copy of the book of Acts, gave cause for encouragement.

"What a difference there was," he remarked, "between Judas and Paul: the one a disciple who betrayed his Master, the other a persecutor who became the most devoted of His followers."

A Buddhist priest, too, hearing Mr. Taylor preach at a street corner, made the evangelist, Tsiu, rejoice by coming daily with intelligent questions. A third who dropped in out of curiosity and was welcomed by one of the young men, was so touched by the kindly spirit behind the poor attempt at Chinese that he came again and soon joined the little group who every morning were to be found in the guest hall, reading the Scriptures.

With the Chinese New Year, early in February (1867), came golden opportunities. A dispensary had by that time been opened, precursor of all the medical work for which Hangchow has become famous. With much else upon his hands, it was not easy for Mr. Taylor to attend to scores of patients daily; but there was no other doctor nearer than Ningpo or Shanghai, and his heart went out to the people in their sufferings. From far and near the patients came with every variety of complaint both of body and soul, and when holiday makers were added at the New Year season, the doctor and his helpers were overwhelmed with guests.

All this, needless to say, was a great joy to Mr. Berger and the friends at home. That within six months of their arrival the *Lammermuir* party should not only be settled in the interior, but that they should be cheered with so much of blessing in their rapidly growing work, was a wonderful answer to the prayers that had been going up on their behalf. No less strenuous than their own was the life Mr. and Mrs. Berger were living in the service of the mission. Already advanced in years, it was not easy for them to turn their quiet home into a mission center, using as offices both dining room and study; to encumber the billiard room with packing cases; to receive at their table candidates for China and friends of the missionaries; to direct wrappers, and send out with their own hands the *Occasional Paper;* to attend to a large correspondence, keep accounts, transmit money, arrange for the outgoing of new workers, help with their preparations, fit up their cabins, see them off from any port at any hour of the day or night, and correspond with those already on the field. Yet all this they did with the loving interest of a father's and mother's heart. When it became necessary they went further and adapted a cottage on their grounds for the young men candidates and another for a tutor who gave secretarial help.

How Mr. Berger could find time, amid the claims of business as well as these self-imposed tasks, to write regularly and freely to Mr. Taylor as he did is a marvel. He seems never to have missed a mail. A whole volume of his letters—thin, foreign paper stitched into a leather binding—has been preserved, covering a period of about two years from the sailing of the *Lammermuir*. Reflecting the sympathy and eager interest with which mail after mail was received, this correspondence deals with varied questions, from important spiritual principles to details concerning individual workers. Penned in joy and sorrow, as the tidings from China were cheering or otherwise, these letters breathe a faith and love that were unchanging and form a veritable storehouse of wisdom, helpfulness, and encouragement.

Chapter 9

Treasures of Darkness

Little reference has hitherto been made to an element that entered largely into Mr. Taylor's experience: he was the tenderest of fathers. His children meant more to him than is usually the case with a very busy man, and his delight in them from their infancy was second only to his sense of responsibility for their training. It had cost him much to bring them to China, and journeys that involved an absence from home of weeks at a time, with no means of communication save by special messenger, were a real test both to him and to those left behind.

A tiny sheet of pink note paper with a flower painted in one corner followed Mr. Taylor on his first journey. The single word "Papa" in a large round hand on the envelope showed from whom it came, but the worn, travel-stained condition of the little missive, as one handles it now, is more eloquent than the loving words:

> Dear Papa, I hope God has helped you to do what you wanted, and that you will soon come back. I have a nice bead mat for you when you come home...dear, *dear* Papa.

Carried in her father's pocketbook for many a long year, Gracie's little letter, probably the first she ever wrote, tells of the hard life he led no less than of his tender love for her. She was the eldest of his flock, the precious link with early years when he had first met, loved, and married her mother in Ningpo. Three sons had been given to them in England, followed by the baby sister, whose arrival brought special joy to Gracie's heart. But though all were equally dear to their parents, there was about the little maiden of eight years old a peculiar charm. On the *Lammermuir*, the wonderful change in some of the sailors when they came to know and love the Lord Jesus had so impressed her that she too gave her heart to the Savior as never before. Her deeply spiritual nature had developed like a flower in the sunshine, under the consciousness of His love, so that toward the end of this first summer in Hangchow her father could write to the grandparents:

> I do wish you had seen her lately. Since her conversion she had become quite another child. Her look was more soft, more sweet, more happy.

That first summer was intensely hot, and when the thermometer stood at 103 degrees indoors it seemed time to seek relief. The children were all suffering, and Mrs. Taylor was so ill that it was with difficulty she could be taken out of the city. A boat trip of six miles brought them to the hills, where, amid the ruins of a once famous temple, accommodation had been found. A couple of sheds, or long narrow buildings, were still habitable, in addition to the hall that held idols, and in the former—the priests being willing to turn an honest penny—the Hangchow party established themselves. The hills were lovely, though the glory of azaleas, wisteria, and other spring flowers had passed away. Pines, oaks, and elms afforded welcome shade, while mountain streams made music, and as far as eye could see there was one unbroken sweep of higher or lower ranges, canals, and rivers, with the Hangchow

Bay and the open sea beyond. It would have been a paradise as compared with the city, but for the illness of several of the party and the sorrowful sights and sounds of idol worship close at hand.

As they left their boats the first day and were going up the steep stone path made for pilgrims, little Gracie noticed a man making an idol.

"Oh, Papa," she said earnestly, "he doesn't know about Jesus, or he would never do it! Won't you tell him?"

Her hand clasped in his, Mr. Taylor did so, the child following with eager interest. Farther on they came to a shady place and sat down to rest. Gracie's thoughts were still full of what had happened, and she seemed relieved when her father suggested that they should pray for the man they had been trying to help. Of this occasion, Mr. Taylor later recalled when every memory of her was precious:

> We sang a hymn, and then I said, "Will you pray first?" She did so, and never had I heard such a prayer. She had seen the man *making an idol:* her heart was full, and she was talking to God on his behalf. The dear child went on and on, pleading that God would have mercy upon the poor Chinese and would strengthen her father to preach to them. I never was so moved by any prayer. My heart was bowed before God. Words fail me to describe it.

And now, a week later, how dark the shadow that had fallen on that father's heart! He wrote to Mr. Berger on August 15:

> Beloved brother, I know not how to write or how to refrain. I seem to be writing, almost, from the inner chamber of the King of Kings.

Surely this is holy ground. I am trying to pen a few lines by the couch on which my darling little Gracie lies dying. Her complaint is hydrocephalus. Dear brother, our flesh and our heart fail, but God is the strength of our heart and our portion forever.

It was no vain nor unintelligent act when, knowing this land, its people and climate, I laid my wife and children, with myself, on the altar for this service. And He Whom so unworthily, with much of weakness and failure, yet in simplicity and godly sincerity, we are and have been seeking to serve, and not without some measure of success—He has not left us now.

"Who plucked this flower?" said the gardener.

"The Master," answered his fellow workman. And the gardener held his peace.

It was not that there was any questioning of the dealings of God with them or their precious child. But the loss was so great, so overwhelming! Hudson Taylor wrote to his mother in September:

Except when diverted from it by the duties and necessities of our position, our torn hearts will revert to the one subject, and I know not how to write to you of any other. Our dear little Gracie! How we miss her sweet voice in the morning, one of the first sounds to greet us when we woke—and through the day and at eventide! As I take the walks I used to take with her tripping at my side, the thought comes anew like a throb of agony, "Is it possible that I shall never more feel the pressure of that little hand, never more hear the sweet prattle of those dear lips, never more see the sparkle of those bright eyes?" And yet she is not *lost.* I would not have her back again. I am thankful *she* was taken, rather than any of the others, though she was the sunshine of our lives....But she is far holier, far happier than she could ever have been here.

I think I never saw anything so perfect, so beautiful, as the remains of that dear child. The long, silken eyelashes under the finely arched brows; the nose, so delicately chiseled; the mouth, small and sweetly expressive; the purity of the white features; the quiet composure of the countenance—all are deeply impressed on heart and memory. Then her sweet little Chinese jacket, and the little hands folded on her bosom, holding a single flower—oh, it was passing fair! and so hard to close forever from our sight.

Pray for us. At times I seem almost overwhelmed with the internal and external trials connected with our work. But He has said, "I will never leave thee, nor forsake thee" (Heb. 13:5), and "My strength is made perfect in weakness" (2 Cor. 12:9). So be it.

Meanwhile, the great, waiting land, in all its need and darkness, was not forgotten. Difficulties had been more and trials heavier than had been anticipated, but even as Mr. and Mrs. Taylor gave back the little one they so tenderly loved to Him whose loan she had been, they consecrated themselves afresh to the task of reaching inland China with the Gospel. At the bedside of their dying child in the temple, Duncan, the steadfast Highlander, Mr. Taylor's chief companion on pioneering journeys, had been keeping watch, giving much comfort to the grieving family.

The sorrowful days of summer then gave place to the joy of harvest. To Mr. Taylor's great thankfulness, he had been joined by his old friend Wang Lae-djün of Ningpo, who was by this time an experienced Christian worker. An engagement with another mission had detained him, but no sooner was he free than he came over to see if he could be of use to those to whom he owed everything spiritually. Twice already baptisms had taken place at Hangchow, and there was quite a group of believers who needed pastoral care. This Mr. Taylor was little able to give, with all the other claims upon him, and it was with great thankfulness he recognized in Wang Lae-djün the very helper needed.

And now the little church, inaugurated in July with nineteen members, was growing rapidly under the helpful oversight of its native pastor. Mr. Taylor himself was keeping in close touch with them, preaching on Sundays whenever he could, and seeking to develop a missionary spirit among the Christians. Many glimpses are given in the correspondence of the period of this side of his activities, the more directly missionary work in which he delighted, but upon these we must not dwell.

This brings us to one of the important discoveries Mr. and Mrs. Taylor were making along the lines of women's work. For the new departure of going to the people in their own homes, dressed as they were, and with nothing that could make them feel the Gospel message to be foreign to their own life and surroundings, was justified by results. Miss Faulding wrote that autumn:

> I think if you could see how the people love and trust us you would rejoice. It does so please them to see us liking to be like themselves in outward things. They express the greatest satisfaction and are delighted especially that our shoes and style of hair dressing should be the

same as theirs. Instead of having difficulty in getting access to the people, they come here day after day saying,

"We want you to come to our house and teach us about the religion."

A woman said to me the other day, "Do come, my mother wants to hear...."

I sometimes long that my whole time could be spent in visiting, at others that at least half could be given to the school—for I do so long to see native preachers raised up there, and the boys want training. Then again, we need books so much that if I could spend several hours daily with the teacher I should be glad. The work just seems overwhelming taking this city alone, and how much more so when one looks beyond to provinces full of cities in which there is no missionary! And look beyond we must.

My heart does so well up with joy that I am here, and here among the people to a great extent as one of themselves....Nothing could be more encouraging than our position—so almost more than willingly the people listen. I should think when I go out I often speak to more than two hundred persons....Yet I am never treated in any way rudely, but with all kindness. Sometimes, indeed, it is with difficulty I get out of having to smoke a pipe, while tea and lunch I frequently have to take.

Rich and poor alike welcomed this gentle visitor, and it was not a passing curiosity, for the more she became known, the more she was invited into homes of all sorts. Ladies in mandarins' families sent for her, and she was welcomed even to a Buddhist nunnery, but as of old it was "the common people" who gave most heed to the message.

People came to hear the message because of women such as Miss Faulding—men, women, and children, whether to school or sewing class, dispensary or public meetings. The medical work had done much to attract, but Mr. Taylor, as he watched it all, could not but be profoundly impressed with this new line of things, new at any rate in China. And fuller experience only justified the conclusion. Yet of all the innovations connected with the mission, none met with stronger opposition. The presence of unmarried ladies in the interior at all was, with many, a sufficient ground for condemning the whole work, and determined efforts were made to secure their recall to the coast. It was strongly stated in letters home that to send unmarried ladies to inland stations was a waste of life and energy, as there was no opening for their labors.

Thus they were grappling with big problems, and obtaining, even then, glimpses of developments to which God was leading in His own way. And in the process He was developing them, preparing one and another for the special work that lay before them.

Among all the mercies that crowned the year 1867—the first complete year for the *Lammermuir* party in China—none was greater than the answer to the prayer with which it had opened: "Oh that thou wouldest bless me indeed, and enlarge my coast" (1 Chron. 4:10). The stations occupied by the mission had doubled in number in that short period. At its commencement, the distance between the most widely separated had been only four days' journey, but at its close, Duncan, in Nanking, was as much as twenty-four days, by ordinary means of travel, from Stott in Wen-chow.

This was a considerably enlarged sphere of labor when one remembers that, with the exception of Hangchow, no Protestant missionaries save those of the C.I.M. were settled anywhere away from the coast or the treaty ports.

Very easily, as one can see, might the whole mission have become absorbed in that one coast-board province, small though it was among all the provinces of China. But, providentially, door after door was closed. Riots, disturbances, sickness, and other troubles hindered developments that would have tended in this direction, and gradually, almost insensibly, Mr. Taylor's own way seemed guided northward.

It was not easy after sixteen months in Hangchow to face the thought of leaving the work that had become so dear to them for some desirable city near the Yangtze in which to begin all over again. Fifty baptized believers were gathered already in the little church under Pastor Wang's care, and there were many inquirers. But Mr. and Mrs. McCarthy and Miss Faulding would remain in charge of the station and be quite able to receive and help new workers. Duncan at Nanking was sorely needing relief, and Mrs. Taylor was ready to go either there or anywhere else as the work seemed to require. But much had to be considered as spring came on, and the noon prayer meetings were times of real drawing near to God.

An Open Door

Pleasant enough for the first few weeks was a spring journey up the Grand Canal. Hangchow was left behind on the tenth of April, Mrs. Taylor and the children traveling by houseboat in a measure of comfort. After long confinement within city walls, the freedom and freshness of the country were delightful. Extensive mulberry plantations bordered the canal, with plum, peach, and apricot orchards in bridal array. Wheat and barley covered the valleys, interspersed with great tracts of peas and beans in flower. The canal itself, alive with boat traffic, was an endless interest to the children, while the background of hills refreshed their elders with ever-changing loveliness. And there were many opportunities for coming into friendly relation with other travelers and the people whose homes they were passing day by day.

At one great city en route, Soo-chow, workers of the mission had recently obtained a settlement, and a stay of three weeks enabled Mr. Taylor, who there caught up with the party, to give considerable help in medical and other ways. Beyond this point all was unbroken ground. Hardly a Protestant missionary was resident northward or westward anywhere in the interior besides Mr. Taylor's companion of old, Duncan, who was in Nanking. To join him in his lonely post was Mr. Taylor's intention, unless some more important opening should detain him by the way.

And this was just what happened when Chinkiang was reached—that busy center of population and commerce at the junction of the Grand Canal and the mighty flood of the Yangtze. Being a treaty port, a few foreigners, including the British consul, were living in the settlement outside the native city, and in one of the suburbs the L.M.S. had a chapel in charge of a native preacher. No missionary, however, was to be found nearer than Shanghai, at a distance of twenty-four hours by steamer. Much impressed with the strategic importance of this place, Mr. Taylor set out on foot with a view to renting premises and was soon in treaty for a house inside the city, which was ultimately obtained, though not without serious difficulty and danger. Meanwhile, seeing that the negotiations were likely to be prolonged, he continued his journey across the Yangtze and a few miles up the northern section of the Grand Canal.

And now the travelers were nearing the far-famed city of Yangchow, of which Marco Polo was once governor. Rich, proud, and exclusive, it contained a population of three hundred and sixty thousand, still without any witness for Christ. Life on the water by this time was losing its charm. Spring had given place to summer, and with the intense heat the rainy season had come on. Day and night it poured incessantly, and the children, cooped up in the leaky boat, where nothing could be kept dry, were exposed to serious risks. Waiting upon God very definitely for guidance, it was with no little thankfulness that Mr. and Mrs. Taylor saw the way open before them much more readily than could have been anticipated. Within the city, their native helpers had come into friendly touch with an innkeeper able and willing to receive the whole party. The accommodation he offered, moreover, was not on the ground floor—always more or less malarious at such a season—but five rooms forming an upper story which they could have to themselves. This was so unusual from every point of view that they could not but feel it providential, and, thankfully leaving the crowded junks on the canal, they took possession of their new quarters.

"An open door...a little strength" (Rev. 3:8) and "many adversaries" (1 Cor. 16:9)—it was no new situation for heralds of the Cross, though it was to prove more serious in its outcome than Mr. Taylor at first anticipated. For to begin with, the people seemed friendly. The presence of the mother and children disarmed suspicion. Evidently this foreigner in "civilized" (i.e., Chinese) dress was no commercial or political agent, and curiosity attracted many visitors. The innkeeper, indeed, who had been a little anxious, offered his services as "middleman," if Mr. Taylor wished to rent premises and settle in the city.

Their original success in this area was soon to come to an end. After not being able to settle the matter of the house in which they found themselves living, the missionaries began to realize a change that was coming over the attitude of the people. Friendly visitors had given place to crowds of the lowest rabble about the door, and a set of posters, quite unfit for translation, was as fuel to the fire.

When it looked as if the worst was over, after some rain kept the people from attacking in response to the slanderous handbills, an opportunity occurred for reviving the agitation. A couple of foreigners from Chinkiang, wearing not the native costume adopted by Mr. Taylor's party, but undisguised "foreign dress," came up to visit Yangchow, and were seen in various parts of the city. This was too good a chance to be lost, and no sooner had they left with the impression that all was quiet than reports began to be circulated that children were missing in all directions, entrapped by the "foreign devils." The weather was intensely hot, which always predisposes to excitable gatherings. Children had disappeared, so the people believed; twenty-four at least had fallen prey to the dreaded foreigners. And on the foreigners premises, as was well known, vast stores of treasures were accumulated! Boatloads of goods had been brought in only a few days previously.[1] Courage! Avenge our wrongs! Attack—destroy! Much plunder will be ours!

Forty-eight hours later, in a boat nearing Chinkiang, the letter quoted below from Miss Blatchley to Mrs. Berger was bravely finished.

> We have had to flee from Yangchow. I cannot stop now to describe the last few days, if indeed they are describable—for we must send off our notes, such as we have ready. Next mail must bring further particulars. Meanwhile you will join us in praise to God for saving our lives and limbs, and our *most* valuable property. The rioters sacked every room excepting mine, in which were all our most important papers and the bulk of our money—a considerable sum, three hundred dollars, having reached us from Chinkiang only an hour before the breaking into the house.
>
> Poor Mr. Reid is the most severely hurt of all; a brickbat struck his eye while he was standing ready to catch Mrs. Taylor and me—as we had to escape for our lives by jumping from the verandah roof over the front of the reception hall. Dear Mrs. Taylor hurt her leg very much. I, whose fall was

[1] But for difficulties at Chinkiang there never would have been, humanly speaking, a Yangchow riot. Arriving there with a large quantity of goods and finding no house available, other missionaries with the C.I.M. had come on to Yangchow early in August. Thus, three additional foreigners, and all the paraphernalia needed for a printing press and a second household, had been crowded into Mr. Taylor's premises. No wonder the Yangchow people were tempted with thoughts of plunder!

not broken (as Mr. Reid was wounded, and so disabled from helping me), came down on my back on the stones, and it is only by God's great lovingkindness that I have not a broken spine or skull. I have only a wound on my arm, and that the left arm. It is getting very painful, as it is ulcerating, and I am tolerably bruised all over; but there is so much to be thankful for that this seems as nothing, except that it makes one rather awkward, for I feel so stiff. We have not had time yet to change our blood-stained clothes.

And Mrs. Taylor wrote to the same beloved friend:

I do not know whether I shall be able to give you much idea, by this opportunity, of the perils through which we have passed within the last forty-eight hours. *Our* God has brought us through: may it be to live henceforth more fully to His praise and glory....I believe God will bring His own glory out of this, and I hope it will tend to the furtherance of the Gospel—Yours in a present Savior,

"A present Savior"—how little could the rioters understand the secret of their calmness and strength! Awed by something, what, they did not know, the infuriated mob had been restrained from the worst excesses. Murder, though intended, had been averted again and again, and both Mr. Taylor, exposed to all the fury of the populace on his way to seek help of the authorities, and those he had to leave, who faced the perils of attack and fire in their besieged dwelling, were alike protected by the wonder-working hand of God.

But they were hours of anguish—anguish for the mother as she gathered her children and the women of the party in the upper room that seemed most sheltered; anguish for the father, detained at a distance, hearing from the mandarin's yamen the yells of the rioters bent on destruction. Mrs. Taylor wrote:

> After they were gone (Mr. Taylor and Mr. Duncan) we feebler ones could do nothing, assembled in my room to plead for God's protection, both for ourselves and for those who faced the fury of the stone without. Mr. Rudland and Mr. Reid were doing their best to keep the crowd from entering our premises. I do not know that the throne of grace ever seemed so near to me as that night and the following morning. Not that the closeness of communion with God was greater than at any other time, but I felt able in an especial manner to lay hold of God's *strength*. And earnestly did we plead with Him to raise as it were a wall of fire around my dear husband and Mr. Duncan, and to give His angels to encamp round about them. I specially needed His sustaining grace to keep me quiet and calm and to give me soundness of judgment, that no rash step might be taken, for naturally all looked to me to say what was to be done.

Outwardly as calm as if there were no danger, Mrs. Taylor went through those terrible hours, more than once saving the life of a fellow worker by her presence of mind and perfect command of the language; her heart, meanwhile, was torn with anxiety for the loved one it seemed more than likely they might never see again. As for Mr. Taylor, he had quite an adventure himself:

> But for the protection afforded us by the darkness, we should scarcely have reached the

yamen alive. Alarmed by the yells of the people, the gatekeepers were just closing the doors as we approached, but the momentary delay gave time for the crowd to close in upon us; the as yet unbarred gates gave way to the pressure, and we were precipitated into the entrance hall. Had the gates been barred, I am convinced that they would not have been opened for us, and we should have been torn to pieces by the enraged mob.

Once in the yamen, we rushed into the judgment hall crying "Kiu-ming! Kiu-ming!" (save life! save life!), a cry the Chinese mandarin is bound to attend to at any hour of the day or night.

We were taken to the room of the chief secretary, and kept waiting three-quarters of an hour before we had an audience with the prefect, all the time hearing the yells of the mob a mile or more off, destroying, for aught we knew, not only the property, but possibly the lives of those so dear to us. And at last when we did get an audience, it was almost more than we could bear with composure to be asked as to what we really did with the babies; whether it was true we had bought them, and how many; what was the cause of all this rioting? etc., etc.

At last I told His Excellency that the real cause of all the trouble was his own neglect in not taking measures when the matter was small and manageable; that I must now request him first to take steps to repress the riot and save any of our friends who might still be alive, and afterwards make such inquiries as he might wish, or I would not answer for the result.

"Ah," said he, "very true, very true! First quiet the people and then inquire. Sit still, and I will go to see what can be done."

> He went out telling us to remain, as the only chance of his effecting anything depended on our keeping out of sight, for by this time the number of rioters amounted to eight or ten thousand. The natives estimated them at twenty thousand.
>
> We were kept in this torture of suspense for two hours, when the prefect returned with the ts'ao-fu (governor of the military forces of the city, some three thousand men) and told us that all was quiet; that the ts'ao-fu himself, the sheo-pe (captain of the soldiers who guard the gates), and two local mandarins had been to the scene of the disturbance; that they had seized several of those who were plundering the premises, and would have them punished. He then sent for chairs, and we returned under escort. On the way back we were told that all the foreigners we had left were killed. We had to cry to God to support us, though we hoped this might prove exaggerated or untrue.
>
> When we reached the house, the scene was such as baffled description. Here, a pile of half-burned reeds showed where one of the attempts to fire the premises had been made; there, debris of a broken-down wall was lying; and strewn about everywhere were the remains of boxes and furniture, scattered papers and letters, broken work boxes, writing desks, dressing cases, and surgical instrument cases, smoldering remains of valuable books, etc.—but no trace of inhabitants within.

After a long and agonizing search, it was with unspeakable thankfulness he learned that some, at any rate, of the party were hiding in a neighbor's house. The darkness of the night had favored their escape from their own burning premises. Taken from one room to another as the danger of discovery increased, they had finally been left without a glimmer of light in the innermost apartments. Then it was that suspense about Mr. Taylor was hardest to bear. In the darkness and silence, the uncertainty as to his fate as well as their own was terrible. Mrs. Taylor continued to Mrs. Berger:

> I cannot attempt to describe to you our feelings. How my dear husband and Mr. Duncan were faring or had fared we could not tell. Where they were, why they had not yet returned, whether we ourselves would live till morning, or what would become of us we knew not....But God was our stay, and He forsook us not. This confidence He gave me, that He would surely work good for China out of our deep distress.
>
> At one time we were told that soldiers had arrived from the governor and were driving the rioters away, but still no tidings of my husband! Poor Mr. Reid was laid on the floor of an inner room, and nurse with baby (who happily slept) and Mr. and Mrs. Rudland were there too. The older children were with Miss Desgraz, Miss Blatchley, and myself in the outer room. We did our best to keep them quiet and awake, for we did not know at what moment we might have to flee again.
>
> "Mamma," said one of them, "where shall we sleep tonight as they have burned up our bed?"
>
> I assured him that God would give them somewhere to sleep, little thinking it would be—that very night—in their own nursery.
>
> At last, after a much shorter time than it appeared to us we heard my dear husband's voice outside the door, which had been barred for greater safety. He had had difficulty in finding us, and on his way back from the yamen had heard various reports as to what had happened during his long detention. Some said we were all

killed, others that we had fled, and his heart sickened on nearing the house as he distinguished a smell that proved to be fur-lined garments burning....He told us that the rioters had all been driven out, and he thought we might venture back to our own rooms (which had not been burned down)...for there would be a guard around the premises. How our hearts went up to God in thanksgiving that He had spared us to each other!...A short time before we heard my husband's voice, I had felt encouraged to hope that help was at hand by the fact that my own strength was rapidly ebbing away from loss of blood. I was anxious not to let anyone know how much I was hurt, as I felt it would alarm them, and it seemed most important that all should keep calm.

It was after midnight when we returned. My heart was too full for me to pay much heed to the scene of ruin through which we passed, but at the foot of the stairs my eye fell on a bead mat worked for me by our little Gracie before leaving England. The sight of it at that moment seemed to speak of our Father's love and tenderness in a way that perhaps it would be difficult for another to understand. [It was a year that very day since their little daughter had been taken home from the temple at Pen-shan.] I asked someone to pick it up and give it to me. We found the floor of my room strewn with clothes, etc., which had been turned out of boxes in the search for gold and silver. The leaves of my poor Bible, which I had been unable to take with me, were scattered about in every direction. Kind, loving hands collected them for me. Some, I was told, were found downstairs, and not a leaf is missing.

For the remainder of the night we were in quiet, though for some of us there was no sleep.

Early in the morning the guard retired, and as there was no relay the people began to come in again to plunder, for now there were many entrances. Again my husband had to go to the yamen, and again commenced a season of anxiety similar to, though in some respects more trying than, the night before. Once more my room became our sanctuary...till, just when it seemed as if in another minute the crowd would be upstairs, the alarm was given that the mandarin had come, and his soldiery soon dispersed the people.

In the afternoon of that day we left the city...under an escort of soldiers to see us safely to the Yangtze. I have been much struck by the way in which God used these men—who would have been quite as ready to take our lives as to protect them—for His people's help. As we passed out of the city in chairs, Miss Blatchley heard some of the people say derisively, "Come again! Come again!"

"Yes," I thought, "God will bring us back again, little as you expect it."

The Darkest Hour

It was thankfulness more than anything else that filled the hearts of that little company, wounded and suffering as they were, on the boats that took them to Chinkiang. The mandarins had insisted on their leaving for a time, that the house might be repaired and the people quieted, and with no thought of compensation, still less of revenge, the missionaries looked forward to a speedy return. Homeless and despoiled of almost everything, they rejoiced in having been counted worthy to suffer for the sake of the name, and their hearts were cheered as they recalled the protecting care of God. Had not their lives been spared as by a miracle? Were not the children well and happy? And even the money and more important mission papers were safe, though the room in which they had lain had been open to the rioters.

Upon reaching Chinkiang, homeless and in urgent need of succor, great was the kindness received from the foreign residents. Though the community was small, they managed to put up all the refugees, Mr. and Mrs. Taylor taking a room on the ground floor which, being damp, they considered undesirable for others. Here, in the midst of debris from the riot, they set to work at once on the business and correspondence of the mission, having nine or ten stations and many fellow workers to think of as well as the party with them.

Despite the difficulties in regard to the Yangchow affair, a painful spirit persisted in certain members of the mission. A little group of five, having gone back from its principles, after causing endless trouble, were themselves unhappy in association with it. One of these had to be dismissed now for conduct "utterly inconsistent with the position of a Christian missionary." For more than two years Mr. and Mrs. Taylor had done everything in their power to help this particular brother and his wife to live and work happily in the mission. The suffering they had endured from discourtesy, disloyalty, and untrustworthiness could never be told, and not the least part of it was to see the harmful influence exerted upon others. In severing their connection with the C.I.M., Mr. Taylor realized that he might be opening the door for the retirement of three ladies who from the first had been their confidantes—and so it proved, to the relief of all who had been associated with them, and who had marveled at Mr. Taylor's patience in bearing so long. But the sorrow of his heart was very real over the loss of these workers, and he was conscious of the questions to which it must give rise among the friends of the mission at home.

A letter to Mr. Berger written even before the Yangchow riot showed how the true character of the work was more and more unfolding itself to his mind:

> It is most important that married missionaries should be double missionaries—not half or a quarter or eight-part missionaries. Might we not with advantage say to our candidates: "Our work is a peculiar one. We aim at the interior, where the whole of your society will be Chinese. If you wish for luxury and freedom from care...do not join us. Unless you intend your wife to be a true missionary, not merely a wife, homemaker, and friend, do not join us. She must be able to read and be master of at least one Gospel in colloquial Chinese before you marry. A person of ordinary ability may accomplish this in six months, but if she needs longer there is the more reason to wait until she has reached this point before you marry. She must be prepared to be happy among the Chinese when the duties of your calling require, as they often will, your temporary absence from home. You, too, must master the initial difficulties of the language and open up a station, if none be allotted to you, before you marry. With diligence and God's blessing you may hope to do this in a year or so. If these conditions seem too hard, these sacrifices too great to make for perishing China, do not join our mission. These are small things to some

of the crosses you may be permitted to bear for your dear Master!

China is not to be won for Christ by self-seeking, ease-loving men and women. Those not prepared for labor, self-denial, and many discouragements will be poor helpers in the work. In short, the men and women we need are those who will put Jesus, China, souls first and foremost in everything and at all times; life itself must be secondary—nay, even those more precious than life. Of such men, of such women, do not fear to send us too many. Their price is far above rubies.

The riot and all that grew out of it did but emphasize these considerations and deepen Mr. Taylor's thankfulness for many of the fellow workers already given to him. He rejoiced in the devotion to Christ which had led them to cast in their lot with such a mission, in their love for the Chinese and willingness to live in close touch with them, and in the practical way they were adapting themselves to their surroundings. It could not but be obvious to him, as it was to them, how helpful Mrs. Taylor's quiet, unconscious influence was in this direction.

But the Yangchow difficulties were far from ended. "The devil's growl," as Mr. Spurgeon called it, had yet to come, and an angry growl it was that upset not a few friends of the mission. For the action of the consular authorities to deal with the repercussions of the riots through force gave rise to a storm of indignation at home. Missionaries were making trouble as usual, demanding military support in their ill-judged crusade against ancestral worship. The country would be involved in war before the government had even time to consider the matter! It seems almost incredible, as one looks back upon it, that so much misrepresentation could have found its way into the daily papers, and that, for a period of four or five months, Mr. Taylor and his doings could so largely have occupied the public mind. China, of course, was farther off then than now, and there was far less understanding of its problems. But, even so, the attention the subject evoked and the prejudice displayed were extraordinary. From the "connected narrative" in the *Times* of December 1, 1868, "explaining" the whole situation, to the discussion in the House of Lords on March 9, 1869—in which, after a heated declamation, the Duke of Somerset urged that all British missionaries should be recalled from China—the matter seems hardly to have been absent from the public mind. The vigorous attitude enjoined upon the British representative at Peking by a former government was utterly repudiated now, and there was not much to choose between the accusation heaped upon the consular authorities and upon the missionaries. But Mr. Taylor it was, all through, who had brought the country to the verge of war by his irresponsible conduct.

One result of all these difficulties was, not unnaturally, a falling off in the income of the mission, so that for the first time Mr. Taylor was faced with serious shortness of funds in China. This would have been much more the case if the Lord had not laid it upon the heart and put it into the power of Mr. George Müller largely to increase his gifts. He had been sending regularly to several members of the mission, sometimes as much as twenty-five pounds a quarter, and now, within a day or two of the Yangchow riot (long before he heard of it), he wrote to Mr. Berger asking for the names of others who were thoroughly satisfactory in their work whom he might add to his list. Mr. Berger sent him six names from which to choose, and his choice was to take them all. This was not only a substantial help, it was a great encouragement, for it meant added sympathy and prayer on the part of one who knew the way to the throne. And more and more, Mr. Taylor was feeling the need of just such fellowship.

But "the heart knoweth his own bitterness" (Prov. 14:10), and the load Hudson Taylor was carrying was almost more than he could bear. It was not the work with all its difficulty and trial; when consciously in communion with the Lord, these seemed light. It was not shortness of funds, nor anxiety about those dearest to him. It was just—himself: the unsatisfied longing of his heart, the inward struggle to abide in Christ, the frequent failure and disappointment. So bitter was this experience that even when it was left far behind he could never forget it. This it was that made him always sympathetic with younger workers in their spiritual conflicts, quick to see and make the most of every opportunity to help them. Fellowship with God was to him a great reality, a great necessity. He had known much of it, much too of the terrible void of losing it. "Like a diver under water without air, or a fireman on a burning building with an empty hose," he found himself face to face with heathenism and all the claims that pressed upon him, but alas! too often out of touch with Christ. Had he been responsible for himself only this would have been bad enough, but with all the demands upon him it was unbearable—especially in view of the subject to which his thoughts in common with those of his fellow workers were being directed: deeper spiritual life.

To know of our redemption through Christ, of His love for us, in fuller measure was Mr. Taylor's deepest longing, but oh, how different were the actual experiences of his soul! With the growth of the mission, his way seemed ever more beset with inward and outward perplexity, and with a need for the exercise of faith and grace which he had not faith and grace to meet. Sometimes he was buoyed up by hope, sometimes almost in despair.

Life was too busy, as a rule, for his correspondence to reveal much of the crisis through which he was passing, but early in 1869 he found himself alone on a journey which gave opportunity for one of the old-time letters to his mother. He had brought his family to Ningpo for the time being, while he went to and from among the older stations of the mission. Danger of riots detained him in Tai-chow-fu for a month, while the city was full of students for the yearly examination. Both there and in Wen-chow, where Mr. Stott had weathered persistent storms of opposition, the work was already bearing fruit, and Mr. Taylor had the joy of baptizing the first believers. In a more recently opened station, Ning-hai, he found five candidates for baptism and a general willingness to hear the Gospel, where thirteen months previously there had been neither convert nor preacher. His heart had been so burdened about the place on his former visit that he had definitely prayed that the Gospel might be brought there before long, and now it was cheering to see the answer. But while, writing from that very city, he gave his parents the good news, it was their help he sought in those personal matters of which he could hardly have spoken so freely to any other:

I have often asked you to remember me in prayer, and when I have done so there has been much need of it. That need has never been greater than at the present time. Envied by some, despised by many, hated perhaps by others; often blamed for things I never heard of, or had nothing to do with; an innovator on what have become established rules of missionary practice; an opponent of mighty systems of heathen error and superstition; working without precedent in many respects, and with few experienced helpers; often sick in body, as well as perplexed in mind and embarrassed by circumstances; had not the Lord been specially gracious to me, had not my mind been sustained by the conviction that the work is His and that He is with me in what it is no empty figure to call "the thick of the conflict," I must have fainted and broken down. But the battle is the Lord's, and He will conquer. We may fail, do fail continually, but He never fails. Still I need your prayers more than ever before.

My own position becomes continually more and more responsible, and my need greater of special grace to fill it, but I have continually to mourn that I follow at such a distance and learn so slowly to imitate my precious Master. I cannot tell you how I am buffeted sometimes by temptation. I never knew how bad a heart I had. Yet I do know that I love God and love His work and desire to serve Him only and in all things. And I value above all things that precious Savior in whom alone I can be accepted. Often I am tempted to think that one so full of sin cannot be a child of God at all, but I try to throw it back and rejoice all the more in the preciousness of Jesus, and in the riches of that grace that has made us "accepted in the beloved" (Eph. 1:6). Beloved He is of God; beloved He ought to be of us. But oh, how short I fall here again! May God help me to love Him more and serve Him better. Do pray for me. Pray that the Lord will keep me from sin, will sanctify me wholly, will use me more largely in His service.

The Exchanged Life

Life was, if anything, especially full and busy for Mr. Taylor at this time. The outcry about the Yangchow riots had blown over, allowing him to resume work for the Inland Mission. He had returned from his journey round the older stations to an endless succession of duties that kept him on the move between Yangchow and Chinkiang. Both were now, in a sense, the headquarters of the mission, and the growing church in the former and the demands of the printing press in the latter filled every moment that could be spared from account keeping, correspondence, and directorial matters. There had recently been baptisms in Yangchow, and Mr. Judd, who, along with his wife, had been first to volunteer to be in Yangchow after the riot, was glad of all the help Mr. Taylor could give in caring for the young converts. The heat of summer had taken its toll upon all the party, and Mr. Taylor himself had been laid aside by severe illness in the middle of August, 1869. Now, early in September, he was recovering, and trying to overtake the work that had accumulated. It was no time, surely, for an outstanding crisis in spiritual things!

Yet, oh, how deep the heart-hunger, in and through all else! That did not diminish. It seemed to increase, rather, with all the need there was to minister to others. Leaving a full house in Chinkiang, Mr. Taylor had run up to Yangchow to see a patient and was returning now alone by a little boat chosen less for comfort than for speed. It was early in the morning, and he was eager to be in Chinkiang, where Mrs. Taylor was, in time for breakfast, so as not to lose a moment of the day for work. Coming down the Grand Canal and crossing the Yangtze (two miles wide) he had quiet for thought—thought and prayer. Were it not recorded in his own words, it would be difficult to believe, certainly impossible to imagine, such conflict, suffering, almost despair in spiritual things in one who had long and truly known the Lord. Ah, was it not that very fact that made it possible? Nearness to Christ had been to him so real and blessed that any distance was unbearable. So deeply did he love that any clouding of the Master's face was felt, and felt at once with anguish of heart. It is the bride who mourns the absence of the bridegroom, not one who has been a stranger to His love.

Reaching the little crowded house at Chinkiang, Mr. Taylor made his way as soon as possible to his room to attend to correspondence. There, amid a pile of letters, was one from Mr. McCarthy. We do not know if he was alone as he read it; we do not know just how the miracle was wrought. But—"As I read, I saw it all. I looked to Jesus; and when I saw, oh how joy flowed!"

It was Saturday, September 4, 1869; the house was full, and others were coming; somehow they must be put up and kept over Sunday, for this great joy could not but be shared. As soon as he could break away from his glad thanksgiving, Mr. Taylor went out, a new man in a new world, to tell what the Lord had done for his soul. He took the letters, Mr. McCarthy's and one from Miss Faulding in the same strain, and, gathering the household together in the sitting room upstairs, told what his whole life was telling from that time onward to the glorious end. Other hearts were moved and blessed; the streams began to flow. From that little crowded home in Chinkiang city, they flowed on and out, and are flowing still—"rivers of living water" (John 7:38). For "whosoever drinketh of the water that I shall give him," Jesus said, "shall never thirst; but the water that I shall give him shall be in him a well of water springing up into everlasting life" (John 4:14).

And he did more than tell. Pressed though he was with business matters, his correspondence took on a new tone. Here is one of the first letters written with that tide of joy and life more abundant sweeping through his soul. The penciled lines on half a sheet of notepaper show that he was very busy—but how at leisure in spirit!

> My dear sister—We had a very happy day here yesterday. I was so happy! A letter from Mr. McCarthy on this subject has been blessed to several of us. He and Miss Faulding also seem so happy! He says: "I feel as though the first glimmer of the dawn of a glorious day had risen upon me. I hail it with trembling, yet with trust."
>
> The part specially helpful to me is: "How then to have our faith increased? Only by thinking of all that Jesus is, and all He is for us: His life, His death, His work, He Himself as revealed to us in the Word, to be the subject of our constant thoughts. Not a striving to have faith, or to increase our faith, but a looking off to the Faithful One seems all we need."
>
> Here, I feel, is the secret: not asking how I am to get sap out of the vine into myself, but remembering that Jesus is the Vine—the root,

stem, branches, twigs, leaves, flowers, fruit, all indeed. Aye, and far more too! He is the soil and sunshine, air and rain—more than we can ask, think, or desire. Let us not then want to get anything out of Him, but rejoice in being ourselves in Him—one with Him, and, consequently, with all His fullness. Not seeking for faith to bring holiness, but rejoicing in the fact of perfect holiness in Christ, let us realize that—inseparably one with Him—this holiness is ours, and accepting the fact, find it so indeed. But I must stop.

Six weeks after these experiences, when Mr. Taylor was rejoicing in the abiding fullness of this new life, a letter reached him from England that specially touched his heart. It was from his sister, Mrs. Broomhall, the intimate friend and correspondent of his early years, who, now with a growing family round her, was sore pressed, as he had been himself, by outward responsibilities and inward conflict rather than at rest in spiritual things. With a great longing to help one so dear to him, Mr. Taylor took up his pen to reply. As he wrote, the whole story of his own extremity and deliverance was poured out in a letter that is so precious:

October 17, 1869: So many thanks for your long, dear letter....I do not think you have written me such a letter since we have been in China. I know it is with you as with me—you *cannot*, not you *will* not. Mind and body will not bear more than a certain amount of strain, or do more than a certain amount of work. As to work, mine was never so plentiful, so responsible, or so difficult; but the weight and strain are all *gone*. The last month or more has been, perhaps, the happiest of my life; and I long to tell you a little of what the Lord has done for my soul. I do not know how far I may be able to make myself intelligible about it, for there is nothing new or strange or wonderful—and yet, all is new! In a word, "Whereas [once] I was blind, now I see" (John 9:25).

Perhaps I shall make myself more clear if I go back a little. Well, dearie, my mind has been greatly exercised for six or eight months past, feeling the need personally, and for our mission, of more holiness, life, power in our souls. But personal need stood first and was the greatest. I felt the ingratitude, the danger, the sin of not living nearer to God. I prayed, agonized, fasted, strove, made resolutions, read the Word more diligently, sought more time for retirement and meditation—but all was without effect. Every day, almost every hour, the consciousness of sin oppressed me. I knew that if I could only abide in Christ all would be well, but I *could not*. I began the day with prayer, determined not to take my eye from Him for a moment, but pressure of duties, sometimes very trying, constant interruptions apt to be so wearing, often caused me to forget Him. Then one's nerves get so fretted in this climate that temptations to irritability, hard thoughts, and sometimes unkind words are all the more difficult to control. Each day brought its register of sin and failure, of lack of power. To will was indeed present with me, but how to perform I found not.

Then came the question, "Is there no rescue? Must it be thus to the end—constant conflict and, instead of victory, too often defeat?" How, too, could I preach with sincerity that to those who receive Jesus, "to them gave he power to become the sons of God" (John 1:12) (i.e. godlike), when it was not so in my own experience? Instead of growing stronger, I seemed to be getting weaker and to have less power against sin; and no wonder, for faith and even hope were getting very low. I hated myself; I hated my sin; and yet I gained no strength against it. I felt I *was* a child of God; His Spirit in my heart would cry, in spite of all, "Abba, Father," but to rise to my privileges as a child, I was utterly powerless. I thought that holiness, practical holiness, was to be gradually attained by a diligent use of the means of grace. I felt that there was nothing I so much desired in this world, nothing I so much needed. But so far from in any measure attaining it, the more I pursued and strove after it, the more it eluded my grasp, till hope itself almost died out, and I began to think that, perhaps to make heaven the sweeter, God would not give it down here. I do not think I was striving to attain it in my own strength. I knew I was powerless. I told the Lord so and asked Him to give me help and strength, and sometimes I almost believed He would keep and uphold me. But on looking back in the evening, alas! there was but sin and failure to confess and mourn before God....

All the time I felt assured that there was in Christ all I needed, but the practical question was how to get it out. He was rich, truly, but I was poor; He strong, but I weak. I knew full well that there was in the root, the stem, abundant fatness, but how to get it into my puny little branch was the question. As gradually the light was dawning on me, I saw that faith was the only prerequisite, was the hand to lay hold on His fullness and make it my own. But I *had not this faith.* I strove for it, but it would not come; tried to exercise it, but in vain. Seeing more and more the wondrous supply of grace laid up in Jesus, the fullness of our precious Savior—my helplessness and guilt seemed to increase. Sins committed appeared but as trifles compared with the sin of unbelief which was their cause, which could not or would not take God at His Word, but rather made Him a liar! Unbelief was, I felt, the damning sin of the world—yet I indulged in it. I prayed for faith, but it came not. What was I to do?

When my agony of soul was at its height, a sentence in a letter from dear McCarthy was used to remove the scales from my eyes, and the Spirit of God revealed the truth of *our oneness with Jesus* as I had never known it before. McCarthy, who had been much exercised by the same sense of failure, but saw the light before I did, wrote (I quote from memory):

"But how to get faith strengthened? Not by striving after faith, but by resting on the Faithful One."

As I read I saw it all! "If we believe *not*...he abideth faithful" (2 Tim. 2:13, italics added). I looked to Jesus and saw (and when I saw, oh, how joy flowed!) that He had said, "I will never leave [you]" (Heb. 13:5). "Ah, *there* is rest!" I thought. "I have striven in vain to rest in Him. I'll strive no more. For has *He* not promised to abide with me—never to leave me, never to fail me?" And, dearie, *He never will!*...

Oh, my dear sister, it is a wonderful thing to be really one with a risen and exalted Savior, to be a member of Christ! Think what it involves. Can Christ be rich and I poor? Can your right hand be rich and the left poor? Or your head be well fed while your body starves? Again, think of its bearing on prayer. Could a bank clerk say to a customer, "It was only your hand wrote that check, not you," or, "I cannot pay this sum to your hand, but only to yourself"? No more can your prayers, or mine, be discredited *if offered in the name of Jesus* (i.e. not in our own name, or for the sake of Jesus merely, but on the ground that we are His, His members) so long as we keep within the extent of Christ's credit—a tolerably wide limit! If we ask anything unscriptural or not in accordance with the will of God, Christ Himself could not do that; but, "If we ask any thing according to his will, he heareth us: and...we know that we have the petitions that we desired of him" (1 John 5:14–15).

The sweetest part, if one may speak of one part being sweeter than another, is the *rest* which full identification with Christ brings. I am no longer anxious about anything, as I realize this; for He, I know, is able to carry out *His will,* and His will is mine. It makes no matter where He places me, or how. That is rather for Him to consider than for me; for in the easiest positions He must give me His grace, and in the most difficult His grace is sufficient. It little matters to my servant whether I send him to buy a few cash worth of things, or the most expensive articles. In either case he looks to me for the money and brings me his purchases. So, if God place me in great perplexity, must He not give me much guidance; in positions of great difficulty, much grace; in circumstances of great pressure and trial, much strength? No fear that His resources will be unequal to the emergency! And His resources are mine, for *He* is mine, and is with me and dwells in me. All this springs from the believer's oneness with Christ. And since Christ has thus dwelt in my heart by faith, how happy I have been! I wish I could tell you, instead of writing about it.

I am no better than before (may I not say, in a sense, I do not wish to be, nor am I striving to be);

but I am dead and buried with Christ—aye, and risen too and ascended; and now Christ lives in me, and "the life which I now live in the flesh I live by the faith of the Son of God, who loved me, and gave himself for me" (Gal. 2:20). I now *believe* I am dead to sin. God reckons me so, and tells me to reckon myself so. He knows best. All my past experience may have shown that it *was* not so, but I dare not say it is not now, when He says it is. I feel and know that old things have passed away. I am as capable of sinning as ever, but Christ is realized as present as never before. He cannot sin, and He can keep me from sinning. I cannot say (I am sorry to have to confess it) that since I have seen this light I have not sinned, but I do feel there was no need to have done so. And further—walking more in the light, my conscience has been more tender; sin has been instantly seen, confessed, pardoned; and peace and joy (with humility) instantly restored: with one exception, when for several hours peace and joy did not return—from want, as I had to learn, of full confession, and from some attempt to justify self.

Faith, I now see, is "the *substance* of things hoped for" (Heb. 11:1, italics added) and not mere shadow. It is not *less* than sight, but *more.* Sight only shows the outward forms of things; faith gives the substance. You can *rest* on substance, *feed* on substance. Christ dwelling in the heart by faith (i.e. His Word of promise credited) is *power* indeed, is *life* indeed. And Christ and sin will not dwell together; nor can we have His presence with love of the world, or carefulness about many things.

And now I must close. I have not said half I would, nor *as* I would had I more time. May God give you to lay hold on these blessed truths. Do not let us continue to say, in effect, "Who shall ascend into heaven? (that is, to bring Christ down from above)" (Rom. 10:6). In other words, do not let us consider Him as afar off, when God has made us *one with Him,* members of His very body. Nor should we look upon this experience, these truths, as for the few. They are the birthright of every child of God, and no one can dispense with them without dishonor to our Lord. The only power for deliverance from sin or for true service is Christ.

Jesus Does Satisfy

That such blessing should be tested by increasing trials is not to be wondered at. Inwardly and outwardly, the period upon which they were entering was to be one of unprecedented distress. In the work, they were to experience the power of the Adversary as never before, while in personal matters, new and deep sorrows awaited them. But for the preparation of heart which unconsciously to themselves had thus been made, things would have gone very differently both with Mr. Taylor and with the mission.

To begin with, the time had come for breaking up that happy family life which meant so much to Mr. and Mrs. Taylor. They dared not risk another summer for their elder children in China, and the delicate health of Samuel, who was only five years old, made it clear that he should go with his brothers and sister. This meant separation from four of their little flock, leaving only the baby born after the Yangchow riot to ease the aching loneliness. For some time it was a question as to whether the mother should not go herself, but the necessity for this seemed averted when Miss Blatchley volunteered to take her place in caring for the children.

To part from her was almost like giving up a daughter, so devoted had she been in sharing all their experiences. But she truly loved the children, and Mr. Taylor was ready to forgo her secretarial help in order that Mrs. Taylor might remain in China. Plan as he might, they could not see far ahead and could only trust the little party to a care infinitely wiser and more tender than their own.

Very painful it was, as the time drew near, to see the parting begin to tell upon the child about whom they were most concerned. Or was it only that his chronic trouble had increased, and that, with care, the voyage would set him up again? Taking the opportunity of a decided improvement, the family set out from Yangchow. The boats were delayed in starting, and hardly had they got clear of the city when the little invalid showed signs of a relapse. All night long they watched beside him, doing everything that could be done under the circumstances. But at dawn the following morning he fell into a deep sleep, and from the turbid waters of the Yangtze he passed without pain or fear to the better land.

Before a driving storm the parents crossed the river, there more than two miles wide, to lay their treasure in the little cemetery at Chinkiang, and then went on with the others to Shanghai. A few weeks later, after taking them all on board the French mail which was to sail at dawn the following morning, Mr. Taylor wrote at midnight:

> I have seen them awake, for the last time in China....Two of our little ones we have no anxiety about; they rest in Jesus' bosom....Though the tears will not be stayed, I do thank God for permitting one so unworthy to take any part in

> this great work, and do not regret having engaged and being engaged in it. It is *His* work, not mine nor yours; and yet it is ours—not because we are engaged in it, but because we are His, and one with Him whose work it is.

This was the reality that sustained, and more than sustained them. Never had there been a more troubled summer in China than that on which they were entering. And yet in the midst of it all, with a longing for their little ones that was indescribable, they never had had more rest and joy in God. Of this time, Mr. Taylor wrote:

> I could not but admire and wonder at the grace that so sustained and comforted the fondest of mothers. The secret was that *Jesus* was *satisfying* the deep thirst of heart and soul.

Mrs. Taylor was at her best that summer, borne up, it would seem, on the very tempest of troubles that raged about them. Sickness was rife in the mission, and before they could reach Chinkiang after parting from the children, news came to them of Mrs. Judd's being there and at the point of death. After days and nights of nursing, Mr. Judd was almost too weary to bear up, when in the courtyard below he heard sounds of an unexpected arrival. Who could it be at that hour of night, and where had they come from? No steamer had passed upriver, and native boats would not be traveling after dark. Besides, it was a wheelbarrow that had been trundled in. A long day's journey on that springless vehicle a woman had come alone, and soon he saw the face of all others he could have longed to see. He had thought them far away, but Mr. Taylor, who could not leave the boat on account of another patient, had consented to Mrs. Taylor's pressing on alone to give what help she could. Nothing but prayer brought the patient through, just as nothing but prayer saved the situation in many an hour of extremity that summer.

It is easy to read, but only those who have passed through like experiences can have any idea of the strain involved. The heat of the summer was excessive, which added to the unrest of the native population. Ladies and children had to be removed from several of the stations, and for a time it seemed as though the Chinese government might insist on their leaving the country altogether. This necessitated much correspondence with officials, both native and foreign, and constant letters of advice and sympathy to the workers most in peril. The accommodation of the little house at Chinkiang was taxed to its utmost, and so great was the excitement, even there, that no other premises could be obtained.

By this time it looked as though all the river-stations might have to be given up. Mr. and Mrs. Taylor were making their home at Chinkiang to be more in the center of things, he sleeping on the floor in the sitting room or passage that she might share their bedroom with other ladies. Yet the troubles of the time were not allowed to interfere with as much work among the people as was possible. Mrs. Taylor, especially, with fewer household and family cares, was seeking to help the little church at Chinkiang. In the hottest days of June she wrote to Miss Blatchley:

> We have been holding classes on Sundays and two or three evenings in the week, having two objects specially in view: first, to interest the

natives, those who can read, in searching the Scriptures, and those who cannot, in learning to do so; and secondly, to set an example to the younger members of the mission who know pretty well that we have no lack of work. It may be a practical proof to them of the importance we attach to securing that the Christians and other natives about us learn to read and understand for themselves the Word of God.

The joy that had come to Mr. Taylor in a deeper apprehension of living, present oneness with Christ seems in no wise to have been hindered by the troubles of the time. The pages of his letter book reveal, in fact, not so much the endless difficulties as the full tide of blessing that carried him through all. Though no detail is overlooked in the business part of the correspondence, letter after letter is taken up with that which was far more important. To Miss Desgraz, for example, he wrote in the middle of June after a careful letter about Yangchow affairs:

And now, my dear Sister, I have the very passage for you, and God has so blessed it to my own soul! John 7:37–39: "If any man thirst, let him come unto me, and drink." Who does not thirst? Who has not mind thirsts or heart thirsts, soul thirsts or body thirsts? Well, no matter which, or whether I have them all—"Come unto Me and" remain thirsty? Ah no! "Come unto Me and drink."

What, can Jesus meet my need? Yes, and more than meet it. No matter how intricate my path, how difficult my service, no matter how sad my bereavement, how far away my loved ones, no matter how helpless I am, how hopeless I am, how deep are my soul yearnings—Jesus can meet all, all, and more than *meet.* He not only promises me rest (Matt. 11:28–30)—ah, how welcome *that* would be were it all, and *what* an all that one word embraces! He not only promises me drink to alleviate my thirst. No, better than that!

"He who trusts me in this matter (who believeth on Me—takes me at my word), out of him shall flow...." (See John 7:38.)

Can it be so? Can the dry and thirsty one not only be refreshed, the parched soil moistened, the arid places cooled, but the land be so saturated that springs well up, streams flow down from it? Even so! And not mere mountain torrents, full while the rains last, then dry again...but "out of his belly shall flow rivers" (John 7:38)—rivers like the mighty Yangtze, ever deep, ever full. In times of drought, brooks may fail, often do; canals may be pumped dry, often are; but the Yangtze *never.* Always a mighty stream; always flowing, deep and irresistible!

How sorely the lesson would be needed by his own heart, in days that were drawing near, he little knew when writing, but the blessed Reality did not fail him.

* * * * *

Mr. and Mrs. Taylor's hearts were filled with love and joy in receiving, meanwhile, a new gift from God. Born on July 7, 1870, this little one was her fifth son and called forth all the pent-up love of his parents' hearts. But the earthly joy of this moment was not to last.

An attack of cholera greatly prostrated the mother, and lack of natural nourishment took its toll upon the child. When a Chinese nurse could be found, it was too late to save the little life, and after one brief week on earth he went back to the home above in which his mother was so soon to join him.

She chose herself the hymns to be sung at the little grave, one of which, "O holy Savior, Friend unseen," seemed especially to dwell in her mind.

> Though faith and hope are often tried,
> We ask not, need not, aught beside;
> So safe, so calm, so satisfied,
> The souls that cling to Thee.
>
> They fear not Satan nor the grave,
> They know Thee near, and strong to save;
> Nor fear to cross e'en Jordan's wave,
> While still they cling to Thee.

Weak as she was, it had not yet occurred to them that for her, too, the end was near. The deep mutual love that bound their hearts in one seemed to preclude the thought of separation. And she was only thirty-three. There was no pain up to the very last, though she was weary, very weary. A letter from Mrs. Berger had been received two days previously, telling of the safe arrival at Saint Hill of Miss Blatchley and the children. Every detail of the welcome and arrangements for their well-being filled her heart with joy. She did not know how to be thankful enough and seemed to have no desire or thought but just to praise the Lord for His goodness. Many and many a time had Mrs. Berger's letters reached their destination at the needed moment; many and many a time had her loving heart anticipated the circumstances in which they would be received, but never more so than with this letter.

"And now farewell, precious Friend," she wrote. "The Lord throw around you His everlasting arms."

It was in those arms she was resting.

At daybreak on Saturday, July 23, she was sleeping quietly, and Mr. Taylor left her a few moments to prepare some food. While he was doing so she awoke, and serious symptoms called him to her side. He later wrote:

> By this time it was dawn, and the sunlight revealed what the candle had hidden—the deathlike hue of her countenance. Even my love could no longer deny, not her danger, but that she was actually dying. As soon as I was sufficiently composed, I said,
>
> "My darling, do you know that you are dying?"
>
> "Dying!" she replied. "Do you think so? What makes you think so?"
>
> I said, "I can see it, darling. Your strength is giving way."
>
> "Can it be so? I feel no pain, only weariness."
>
> "Yes, you are going home. You will soon be with Jesus."
>
> My precious wife thought of my being left alone at a time of so much trial, with no companion like herself, with whom I had been wont to bring every difficulty to the throne of grace.
>
> "I am so sorry," she said, and paused as if half-correcting herself for the feeling.
>
> "You are not sorry to go to be with Jesus?"
>
> Never shall I forget the look with which she answered, "Oh, no! It is not that. You know, darling, that for ten years past there has not been a cloud between me and my Savior. I cannot be sorry to go to Him, but it does grieve me

to leave you alone at such a time. Yet...He will be with you and meet all your need."

But little was said after that. A few loving messages to those at home, a few last words about the children, and she seemed to fall asleep or drift into unconsciousness of earthly things. The summer sun rose higher and higher over the city, the hills, and the river. The busy hum of life came up around them from many a court and street. But within one Chinese dwelling, in an upper room from which the blue of God's own heaven could be seen, there was the hush of a wonderful peace. Of this, Mrs. Duncan wrote:

> I never witnessed such a scene. As dear Mrs. Taylor was breathing her last, Mr. Taylor knelt down—his heart so full—and committed her to the Lord; thanking Him for having given her, and for the twelve and a half years of happiness they had had together; thanking Him, too, for taking her to His own blessed presence, and solemnly dedicating himself anew to His service.

It was just after nine o'clock in the morning when the quiet breathing ceased, and they knew she was "with Christ; which is far better" (Phil. 1:23).

Chapter 10

New Visions

"My thirsty days are all past," Hudson Taylor had felt and said and written that very summer, rejoicing as never before in the Savior's promise, "he that cometh to me shall never hunger; and he that believeth on me shall never thirst" (John 6:35). Would it prove true now—now that the joy of life on its human side was gone, and there was nothing left but aching loneliness and silence? Would it prove true now—when, under the pressure of continued difficulty on every hand, health began to give way, and, sleepless at night, he found himself scarcely able to face the suffering, not to speak of the labors of each new day? If ever the reality of the power of Christ to meet the heart's deepest need was put to the test of experience, it was in this life, swept clean of all that had been its earthly comfort—wife, children, home, health to a large extent—and left amid the responsibilities of such a mission and such a crisis, far away in China.

A few days only before his great bereavement, when there was no thought of immediate danger, Mr. Taylor had written to his mother at home:

> I find increasing comfort in the thought that all things are really in our Father's hand and under His governance. He cannot but do what is best.

And now, after all that had happened, he continued:

I have just been reading over my last letter to you, and my views are not changed, though chastened and deepened. From my inmost soul I delight in the knowledge that God does or deliberately permits *all* things and causes all things to work together for good to those who love Him (Rom. 8:28).

He and He only knew what my dear wife was to me. He knew how the light of my eyes and the joy of my heart were in her. On the last day of her life (we had *no* idea that it would prove the last) our hearts were mutually delighted by the never-old story of each other's love, as they were every day, nearly; and almost her last act was, with one arm round my neck, to place her hand upon my head, and, as I believe, for her lips had lost their cunning, to implore a blessing on me. But He saw that it was good to take her; good indeed for her, and in His love He took her painlessly; and not less good for me who must henceforth toil and suffer alone—yet not alone, for God is nearer to me than ever. And now I have to tell Him all my sorrows and difficulties, as I used to tell dear Maria; and as she cannot join me in intercession, to rest in the knowledge of Jesus' intercession; to walk a little less by feeling, a little less by sight, a little more by faith.

To Mr. Berger he had written some days previously:

And now, dear brother, what shall I say of the Lord's dealings with me and mine? I know not! My heart is overwhelmed with gratitude and praise. My eyes flow with tears of mingled joy and sorrow. When I think of my loss, my heart—nigh to breaking—rises in thankfulness to Him who has spared *her* such sorrow and made her so unspeakably happy. My tears are more tears of joy than of grief. But most of all, I joy in God through our Lord Jesus Christ—in His works, His ways, His providence, in Himself. He is giving me to prove (to know by trial) "what is that good, and acceptable, and perfect, will of God" (Rom. 12:2). I do rejoice in that will. It is acceptable to me; it is perfect; it is love in action. And soon, in that same sweet will, we shall be reunited to part no more. "Father, I will that they also, whom thou hast given me, be with me where I am" (John 17:24).

It was only to be expected that as the days wore on there should be some measure of reaction, especially when illness and long, wakeful nights came. Of these, he recalled:

How lonesome were the weary hours when confined to my room. How I missed my dear wife and the little pattering footsteps of the children far away in England! Then it was I understood why the Lord had made that passage so real to me, "whosoever drinketh of the water that I shall give him *shall never* thirst" (John 4:14, italics added). Twenty times a day, perhaps, as I felt the heart thirst coming back, I cried to Him:

"Lord, you promised! You promised me that I should never thirst."

And whether I called by day or night, how quickly He always came and satisfied my sorrowing heart! So much so, that I often wondered whether it were possible that my loved one who had been taken could be enjoying more of His presence than I was in my lonely chamber. He had literally fulfilled the prayer:

> Lord Jesus, make Thyself to me
> A living, bright Reality;
> More present to faith's vision keen
> Than any outward object seen;
> More dear, more intimately nigh,
> Than e'en the sweetest earthly tie.

What more can be added to experiences so sacred? Were it not that the correspondence of the period is too precious to be passed over, one would hesitate to dwell upon the intimacies of this stricken soul with its God. But letters remain that have a message, surely, for such days as ours. Let them tell their own story.

To Mr. Berger:

> It is Sunday evening. I am writing from Mr. White's bungalow. The cool air, the mellow, autumnal beauty of the scene, the magnificent Yangtze—with Silver Island, beautifully wooded, reposing, as it were, on its bosom—combine to make one feel as if it were a vision of dreamland rather than actual reality. And my feelings accord. But a few months ago my home was full, now so silent and lonely—Samuel, Noel, my precious wife, with Jesus; the elder children far, far away, and even little T'ien-pao in Yangchow. Often, of late years, has duty called me from my loved ones, but I have returned, and so warm has been the welcome! Now I am alone. Can it be that there is no return from this journey, no homegathering to look forward to! Is it real, and not a sorrowful dream, that those dearest to me lie beneath the cold sod? Ah, it is indeed true! But not more so than that there is a homecoming awaiting me which no parting shall break into, no tears mar....Love gave the blow that for a little while makes the desert more dreary, but

heaven more homelike. “I go to prepare a place for you” (John 14:2), and is not our part of the preparation the peopling it with those we love?

And the same loving Hand that makes heaven more homelike is the while loosening the ties that bind us to this world, thus helping our earth-cleaving spirits to sit looser, awaiting our own summons, whether personally to be “present with the Lord” (2 Cor. 5:8), or at “the glorious appearing of the great God and our Saviour” (Titus 2:13). “Even so, come, Lord Jesus” (Rev. 22:20), come quickly! But if He tarry—if for the rescue, the salvation of some still scattered upon the mountains He can wait the full joy of having all His loved ones gathered to Himself—surely we, too, should be content, nay, thankful, a little longer to bear the cross and unfurl the banner of salvation. Poor China, how great her need! Let us seek to occupy a little longer.

To Miss Blatchley:

Nearly three weeks have passed since my last letter to you: a little lifetime it has been....I cannot describe to you my feelings; I do not understand them myself. I feel like a person stunned with a blow, or recovering from a faint, and as yet but partially conscious. But I would not have it otherwise, no, not a hair’s breadth, for the world. My Father has ordered it so—therefore I know it is, it must be best, and I thank Him for so ordering it. I feel utterly crushed, and yet “strong in the Lord, and in the power of his might” (Eph. 6:10). Oft-times my heart is nigh to breaking...but withal, I had almost said, I never knew what peace and happiness were before—so much have I enjoyed in the very sorrow....

I think I sent you a few weeks ago a copy of some notes on John 7:37; precious thoughts they have been to me, and needed and true. I now see more and deeper meaning in them than then. And this I know: only a thirsty man knows the value of water, and only a thirsty soul the value of the living water.

I could not have believed it possible that He could *so* have helped and comforted my poor heart.

Thursday, Friday, and Saturday were all spent in bed, and part of yesterday—ague and affection of the liver this time. It throws me back very much, but the Lord's will be done. Yesterday...in the cold stage of the ague, I was shaking until the bed shook under me, but I enjoyed such a vivid realization that I was altogether the Lord's, purchased not with silver and gold—that I had not a particle of property, so to speak, in myself—that it filled my heart to overflowing. I felt, if He wanted me to shake, I could shake *for Him;* if to burn with fever, I could welcome it for His sake.

By the end of the month (August) the youngest of Mr. Taylor's children, the motherless baby alone left to him in China of his family, was hanging between life and death. As the only hope of saving him, his father took him with Mrs. Duncan's kind help to Ningpo and the island of Pu-du. A fortnight spent there, however, proved an anxious time, and to his parents in Barnsley Mr. Taylor wrote (September 25):

T'ien-pao has not improved so much as I had hoped. May the Lord help me to be patient and trustful. Long-continued anxiety and weariness from want of rest; sorrow from repeated bereavements and trouble in the work, from the state of China and the timidity of the workers; and other trials from without and within do make one feel the need of a strong arm to lean upon—aye, and a tender one too. And here, thank God, our great need is just met. "As one whom his mother comforteth" (Isa. 66:13), so He comforts us. Strengthened by His power, though troubled on every side, we are not forsaken, nor left to doubt either the wisdom or love of Him who is at the helm.

To his children, Hudson Taylor wrote:

You do not know how often Papa thinks of his darlings and how often he looks at your photographs till the tears fill his eyes. Sometimes he almost fears lest he should feel discontented when he thinks how far away you are from him; but, then, dear Jesus, who never leaves him, says: "Don't be afraid. I will keep your heart satisfied. You know it was your Father in heaven who took them to England, and who took Mamma to her little Noel, Samuel, and Gracie in the better land." Then I thank Him and feel so glad that Jesus will live in my heart and keep it right for me.

I wish you, my precious children, knew what it was to give your hearts to Jesus to keep every day. I used to try to keep my own heart right, but it would be always going wrong; and so at last I had to give up trying myself, and accept Jesus' offer to keep it for me. Don't you think that is the best way? Perhaps sometimes you think: "I will try not to be selfish, or unkind, or disobedient."

And yet, though you really try, you do not always succeed. But Jesus says, "You should trust that to Me. I would keep that little heart, if you could trust Me with it." And He would, too.

Once I used to try to think very much and very often about Jesus, but I often forgot Him; now I trust Jesus to keep my heart remembering Him, and He does so. This is the best way. Ask dear Miss Blatchley to tell you more about this way, and pray God to make it plain to you, and to help you so to trust Jesus.

To keep their confidence and love, even at so great a distance, Mr. Taylor toiled many an hour long after body and mind craved rest. Returning to Shanghai, for example, amid other letters penned in his comfortless, third-class quarters were the following:

My Darling Treasures—It is not very long since my last letter, but I want to write again. I wonder if you will try to write me a little answer?...I have been thinking tonight—if Jesus makes me so happy by always keeping near me, and talking to me every minute or two though I cannot see Him, how happy darling Mamma must be! I am so glad for her to be with Him....I shall be so glad to go to her when Jesus thinks it best. But I hope He will help me to be equally willing to live with Him here, so long as He has any work for me to do for Him and for poor China.

Now, my darling children, I want you to love Jesus very much, and to *know* that *He* really does love you very much. Don't you think your far-off, dear Papa would be very pleased to see you and talk to you, and to take you on his knee and kiss you? You know he would! Well, Jesus will always be *far more pleased* when you think of Him with loving thoughts and speak to Him with loving words. Don't think of Him as some dreadful being. Think of Him as very good and very great, able to do everything, but as very gentle and very kind. When you wake, say to Him, either aloud or in your hearts:

"Good morning, dear Jesus. I am so glad you have been by me all night, and have taken care of me. Teach me how much you love me. Take care of my heart; make it think good thoughts. Take care of my lips; only let them speak kind, good words. Help me always to know what is right and to do it."

He likes us to talk to Him. When I am walking alone, I often talk aloud to Him. At other times I talk to Him in my heart. Do not forget, my darling children, that He is *always* with you. Awake or asleep, at home or elsewhere, He is *really* with you, though you cannot see Him. So I hope you will try not to grieve so constant and kind a friend.

And to Mrs. Berger he wrote:

No language can express what He has been and is to me. Never does He leave me; constantly does He cheer me with His love. He who once wept at the grave of Lazarus often now weeps in and with me. He who once on earth rejoiced in spirit and said, "Even so, Father: for so it seemed good in thy sight" (Matt. 11:26), daily, hourly, rejoices in spirit in me, and says so still. His own rest, His own peace, His own joy He gives me. He kisses me with the kisses of His love, which are better than wine. Often I find myself wondering whether it is possible for her, who is taken, to have more joy in His presence than He has given me. If He has taken her to heaven, He has also brought heaven here to me, for He is heaven. There is no night, no gloom, in His presence. In His presence there is "fulness of joy" (Ps. 16:11).

At times He does suffer me to realize all that was, but is not now. At times I can almost hear again the sweet voice of my Gracie, feel the presence of little Samuel's head on my bosom. And Noel and his mother—how sweet the recollection, and yet how it makes the heart ache!...And then, He who will soon come and wipe away every tear, comes and takes all bitterness from them...and fills my heart with deep, true, unutterable gladness. I have not to seek Him now; He never leaves me. At night He smoothes my pillow; in the morning He wakes my heart to His love. "I will be with thee all day long: thou shalt not be alone, nor lonely." I never was so happy, dear Mrs. Berger; I know you sympathize, and I feel I must tell you of His love.

Meanwhile, there was no lessening of the pressure of outward difficulties. Politically, the aspect of affairs had for months been darker than Mr. Taylor had ever known it in China. The Tien-tsin massacre, in which twenty-one foreigners had lost their lives, including the French consul and Sisters of Mercy, was still unsettled, and the Chinese authorities, knowing that Europe was involved in war, took no steps to allay antiforeign feeling. Mr. Taylor had written of it:

In the event of any riot now, not only a few plunderers are to be feared; all the people are roused....Unless something is done about the Tien-tsin murders before long, I fear you will learn of even more serious troubles. The Chinese generally are satisfied that only consciousness of guilt, and weakness, have prevented vengeance from reaching the perpetrators of those crimes: in other words, that foreigners do really eat children, etc., and are now unable to defend themselves.... But the Lord reigns.

It was scarcely to be wondered at that the long strain of excitement and danger should tell on the nerves, and even the spiritual life of lonely missionaries; but it was no little sorrow to Mr. Taylor when an inland station was abandoned that might have been held, and when some dear fellow workers seemed to fail in faith and courage. He knew the weakness of his own heart too well to be harsh toward others and sought, as far as in him lie, to strengthen their hands in God. The last day of the year was set apart as usual for prayer and fasting, in arranging for which Mr. Taylor wrote to the members of the mission:

> The present year (1870) has been in many ways remarkable. Perhaps every one of our number has been more or less face to face with danger, perplexity, and distress, but out of it all the Lord has delivered us. And some of us, who have drunk of the cup of the Man of Sorrows more deeply than ever before, can testify that it has been a most blessed year to our souls and can give God thanks for it. Personally, it has been alike the most sorrowful and the most blessed year of my life, and I doubt not that others have to a greater or lesser extent had the same experience. We have put to the proof His faithfulness, His power to support in trouble and to give patience under affliction, as well as to deliver from danger. And should greater dangers await us, should deeper sorrows come than any we have yet felt, it is to be hoped that they will be met in a strengthened confidence in our God.
>
> We have had great cause for thankfulness in one respect: we have been so placed as to show

the native Christians that our position as well as theirs has been, and may be again, one of danger. And they have been helped, doubtless, to look from "foreign power" to God Himself for protection, by the facts that (1) the former has been felt to be uncertain and unreliable, both with regard to themselves and to us, and (2) that we have been kept in calmness and joy in our various positions of duty. If in any measure we have failed to improve for their good this opportunity, or have failed to rest for ourselves in God's power to sustain in or protect from danger, as He sees best, let us humbly confess this and all conscious failure to our faithful, covenant-keeping God....

I trust we are all fully satisfied that we are God's servants, sent by Him to the various posts we occupy, and that we are doing His work in them. He set before us the open doors into which we have entered, and in past times of excitement He has preserved us in them. We did not come to China because missionary work here was either safe or easy, but because *He* had called us. We did not enter upon our present positions under a guarantee of human protection, but relying on the promise of *His* presence. The accidents of ease or difficulty, of *apparent* safety or danger, of man's approbation or disapproval, in no wise affect our duty. Should circumstances arise involving us in what may seem special danger, I trust we shall have grace to manifest the reality and depth of our trust in Him, and by our faithfulness to our charge *prove* that we are followers of the Good Shepherd, who did not flee from death itself....But if we would manifest this calmness *then,* we must seek the needed grace *now.* It is too late to look for arms and begin to drill when in presence of the foe.

With regard to funds Mr. Taylor continued:

> I need not remind you of the liberal help which, in our need, the Lord has sent us direct from certain donors, nor of the blessed fact that He abideth faithful, and cannot deny Himself (2 Tim. 2:13). If we are really trusting *in Him* and seeking *from Him,* we cannot be put to shame; if not, perhaps the sooner we find the unsoundness of any other foundation, the better. The mission funds, or the donors, are a poor substitute for the living God.

So great was the pressure on Mr. Taylor at this time that he wrote early in December that he had never known anything like it, save just before leaving England with the Lammermuir party.

* * * * *

March winds, tossing the big elms at Saint Hill and sweeping round the house that had so warmly welcomed Mr. Taylor on his return from China, did but make the fireside more homelike when at length he had time to sit down quietly and talk over with Mr. and Mrs. Berger all that was on their hearts. Six years almost had elapsed since the outgoing of the Lammermuir party, years of wonderful progress considering the initial difficulties. The mission, which up to that time had had but two stations and seven members, now numbered more than thirty foreign and fifty native workers in thirteen central stations at an average distance of a hundred miles apart. Nothing could have exceeded, as we have seen, the devotion with which Mr. and Mrs. Berger had watched over its interests, giving their time and substance, their home, themselves indeed to its service. And now, all that must change. The love and prayers would continue, but to younger hands must be committed the task that had proved too much for their strength. Saint Hill was to be sold, its beloved owners finding it needful to winter abroad, and to them, no less than to Mr. Taylor, the parting was painful, and the position full of problems. For who was to take their place and bear all the responsibility of the home work of the mission? Who would edit its *Occasional Paper*, test and train its candidates, carry on its correspondence, keep in touch with its friends, and do all the thousand and one things they had done without expense to its funds, prompted by a love that felt it never could do enough? Such cooperation could no more be replaced than parental care in a family, and the need for the change had come so suddenly that Mr. Taylor had no plans in view. The work in China was now a large one, entailing an expenditure of about three hundred pounds a month. His own health was much impaired by those six strenuous years, and rest of mind and body would have been grateful, in view especially of a speedy return to the front. But the home base could not be neglected. Unequal as he felt to the task, there was nothing for it but to take up the entire responsibility himself, looking to the Lord to liberate him when and as He should see fit. "Thou remainest" (Heb. 1:11) was a certainty that meant much to Hudson Taylor in those days.

Writing to his parents, a few weeks later, Mr. Taylor used note paper bearing the modest heading,

China Inland Mission,
6 Pyrland Road,
Newington Green, N.

It was a far cry from Saint Hill to a little suburban street on the outskirts of London, such as Pyrland Road was in those days, and the change from Mr. Berger's library to the small back bedroom which had to do duty as study and office in one was equally complete. But how dear and sacred to many a heart is every remembrance of number six and the adjacent houses—numbers four and two—acquired as need arose. For more than twenty years the entire home work of the mission was carried on from this center, a few steps only from its present quarters. The weekly prayer meeting was held in the downstairs rooms, two of which could be thrown together, and many a devoted band of missionaries, including "the Seventy" and "the Hundred," were sent forth from these doors, from which no suitable candidate for work in China was ever turned away. But we are running far ahead of the small beginnings of 1872, when Mr. Taylor was himself the whole executive of the mission, and they are well to be recalled by one who cherishes a vivid memory of those early days.

In the busy world of London, a bright lad full of life and spirits had given his heart to the Lord, and his life also, for whatever service He might appoint. Hearing an address from Mr. Meadows, recently returned from China, this lad, Mr. F. W. Baller, had a strong desire to learn more about the Inland Mission, little thinking that he would one day be its chief sinologue as well as one of its most useful workers:

> After a good deal of thought and prayer, I determined to seek an interview with Mr. Taylor, and in company with a friend started out one Saturday afternoon for the north of London, to

find Pyrland Road, where the headquarters of the mission were located. When we reached the place, we found that but half the street was built, and away to the north stretched open fields. ...The house we sought was number six, and on reaching it we were shown into the room where the meeting was to be held. Strictly speaking it was two rooms, divided by folding doors, but these were thrown open and the two rooms turned into one. A large harmonium stood at one side, and various Chinese articles were arranged in other parts of the room, but beyond this there was little either of furniture or decoration. A large text, "My God shall supply all your need" (Phil. 4:19), faced the door by which we entered, and, as I was not accustomed to seeing texts hung on walls in that way, decidedly impressed me. Between a dozen and twenty people were present.

Mr. Taylor opened the meeting by giving out a hymn, and, seating himself at the harmonium, he led the singing. His appearance did not impress me. He was slightly built and spoke in a gentle voice. Like most young men, I suppose I associated power with noise and looked for great physical presence in a leader. But when he said, "Let us pray," and proceeded to lead the meeting in prayer, my ideas underwent a change. I had never heard anyone pray like that. There was a simplicity, a tenderness, a boldness, a power that hushed and subdued one, and made it clear that God had admitted him into the inner circle of His friendship. He spoke with God face to face, as a man talketh with his friend. Such praying was evidently the outcome of long tarrying in the secret place and was as a dew from the Lord. I have heard many men pray in public since then, but the prayers of Mr. Taylor and the prayers of

Mr. Spurgeon stand all by themselves. Who that heard could ever forget them? It was the experience of a lifetime to hear Mr. Spurgeon pray, taking, as it were, the great congregation of six thousand people by the hand and leading them into the Holy Place, and to hear Mr. Taylor plead for China was to know something of what is meant by "the effectual fervent prayer of a righteous man" (James 5:16).

The meeting lasted from four to six o'clock, but seemed one of the shortest prayer meetings I had ever attended. Most present took part audibly. There were no long, awkward pauses, but the Spirit of the Lord, the Spirit of liberty, was manifestly present. The meeting over, tea was served, giving an opportunity for friendly intercourse. I introduced myself to Mr. Taylor, who asked me to stay till others were gone, when he would see me alone. This he did, taking me upstairs to a room on the first floor. He was the soul of kindness—drawing me out, making me feel quite at home, and encouraging the hope that I might one day see China and labor there. This was more indeed than I had anticipated when I set out to seek him. My idea was that perchance I might some day go as a helper to a missionary; to be a missionary myself seemed too great an honor....Seeing I was young, scarcely twenty, Mr. Taylor gave me some good advice as to what to do until the Lord's way should be made plain. The interview over, I went home with a light heart, filled with gratitude to God for His goodness in thus encouraging me to hope in Him.

Longing to press forward with the great task before the mission, it must have been difficult indeed for Mr. Taylor to curb himself to the routine of office work as the days and weeks went by. He was not in haste to rush into new arrangements, having no indication as to what might be the mind of the Lord. But when prayer for the right helpers seemed to bring no answer, and the work to be done kept him busy morning, noon, and night, it would have been so easy to be impatient or discouraged! But in the dark days of 1870 he had learned some deep lessons about waiting for, as well as waiting upon God.

The deepened current of Mr. Taylor's own life could not but be felt throughout the circle of the mission. His chief reason for settling in North London had been to be in touch with "Mildmay" and all it stood for—the far-reaching institutions founded by the Rev. W. Pennefather, vicar of the parish, whose ministry he greatly valued. The annual conference convened by him for Christians of all denominations was still the only one of its kind in England and made the neighborhood a gathering ground for spiritually-minded people to whom oneness in Christ was more than minor differences. Mr. Taylor had been in touch with the conference from its early days, and now that he was a near neighbor, Mr. Pennefather soon discovered qualities that fitted him to take a leading place among its speakers. The meetings of 1872 were largely attended, visitors coming from the Continent as well as from all parts of the United Kingdom to be present. Two thousand five hundred people crowded the great hall daily, and among the ministers on the platform were D. L. Moody and the leaders of the movement for Scriptural holiness, which had already brought so much blessing through the pages of *The Revival*. It was a surprise to Mr. Taylor, and doubtless to many who heard him, that a missionary, comparatively young and little known, should be asked to give the opening address, but the promise he had learned to claim was fulfilled that day in his experience as never before—"[from him] shall flow rivers of living water" (John 7:38).

Not the great meetings, however, or that address so full of blessing, made the deepest impression on a young visitor from Barnstaple who was staying at Pyrland Road. Memorable as they were, she was more interested and even more helped by the family life she was sharing day by day.

The place at Mr. Taylor's side that had been so empty was now taken by one fitted in every way to be a help and comfort. It had been his loved one's wish, for his own sake, as well as that of the children and the mission, that Mr. Taylor should marry again, and very unexpectedly his thoughts had been turned in that direction. Miss Faulding, the life, by God's blessing, of the women's work in Hangchow, had been obliged to come home on furlough, and traveling by the same steamer—other arrangements having fallen through at the last moment—Mr. Taylor found the regard he had long felt for her developing into something more than friendship. The marriage had not been long delayed, and he was thankful for the children to see as much of her as possible before she returned with him to China. But though it was the home of a bride, the arrangements at Pyrland Road were just as simple as in the early days, and Mr. and Mrs. Taylor were carefully economizing in order to add to the funds of the mission.

This visitor from Barnstaple, Miss Soltau, had come up with the earnest desire to give her life to China and was in no way deterred by the real self-sacrifice she saw at the heart of things. Hudson

Taylor, valued and sought after among the leaders of the conference, and Hudson Taylor in the little office and daily prayer meeting of the mission house close by, might seem to be living two very different lives; but the reality of the one explained to her the growing influence of the other, and she carried home many a lesson. She wrote long after:

> I remember dear Mr. Taylor's exhortation to keep silent to all around and let our wants be known to the Lord only. One day when we had had a small breakfast and there was scarcely anything for dinner, I was so thrilled to hear him singing the children's hymn:
>
> Jesus loves me, this I know,
> For the Bible tells me so.
>
> Then he called us all together to praise the Lord for His changeless love, to tell our needs and claim the promises—and before the day was over we were rejoicing in His gracious answers.

Far from discouraged by the shortness of funds after Mr. Berger's retirement, Mr. Taylor was praying and planning more definitely than ever for advance to the unreached interior of China. During the week of the conference a few special friends were at Pyrland Road between the meetings, and standing before the large map in the sitting room, their hearts were moved by the thought: How are these Christless millions to be reached? Miss Soltau was of the number, and well remembered Mr. Taylor saying:

"Have you faith to join me in laying hold upon God for eighteen men to go two and two to those unoccupied provinces?"

They knew what he meant, and then and there covenanted with one another to pray daily in definite faith for this, until the Lord should bring it to pass. Then all joined hands, and Mr. Taylor led in a prayer never to be forgotten.

* * * * *

It was about this time that, from unexpected quarters, guidance began to come as to the future management of the home side of the mission. It was but natural that Mr. Taylor had, perhaps unconsciously, been looking for helpers who, like Mr. and Mrs. Berger, could assume the whole responsibility. But none such were forthcoming. The burden, meanwhile, of directing the work in China from a distance, as well as attending to all that had to be done at home, was very heavy. He was toiling far beyond his strength. "The thing that thou doest is not good," wrote two old friends, businessmen in London; "thou wilt surely wear away...thou art not able to perform it thyself alone" (Exod. 18:17–18). They urged the advice of Jethro—to divide among a number such responsibility as could be delegated, offering themselves a measure of help with correspondence, account keeping, etc.

At Greenwich also, one evening in July, the matter was brought up still more definitely. Mr. Taylor was visiting Mr. and Mrs. Richard Hill, who would gladly have given themselves to the work of the mission had family claims permitted. As it was, Mr. Hill suggested the formation of a council of Christian friends, not to take any responsibility with regard to the management of affairs on the field, but to divide among themselves the home work of the mission, thus setting Mr. Taylor free to return to China.

This suggestion, reinforced by Mr. Hill's offer to become honorable secretary to such a council, proved a seed thought. The more Mr. Taylor considered it, the more he saw that it was simply an enlargement of the plan upon which the C.I.M. had been worked from the beginning. A council, not a committee of management, could undertake many of Mr. Berger's former responsibilities. Mr. Taylor was planning to leave Miss Blatchley in charge of his children at Pyrland Road. Intimately acquainted with the work both at home and in China, she would be of the greatest assistance to the council and would be able to keep up the prayer meeting and provide a center for returning missionaries. Passing through her hands, the daily correspondence could be attended to, and only necessary letters forwarded to the secretary, while the council would deal with candidates and with funds, keeping in touch with the friends of the mission through its *Occasional Paper*.

Quietly, thus, the way opened. A meeting was held and the council was practically formed in one night (August 6, 1872), a council which in the goodness of God so faithfully stood behind the work for more than forty-five years.

It was not a large balance Mr. Taylor was able to hand over to the secretaries when he set out for China a couple of months later. A little over twenty-one pounds was all they had in hand; but there was no debt, and they had all the promises of God for the future, as in the past. With regard to the new arrangements, Mr. Taylor wrote to the friends of the mission:

> We trust none will think that because the form of the home work is changed the character

of the work itself is altered. Now that the mission has grown, more workers are needed at home, as abroad. But the principles of action will be the same. We shall seek pecuniary aid from God by prayer, as heretofore. He will put it into the hearts of those He sees fit to use to act as His channels. When there is money in hand, it will be remitted to China; when there is none, none will be sent; and we shall not draw upon home, so that there can be no going into debt. Should our faith be tried, as it has been before, He will prove Himself faithful, as He has ever done; nay, should our faith fail, His faithfulness will not—for it is written, "If we believe not, yet he abideth faithful" (2 Tim. 2:13).

He continued:

In the work itself our aim will be, as heretofore, to encourage as much as possible the gifts of the native Christians, and to lead them on to an ever-deepening knowledge of and love for the Word of God, so that as soon as possible they may be able to stand alone. We shall seek, by God's help, to plant the standard of the cross in new and unoccupied regions, to get as near to the people, and to be as accessible to them as possible, that our *lives* may commend the Gospel to the heathen whom we endeavor by word to instruct; and you will seek grace and wisdom from God, that it may really be so. Pray that we may daily follow Him who took our nature that He might raise us to be partakers of the divine nature. Pray that this principle of becoming one with the people, of willingly taking the lowest place, may be deeply inwrought in our souls and expressed in our deportment.

Things Will Soon Look Up

After an absence from China of a year and three months, Mr. Taylor was prepared to find matters needing a good deal of attention. It had not been possible to leave anyone in charge of the whole work, none of the members of the mission having sufficient experience to fit them for such a position. Mr. C. T. Fishe, who had received and forwarded remittances and given much help in business matters, had been laid aside by a long, most serious illness, and others too had been incapacitated in a similar way. That there would be much to see to and put in order on his arrival Mr. Taylor well knew, and the voyage had been made the most of for preparation of spirit, soul, and body. And now the yellow waters of the Yangtze were around them as they lay at anchor, waiting for the fog to clear before they could proceed up the river to Shanghai. Embracing the opportunity for letters, Mr. Taylor wrote to his mother that November day (1872):

> I should tremble indeed, had we not God to look to, at the prospect of being so soon face to face with the difficulties of the work. Even as it is, I can scarcely help feeling oppressed: "Lord, increase [*my*] faith" (Luke 17:5). Do pray earnestly for me. One more unworthy there could not be. And oh, how I feel my utter incapacity to carry on the work aright! May the mighty God of Jacob ever be my help....I can form no conception as to what our course may be, or whether it will take us N., S., E., or W. I never felt so fully and utterly cast on the Lord, but in due time He *will* lead us on.

Met by Mr. Fishe on arrival, the travelers learned that although there was cause in the southern stations especially for encouragement, the need for Mr. Taylor's presence was even greater than they had anticipated. Duncan of Nanking had been obliged, through failing health, to relinquish the post he had so bravely held, and even then was on his way home, as it proved, to die. The absence of the Judds on furlough, and Mr. Fishe's illness, had left the work in the Yangtze valley with little supervision, and it was important to send someone to take charge without delay. Transferring themselves and their belongings to a native boat, Mr. and Mrs. Taylor set out forthwith for Hangchow. Warm was the welcome that awaited them in the old home from Mr. and Mrs. McCarthy and the members of the church, many of whom owed their spiritual life, under God, to the one who returned to them now as a bride. Mr. McCarthy's six years in China qualified him for larger responsibilities, and leaving Hangchow to Pastor Wang, with help from Mr. and Mrs. Taylor, he willingly undertook the difficult work on the Yangtze (in An-hwei).

And now began an experience for the leader of the mission such as he had never known before to anything like the same extent. Not only were certain stations undermanned through the absence of senior workers, sickness and trial of various sorts had taken a toll on those who remained, while native leaders had grown cold, some having even lapsed into open sin. The tidings that came to him were to a large extent discouraging, and as he began to move from place to place, Mr. Taylor found plenty of cause for humiliation before God.

In the wintry weather, with snow deep on the ground, he set to work at once, leaving Mrs. Taylor at Hangchow for a time. Lonely indeed must it have seemed to open the empty house at Chinkiang, his once happy home, and gather the Christians together for little services with no companion but the evangelist. It was just by getting into close touch with the native helpers, however, that he hoped to cheer and strengthen them, and for this he laid himself out in center after center. Joined by Mrs. Taylor, he spent three months in Nanking, giving much time to direct missionary work. He followed this with a similar sojourn in Yangchow and Chinkiang, before he went on upriver to the newer stations.

He wrote to Miss Blatchley around the New Year:

> If you are ever drinking at the Fountain, what will your cup be running over with? Jesus, Jesus, Jesus!

That it was so in his own case is manifest. Amid much that was difficult and disappointing, amid cold, discomfort, weariness, it was a full cup he carried in this sense, and the overflow was just what was needed. It was so real and unmistakable, the joy of his heart in the Lord, and it did good like a medicine wherever he went. Most people need encouraging, not preaching at or an attitude of condemnation, and tired missionaries no less than Chinese converts responded to a loving spirit full of joy in an all-sufficient Savior.

So the visits accomplished their object and were continued until Mr. Taylor had been, once at any rate, to every station and almost every out-station in the mission. Not content with this, he sought out the native workers in each place, so that the evangelists, colporteurs, teachers, and Bible women, almost without exception, came under his influence.

But it was work that cost, carried on under special difficulties, for Mr. Taylor had all his correspondence and directorial duties to attend to at the same time. It meant constant traveling, through summer heat as well as winter cold, and involved long separations from Mrs. Taylor, who could not always accompany him. At times they were together in stations that needed an extended visit, or she would stay on where there was sickness, to give help in nursing or among the women. How glad they were of his medical knowledge in those days, for it gave opportunity for really serving their fellow workers as well as the native Christians. Needless to say it added to Mr. Taylor's burdens, as when he reached a distant station on the Yangtze to find eighty-nine letters awaiting him and took time to send, the very next day, a page or more of medical directions about "A-liang's baby," A-liang being a valued helper at Chinkiang. But whether it meant longer letters or extra journeys, or the strain of nursing and medical responsibility, he was thankful for any and every way in which he could help. Capacity for usefulness, the power really to serve others, was the privilege he desired most.

And such an outpouring of heart and life could not but tell. To his parents, he wrote:

> The Lord is prospering us and the work is steadily growing, especially in that most important department, *native help.* The helpers themselves need much help, much care and instruction, but they are becoming more efficient as well as more numerous, and the future hope for China lies, doubtless, in *them.* I look on foreign missionaries as the scaffolding round a rising building; the sooner it can be dispensed with the better—or

rather, the sooner it can be transferred to other places, to serve the same temporary purpose.

As to difficulties and sorrows, their name is legion. Some spring from the nature of the work, some from the nature of the workers. Here Paul and Barnabas cannot see eye to eye; there Peter so acts as to need public rebuke; while elsewhere exhortation is needed to restore a wanderer or quicken one growing cold....But it is the Lord's work, and we go on from day to day. He is competent to meet all matters that may arise, as and when they crop up.

Sorely was this faith needed when, after nine months in the Yangtze valley, Mr. Taylor turned his attention to the southern stations, in the province of Che-kiang. Not that the work was discouraging; on the contrary, there was much to cheer in some directions. But it was there the unexpected tidings reached him of the complete breakdown of Miss Blatchley's health. Apart altogether from sorrow in the thought of her removal was the serious question as to how her place was to be filled. Gifted, devoted, and with some experience, matters had tended more and more to come into her hands. Not only was she keeping the mission house going, and the weekly prayer meeting, she was editing and sending out the *Occasional Paper,* dealing with correspondence to a considerable extent, and caring for the children she had received as a sacred charge from their mother, the friend she had supremely loved. All this made it difficult indeed to see how her place could be filled, and Mr. Taylor, unable for the present to return home, could do nothing.

It seemed the last drop in a full cup, for already, in addition to the burdens upon him in

China, he was tried and perplexed by the irregularity as well as diminution of supplies from home. It was but natural that Mr. Berger's retirement should continue to be felt in these and other ways. The work had grown up in his hands. To the friends and supporters of the mission he seemed almost as much a part of it as Mr. Taylor himself. His extensive business had given him a familiarity with financial and practical matters that was invaluable, and the needs of the workers in China had been upon his heart day and night. This could not be so to the same extent with other friends, no matter how interested and anxious to help. The members of the C.I.M. council, moreover, were all new to their responsibilities. They did what they could, with no little sacrifice and devotion, but they had experience to gain.

Meanwhile, it was in China that the difficulties of the situation were most acutely felt. Mr. Taylor did what was possible by correspondence, and irregularities that could not be dealt with in that way had just to be taken to the Lord in faith and prayer. Small though the mission was in those days, comparatively, there were fifty buildings to be kept up and a hundred workers to be provided for, including missionaries' wives and native helpers. There were all the children besides, in families and schools, making fully a hundred and seventy mouths to feed daily. Traveling expenses were also a serious item, with a work extending to five provinces and furloughs involving the expensive journey to England. Altogether, Mr. Taylor's estimate of a hundred pounds a week as a working average could not be considered extravagant. Indeed it was only with most careful planning and economy that the work could be carried on vigorously upon that sum.

But there were many weeks and even months in which little or nothing was forwarded to him for the general purposes of the mission. Funds were not coming in plentifully at home, and many gifts—such as those of Mr. Müller and Mr. Berger—were sent directly to the workers or to Mr. Taylor for transmission. This left but little for the general fund, from which home expenses had to be met, as well as the current outlay for all but specially supported workers in China.

And now, in addition to this long-continued shortness of funds and all the other difficulties of the work, had come the keen personal sorrow of Miss Blatchley's illness. Concern about his children, too, was very real. Who was caring for them, or how they would be provided for if she were taken, he did not know. And before he and Mrs. Taylor could be with them again, many months must elapse. He wrote to his mother:

> No words can express my sorrow for what I fear will be the end of this attack of illness. I feel it selfish to sorrow for what will be infinite gain to one so ready for the change; but, "Jesus wept" (John 11:35), and He is unchanged and can sympathize still in our grief and pain in bereavement. This has been long foreseen, but I did not expect it so suddenly. I thought the disease was so far quiescent that dear Emily [Miss Blatchley] might be spared till we once more visited England, and that ours might have been the privilege of ministering to her as long as human ministry could avail. The Lord seems to see it best otherwise, and we *will* trust Him. He cannot err, nor fail to do the kindest, the best thing every way—for her, for us, for ours. He will show His care for His own work.

Chapter 11

Obedience to the Heavenly Call

It was not until many years later, when Mr. Taylor could look back over all the way in which the Lord had led him, that he was impressed with the fact that every important advance in the development of the mission had sprung from or been directly connected with times of sickness or suffering which had cast him in a special way upon God. It was to be so now, as though a deeper preparedness of spirit were needed, before he could be trusted with the answer to the following prayer:

> Asked God for fifty or a hundred additional native evangelists, and as many foreign superintendents as may be needed, to open up the four Fus and forty-eight Hsiens still unoccupied in Che-kiang; also for the men to break into the nine unoccupied provinces. Asked in the name of Jesus. I thank Thee, Lord Jesus, for the promise whereon Thou hast given me to rest. Give me all needed strength of body, wisdom of mind, grace of soul to do this Thy so great work. Amen.

There was quite enough, as far as outward experiences went, to account for the serious illness that overtook him before he could get back to his temporary quarters at Feng-hwa. In the depth of winter he had been almost incessantly on the road for weeks past, bearing an unusual strain even for him, physically and mentally. So persistent had been the calls upon him, that he had scarcely seen

Mrs. Taylor for three months. Ten weeks out of twelve had been spent apart, though they were planning, as well as longing, to meet. About the middle of December 1873 they had found one another at last, in the empty mission house at Fenghwa, and had actually had the joy of being alone together, strange to say, for the first time! The little honeymoon was soon broken into, however, by a call for help in serious illness.

Only waiting until the coolie could arrive with his belongings, whom he had outdistanced in his eagerness to be with his loved one again, Mr. Taylor set out once more to cross the mountains. It was a desperate business facing January storms on those heights, more than one of which could only be scaled by steps literally cut in the rock. Anxieties pressed sorely upon him with regard to Miss Blatchley and his children at home, as well as in connection with the shortness of funds in China.

The overtaxed physical powers at length gave way, and his patients were no sooner convalescent than Mr. Taylor himself came down with fever and was so ill as to be hardly able to get back to Fenghwa. Now, how unpromising seemed the sequel to that step of faith! Week after week he lay in helplessness and suffering, able to do nothing but wait upon the Lord. Of all that in His providence was drawing near, Hudson Taylor was unconscious. He only knew that God had given him to see something of the purposes of His heart, that he was sharing in some measure the compassion of Christ for the lost and perishing, and that the love of which he felt the yearnings was His own infinite love. That that love, that purpose, would find a way to bless, he could not doubt. So he just prayed on—holding in faith to the heavenly vision, ready to go forward when and as the Lord should open the way. Never had advance seemed less possible. But in the Bible beside him was the record of that transaction of his soul with God, and in his heart was the conviction that even for the inland provinces—the western branch of the mission he longed to plant, as a stepping-stone to the far interior—God's time had almost come.

And then, as he lay there slowly recovering, a letter was put into his hands that had been two months on its way from England. It was from an unknown friend, a Mrs. Grace of Wycombe, Buckinghamshire, who had only recently become interested in the mission:

> My dear Sir, *I bless God,* in two months I hope to place at the disposal of your council, for *further* extension of Inland China mission work, £800. Please remember, for *fresh* provinces....I think your receipt form beautiful—"The Lord our Banner: the Lord will provide." If faith is put forth and praise sent up, I am sure that Jehovah of Hosts will honor it.

Eight hundred pounds for "fresh provinces," for "further extension" of inland work—hardly could the convalescent believe he read rightly! Could anyone have penned those words who did not know the exercise of soul he had been passing through all those months? The very secrets of his heart seemed to look back at him from that sheet of foreign note paper. Even before the prayer recorded in his Bible, the letter had been sent off, and now, just when it was most needed, it had reached him with its wonderful confirmation.

From his sickroom back to the Yangtze valley was the next step, and those spring days witnessed a happy gathering at Chinkiang. There, as in almost all the stations, new life had come to the little company of believers. Young converts were being received into the church, and native leaders were growing in grace and usefulness. Older missionaries were more hopeful, amid the needs of their great districts, and the young men, who had made good progress with the language, were eager for pioneering work. As many as could leave their stations came to meet Mr. Taylor for a week of prayer and conference before he and Mr. Judd set out to seek, up the great river, a home for the new western branch.

It was not any improvement in the state of funds that accounted for the new note of joy and confidence. To his mother, Mr. Taylor wrote:

> I feel no anxiety, though for a month past I have not had a dollar in hand for the general purposes of the mission. The Lord will provide.

Quoting again the hymn they were singing daily at the conference—"In some way or other, the Lord will provide"—he wrote to Miss Blatchley a little later:

> I am sure that if we will but wait, the Lord *will* provide....We go shortly, that is, Mr. Judd and myself, to see if we can procure headquarters at Wu-chang from which to open up western China, as the Lord may enable us. We are urged on to make this effort now, though so weak-handed, both by the needs of the unopened provinces and by our having funds for commencing work in them, while we have none for the general work....I cannot conceive how we shall be helped through next month, though I fully expect we shall be. The Lord cannot and will not fail us.

To Mrs. Taylor he had written during April: "The balance in hand yesterday was sixty-seven cents! The Lord reigns; herein is our joy and confidence." And to Mr. Baller he added, when the balance was still lower, "We have this and all the promises of God."

One thing that concerned Mr. Taylor more at this time than shortness of supplies was the fear lest, in their desire to help, friends at home should be tempted to make appeals in meetings, or even more personally, for funds. To one and another he wrote very earnestly on the subject, begging that this might not be done. The trial through which they were passing was no reason, to his mind, for changing the basis on which they had been led to found the mission. In acknowledging one of Mr. George Müller's generous contributions, he had written early in April:

> The work generally is very cheering, and we feel happier than ever in the Lord and in His service. Our faith never was so much tried, His faithfulness never so much experienced.

And this position was to him far more safe and blessed, as long as the trial was permitted, than the alternative of going into debt or making appeals to man. How truly this was the case may be seen from the following letter to a member of the council, written just after the Conference at Chinkiang (April 24, 1874):

> I am truly sorry that you should be distressed at not having funds to send me. May I not say, "Be careful for nothing" (Phil. 4:6). We should use all care to economize what God does send us, but when that is done, bear no care about real or apparent lack. After living on *God's*

faithfulness for many years, I can testify that times of want have ever been times of special blessing or have led to them. I do beg that never any appeal for funds be put forward, save to God in prayer. When our work becomes a begging work, it dies. God is faithful, must be so. "The LORD is my shepherd; I shall not want" (Ps. 23:1). He has said, "Take no thought [anxiety] for your life, what ye shall eat, or what ye shall drink, nor yet for your body, what ye shall put on. But seek ye first [to promote] the kingdom of God, and [to fulfill] His righteousness; and *all these things shall be added unto you.*" (See Matthew 6:31–33.)

"[Obedience] is better than sacrifice, and to hearken than the fat of rams" (1 Sam. 15:22). It is doubting, beloved Brother, not trusting, that is tempting the Lord.

At this very time, it is interesting to notice, Mr. and Mrs. Taylor were themselves giving largely to the work in various ways. A considerable proportion of all they received for their own use was passed on to fellow workers, and a property yielding an income of four hundred pounds a year, which had recently come to Mrs. Taylor from a relative, was joyfully set apart for the Lord's service. The intimate friend to whom Mr. Taylor was writing had questioned the wisdom of this course, which led to one of the few references he ever made to the subject. Anxious that their position should not be misunderstood, he continued in this letter:

As to the property my dear wife has given to the Lord for His service, I most cordially agreed with her in the step, and do so now. I believe that in so doing she has made hers forever that which was her Master's, and only entrusted to her so to use. It is not a modern question, this of principal or interest, endowment or voluntary support, and we cannot expect *all* to see alike on the subject. We might capitalize the annual income of the mission and use only the interest, but I fear the income would soon be small and the work not very extensive.

But you may, I think, be mistaken as to our thought and intention, as well as with regard to the nature of the property. The whole cannot be realized, half of it being reserved to provide annuities....At present, all we have is about four hundred pounds of annual interest, payable in varying quarterly sums. We do not propose to put either principal or interest into the general fund (though we might be led to do so), but to use it, equally avoiding stint or lavishness, as the Lord may direct, for special purposes not met by the general fund. We are neither of us inexperienced, unacquainted with the value of money, or unaccustomed either to its want or possession. There are few more cool and calculating, perhaps, than we are, but in all our calculations we calculate on God's faithfulness, or seek to do so. Hitherto we have not been put to shame, nor have I any anxiety or fear lest we should be in the future.

Never has our work entailed such real trial or so much exercise of faith. The sickness of our beloved sister, Miss Blatchley, and her strong desire to see me; the needs of our dear children; the state of the funds; the changes required in the work to admit of some going home, others coming out, and of further expansion; and many other things not easily expressed in writing would be crushing anxieties if we were to bear them. But the Lord bears us and them too and makes our hearts so very glad in Himself—not Himself plus a bank balance—that I have never known greater freedom from anxiety and care.

The other week when I reached Shanghai, I was in great and immediate need. The mails were both in—no remittance! and the folios showed no balances at home. I cast the burden on the Lord. Next morning on waking I felt inclined to trouble, but the Lord gave me a word, "I know their sorrows; and I am come down to deliver....*Certainly* I will be with thee" (Exod. 3:7–8, 12, italics added); and before 6 A.M. I was as sure that help was at hand as when, near noon, I received a letter from Mr. Müller which had been to Ningpo and was thus delayed in reaching me and which contained more than three hundred pounds.

My need now is great and urgent; God is greater and more near, and because *He is*, and is *what He is,* all must be, all is, all will be well. Oh, my dear Brother, the joy of knowing the living God, of seeing the living God, of resting on the living God in our very special and peculiar circumstances! I am but His agent. He will look after His own honor, provide for His own servants, and supply all our need according to His own riches—you helping by your prayers and work of faith and labor of love. As to whether He will make the widow's oil and meal go a long way, or send her more—it is merely a question of detail; the result is sure. The righteous shall not be forsaken, nor his seed beg their bread. In Christ, all the promises are Yea and Amen.

Out of Weakness Were Made Strong

It was a memorable day for Hudson Taylor when he set out with his like-minded companion,

Mr. Judd, to follow the mighty Yangtze, if not to its upper waters, at any rate to its confluence with the tributary Han, where the area of mid-China formed the farthest outpost of Protestant missions. Six hundred miles from the coast, this great center of culture and commerce lay far beyond any inland station he had yet visited, but northward, westward, southward of it stretched the nine unopened provinces, from the tropical jungles of Burma to the barren steppes of Mongolia and the snowy ramparts of Tibet. Vast was that waiting world, and vast the longings with which Hudson Taylor turned his face—as he had long turned his heart—toward its silent appeal.

Meanwhile in England, very different were the experiences of those most closely connected with the work. Tenderly cared for by Miss Soltau, Mrs. Duncan, and others, Miss Blatchley still lingered, but it was in great weakness and suffering, and the ebb tide of her life seemed to leave the cause she had so faithfully served almost stranded.

It had been to Mr. Taylor, as we have seen, a keen sorrow that he could not hasten home when he first heard of this illness, to relieve the beloved friend to whom he and his, as well as the mission, owed so much. But month after month had gone by, and it was not until he had seen Mr. Judd in possession of suitable quarters at Wu-chang that the way began to open for his return to England. But even before he could leave China, the one he so hoped to succor had set out on a longer journey. For her, all need of human help was past.

Strange and sorrowful was the homecoming in October 1874, to find Miss Blatchley's place empty, the children scattered, the Saturday prayer meeting discontinued, and the work almost at a standstill.

But, even then, the lowest ebb had not been reached. When on his way up the Yangtze some months previously, a fall had severely shaken Mr. Taylor. Slipping on one of the top steps of the gangway of the boat in which he was traveling, Mr. Taylor had fallen heavily to the bottom, coming down upon his heels, and a sprained ankle had been only a small part of the damage. Extreme pain in the back disabled him for several days, and even when the ankle was well he still needed the help of crutches. Concussion of the spine often develops slowly, and it was not until he had been at home a week or two that the rush of London life, with constant traveling by train and omnibus, began to tell. Then came gradual paralysis of the lower limbs, and the doctor's verdict that consigned him to absolute rest in bed. Stricken down in the prime of his days, he could only lie in that upstairs room conscious of all there was to be done, of all that was not being attended to—lie there and rejoice in God.

Yes, rejoice in God! With desires and hopes as limitless as the needs that pressed upon his heart; with the prayer he had prayed, and the answers God had given; with opportunities opening in China, and a wave of spiritual blessing reviving the churches at home that he longed to see turned into missionary channels; with the "sentence of death" (2 Cor. 1:9) in himself, and only the faintest hope that he would ever stand or walk again; the deepest thing of all was that unquestioning acceptance of the will of God as wise, as kind, as best. Certain it is that from that quiet room, that room of suffering, sprang all the larger growth of the China Inland Mission.

A little bed with four posts was now the sphere to which Hudson Taylor found himself restricted, he who had hoped to do so much on this visit to England. Were not the receiving home in Shanghai and the chain of river stations ready for the pioneers? Was not money in hand for their initial expenses? Was not the home department calling for entire reorganization? If ever strenuous, active effort had been needed, it was surely at this juncture, and a little bed with four posts was his prison, or shall we say, his opportunity? Between the posts at the foot of the bed hung a map—though he hardly needed it—a map of China. And round about him day and night was the Presence to which he had fullest access in the name of Jesus.

Long after, when the prayers that went up from that bed of pain had been more than answered, and the workers of the mission were preaching Christ far and wide throughout inland China, a well-known leader of the Scottish church said to Mr. Taylor:

"You must often be conscious of the wonderful way God has prospered you in the C.I.M. I doubt if any man living has had a greater honor."

"I do not look upon it in that way," was the quiet answer. Then, turning to his friend he said earnestly: "Do you know I sometimes think that God must have been looking for someone small enough and weak enough for Him to use, so that all the glory might be His, and that He found me."

The outlook did not brighten as the year drew to a close. Mr. Taylor was less and less able to move, even in bed, and at last could only turn from side to side with the help of a rope firmly fixed above him. At first he had managed to write a little but now could not even hold a pen, and circumstances deprived him of Mrs. Taylor's help for the time being. Then it was, with the dawn of 1875, that a little paper found its way into the Christian press entitled: "APPEAL FOR PRAYER: On behalf of more than a hundred and fifty millions of Chinese."

It briefly stated the facts with regard to the nine unopened provinces; that friends of the C.I.M. had long been praying for men to go as pioneer evangelists to these regions; that recently four thousand pounds had been given for the purpose; and that among the converts in the older stations of the mission, were some from the far interior who were earnestly desiring to carry the Gospel to the districts from which they had come. It continued:

> Our present, pressing need is of more missionaries to lead the way. Will each of your Christian readers at once raise his heart to God and spend one minute in earnest prayer that God will raise up, this year, eighteen suitable men to devote themselves to this work?

It did not say that the leader of the mission was to all appearances a hopeless invalid. It did not refer to the fact that the four thousand pounds recently given had come from his wife and himself, part of their capital, the whole of which they had consecrated to the work of God. It did not mention that for two and a half years they and others had been praying daily for the eighteen evangelists, praying in faith. But those who read the appeal felt the influence of these things, and much besides, and were moved as men are not moved by sayings and doings that do not have their roots deep in God.

So before long, Mr. Taylor's correspondence was largely increased, as was also his joy in dealing with it—or in seeing, rather, how the Lord dealt with it and with all else that concerned him. He wrote of this time:

> The mission had no paid helpers, but God led volunteers, without prearrangement, to come in from day to day to write from dictation, and thus letters were answered. If one who called in the morning could not stay long enough to answer all, another was sure to come, and perhaps one or two might look in in the afternoon. Occasionally, a young friend who was employed in the city would come after business hours and do any needful bookkeeping or finish letters not already dealt with. So it was day by day. One of the happiest periods of my life was that period of forced inactivity, when one could do nothing but "rest in the LORD, and wait patiently for him" (Ps. 37:7) and see Him meeting all one's need. Never were my letters, before or since, kept so regularly and promptly answered.
>
> And the eighteen men asked of God began to come. There was first some correspondence; then they came to see me in my room. Soon I had a class studying Chinese at my bedside. In due time the Lord sent them forth, and then the dear friends at Mildmay began to pray for my restoration. The Lord blessed the means used, and I was raised up. One reason for my being laid aside was gone. Had I been well and able to move about, some might have thought that my urgent appeals, rather than God's working, had sent the eighteen men to China. But utterly laid aside, able only to dictate a request for prayer, the answer to our prayers was the more apparent.

When he was so far recovered that the physicians wished him to sit up for an hour or two daily, he could scarcely find time to do so, as several letters record. Every moment was taken up with interviews, with correspondence through his willing helpers, and with care for the work in China. The weekly prayer meeting was now held in his room, and the council gathered from time to time at his bedside.

By this time a marked change had come over the spirit of the scene at Pyrland Road. Instead of a deserted house, many were coming and going. The first party of the eighteen had already sailed, and candidates overflowed all the accommodation available for their reception. Another house, indeed, had to be taken for this purpose, for in answer to the "Appeal for Prayer" published in January, no fewer than sixty offers of service were received during the year. How important Mr. Taylor felt it that no hasty decisions should be made, may be judged from the following letter used in his correspondence with candidates at this period. If their response to this faithful statement of the case warranted the hope that they would work happily in the mission, they were invited to spend a longer or shorter time at Pyrland Road for personal acquaintance:

> While thankful for any educational advantages that candidates may have enjoyed, we attach far greater importance to spiritual qualifications. We desire men who believe that there is a God and that He is both intelligent and faithful, and who therefore trust Him; who believe that He is the rewarder of those who diligently seek Him, and are therefore men of *prayer*. We desire men who believe the Bible to be the Word of God, and who, accepting the declaration, "All power is given unto me" (Matt.

28:18), are prepared to carry out, to the best of their ability, the command, "Go...teach all nations" (Matt. 28:19), relying on Him who possesses "all power" and has promised to be with His messengers always, rather than on foreign gunboats, though they possess some power; men who are prepared, therefore, to go to the remotest parts of the interior of China, expecting to find His arm a sufficient strength and stay. We desire men who believe in eternity and live for it; who believe in its momentous issues, whether to the saved or to the lost, and therefore cannot but seek to pluck the ignorant and the guilty as brands from the burning.

The mission is supported by donations, not subscriptions. We have, therefore, no guaranteed income and can only minister to our missionaries as we ourselves are ministered to by God. We do not send men to China as our agents. But men who believe that God has called them to the work, who go there to labor for God, and can therefore trust Him whose they are and whom they serve to supply their temporal needs, we gladly cooperate with—providing, if needful, outfit and passage money, and such a measure of support as circumstances call for and we are enabled to supply. As may be seen from the last *Occasional Paper*, our faith is sometimes tried, but God always proves Himself faithful, and at the right time and in the right way supplies all our need.

One third of the human family are in China, needing the Gospel. Twelve millions there are passing beyond the reach of that Gospel every year. If you want hard work and little appreciation; if you value God's approval more than you fear man's disapprobation; if you are prepared to take joyfully the spoiling of your goods, and seal your testimony, if need be, with your blood; if you can pity and love the poor Chinese in all their mental and moral degradation, as well as literal filth and impurity; you may count on a harvest of souls now and a crown of glory hereafter "that fadeth not away" (1 Pet. 5:4), and on the Master's *"Well done"* (Matt. 25:21, 23, italics added).

You would find that, in connection with the China Inland Mission, it is no question of "making the most of both worlds." The men, the only men who will be happy with us, are those who have this world under their feet, and I do venture to say that such men will find a happiness they never dreamed of or thought possible down here. For to those who count "all things" but dross and dung for "the excellency of the knowledge of Christ Jesus [our] Lord" (Phil. 3:8), He does manifest Himself in such sort that they are not inclined to rue their bargain. If, after prayerfully considering the matter, you still feel drawn to engage in such work, I shall be only too glad to hear from you again.

Young men and women who came to Pyrland Road on probation, encouraged rather than daunted by the spirit of the above letter, soon found occasion to rejoice in God as the hearer and answerer of prayer. Such, for example, was the experience in May that followed the sailing of Mr. George King for China. It had been difficult to spare him, for, busy though he was in the city during the day, he had been one of Mr. Taylor's most faithful helpers both before and after office hours.

"Perhaps the Lord will lessen the amount of correspondence for a time," said the latter, "unless He sends us unexpected help."

The correspondence lessened. Mr. King sailed on the fifteenth, and for a week or two the work was so far reduced as to continue to be manageable.

On the morning of the twenty-fifth, however, when the household gathered for noonday prayer, Mr. Taylor called attention to the fact that this lessening of correspondence had involved a lessening of contributions also.

"Let us ask the Lord," he suggested, "to remind some of His wealthy stewards of the needs of the work."

A remarkable experience soon followed. It was early in June, and Mr. Taylor was returning from Brighton, where he had taken part in a memorable convention on scriptural holiness. Waiting for his train at the station, he was accosted by a Russian nobleman who had been attending the meetings, and who, on learning that Mr. Taylor was going to London, suggested that they should find seats together.

"But I am traveling third class," said the missionary.

"My ticket admits of my doing the same," was the courteous reply. And they seem to have found a carriage alone together, for presently Count Bobrinsky took out his pocketbook with the words:

"Allow me to give you a trifle toward your work in China."

Glancing at the banknote as he received it, Mr. Taylor felt there must be some mistake—it was for no less than fifty pounds.

"Did you not mean to give me five pounds?" he said at once. "Please let me return this note; it is for fifty."

"I cannot take it back," replied the other, no less surprised. "It was five pounds I meant to give, but God must have intended you to have fifty; I cannot take it back."

Impressed with the incident, Mr. Taylor reached Pyrland Road to find a prayer meeting going on. A remittance was about to be sent to China, and the money in hand was short by forty-nine pounds, eleven shillings of the sum it was felt would be required. This deficiency was not accepted as inevitable. On the contrary, it called together those who knew of it for special prayer. Forty-nine pounds, eleven shillings were being asked for in simple faith, and there upon the office table Mr. Taylor laid his precious banknote for fifty pounds. Could it have come more directly from the heavenly Father's hand? "Whoso is wise, and will observe these things, even they shall understand the lovingkindness of the LORD" (Ps. 107:43).

The Faithfulness of God

Mr. Taylor was going back—back to China to speed the pioneers, as he fully hoped and expected, on their far inland journeys. A gracious answer to the prayers of many years had made this possible in the coming of his beloved sister and her husband, Mr. and Mrs. B. Broomhall, into the home department of the work. How real was the faith involved in joining the mission, when at length the way opened, may be judged from the fact that they had by that time a family of ten growing boys and girls. But this was perhaps one of their chief qualifications. What hearts are so large and what hands so free for others as those filled with love and service in which self has no part. Number two Pyrland Road, which became the home of Mr. and Mrs. Broomhall, soon radiated an atmosphere of helpfulness, spiritually and in other ways, that made it for many a long year the best loved center of the mission. Number six was still Mr. Taylor's home, but the two were practically thrown into one, the intervening house being occupied for offices and candidates. Mr. Taylor's little back room was now exchanged for a more cheerful study, and a secretary was installed in the person of Mr. William Soltau, who took over much of his work. Barely waiting to see these arrangements completed, however, and to give time for the preparation of the party of eight who sailed with him, Mr. Taylor set out early in September 1876, notwithstanding the war cloud that hung heavily over the eastern horizon.

Negotiations concerning the murder of a member of a British exploring party had dragged on so long at Peking and had come at last to a stalemate. Nothing would induce the Chinese government to give satisfaction of any sort for this murder, and the British ambassador, having exhausted diplomatic resources, was on the point of retiring to the coast to put the matter into the hands of the admiral. It seemed impossible that war could be averted, and there were many among the friends of the mission who strongly advised against Mr. Taylor's going out.

"You will all have to return," they said. "And as to sending off pioneers to the more distant provinces, it is simply out of the question."

It was indeed a critical juncture. After years of prayer and preparation, evangelists for the unentered provinces had been given, had gone to China, and, having acquired some knowledge of the language, were ready to set forth. Could it be that the iron gate of the last ward—having opened thus far—was again to close, leaving the prayer of faith unanswered? Mr. Taylor did not think so. Indeed he felt as sure that God's time had come, as he was that the men had been given. He was fully aware that in event of war, not the pioneers only, but *all* his fellow workers might have to leave their inland stations. That matters could not look more threatening was obvious. Every effort had failed, and a war that might close the country entirely to missionary effort had all but begun.

But no, prayer had not failed. In the third-class cabin of the French mail ship, as in the prayer meetings at Pyrland Road, fervent supplication was going up to God, that He would overrule the crisis for the furtherance of His own great ends. With Him it is never too late. At the last moment, utterly improbable as it seemed, a change came over the Peking Foreign Office. More alive to the situation than his fellows, the viceroy, Li Hung-chang, hurried to the coast, overtaking the British ambassador just in time to reopen negotiations; and there, at Chefoo, was signed the memorable convention which threw open the door of access at last to the remotest parts of China. This was the news that awaited Mr. Taylor on his arrival in Shanghai, the agreement having been signed within a week of his leaving England, and already three parties of the eighteen had set out and were well on their way to the interior. He wrote:

> Just as our brethren were ready, not too soon and not too late the long-closed door opened to them of its own accord.

And what were the provisions of that notable convention signed at Chefoo on September 13, 1876? As concerned the pioneers, simply these: that foreigners were at liberty to travel in any part of the emperor's dominions; that they did so under his protection, and were to be received with respect and in no way hindered on their journeys. Imperial proclamations were to be posted in every city, giving publicity to these arrangements, and for a period of two years British officials might be sent inland, specially to see that this clause was carried out. As a matter of fact, representatives of the C.I.M. were the first, and for years almost the only foreigners, to avail themselves of this great opportunity. Far and wide they traveled, crossing and recrossing all the provinces of the interior, and penetrating even into eastern Tibet. Thirty thousand miles were thus traversed in the next eighteen months, Scriptures and tracts being everywhere sold or distributed, and friendly relations almost uninterruptedly were maintained. At first, indeed, the missionaries were supposed to be government agents, and their arrival spread dismay in the official breast. For there had been no unseemly haste in issuing the proclamations, and more than one mandarin hit upon the happy expedient of entertaining the visitors with elaborate hospitality, while the city was hurriedly placarded with the belated documents.

For Mr. Taylor, little that he had planned was to be accomplished during the first few months after his arrival. A chill caught in the China Sea led to serious illness. He was able to go upriver as far as Chinkiang, but there he had to learn many a lesson of patience, as he found himself needed at nearly every station in the mission and unable to do more than pray and help by correspondence.

Yet overwork seemed almost inevitable; for Mr. C. T. Fishe, in broken health, had gone home on furlough, and there was no one else to take his place as secretary to the mission in China. This meant long hours daily at office work, besides Mr. Taylor's directorial duties and the oft-recurring claims of *China's Millions,* of which he was editor. This innovative monthly illustrated paper gave news of pioneer journeys, conversions, and progress in the older stations, along with up-to-date pictures and spiritually helpful articles penned by Mr. Taylor himself.

Despite absence from home and loved ones, and the limitations of ill health which he was feeling keenly, Mr. Taylor was enabled so to cast his burdens on the Lord that, as he wrote to Mr. Hill in February 1877, he "could not but rejoice seven days a week." Whenever work permitted, he was in the habit of turning to a little harmonium for refreshment, playing and singing many a favorite hymn, but always coming back to—

> Jesus, I am resting, resting, in the joy of what Thou art;
> I am finding out the greatness of Thy loving heart.

Some around him could hardly understand this joy and rest, especially when fellow workers were in danger. A bundle of letters arriving on one occasion, as Mr. Nicoll relates, brought news of serious rioting in two different stations. Standing at his desk to read them, Mr. Taylor mentioned what was happening and that immediate help was necessary. Feeling that he might wish to be alone, the younger man was about to withdraw, when, to his surprise, someone began to whistle. It was the soft refrain of the same well-loved hymn: *Jesus I am resting, resting, in the joy of what Thou art...*

Turning back, Mr. Nicoll could not help exclaiming, "How can you whistle, when our friends are in such danger!"

"Would you have me anxious and troubled?" was the long-remembered answer. "That would not help them and would certainly incapacitate me for my work. I have just to roll the burden on the Lord."

Day and night that was his secret: "just to roll the burden on the Lord." Frequently, those who were wakeful in the little house at Chinkiang might hear, at two or three o'clock in the morning, the soft refrain of Mr. Taylor's favorite hymn. He had learned that, for him, only one life was possible—just that blessed life of resting and rejoicing in the Lord under all circumstances, while He dealt with the difficulties inward and outward, great and small.

Chapter 12

Bearing Fruit

Hudson Taylor was preparing to begin a new phase of work in the far interior of China. Within a few years' time, young couples had left for the interior, beginning work for the first time among the women of the western and northwestern provinces. What that work would mean Mr. Taylor largely realized, and how great would be the need for sisterly help and companionship. Never in all the history of the mission had he been called to take a step which cast him more in faith upon the living God. What, send women—unmarried women, young and defenseless—into all the dangers and privations, the hardship and loneliness of life in the far interior of China? Let them take those perilous journeys of weeks and months at a time, and condemn them to isolation in crowded cities, hundreds of miles from any other foreigner? The responsibility was great indeed, and he felt it keenly. He was but a servant, however, not the Master. And if women were waiting to go at the Master's call, surely the time had come to help them rather than hinder. He wrote of this:

> None can be more anxious than myself to see women's work commenced in the interior of the various provinces. This has long been the consuming desire of my heart.

Did the vision come to him as he traveled and passed the very cities which were to witness the loving, self-sacrificing labors of girls then free and happy in far-off Christian homes: the vision of lives laid down for Jesus' sake, quietly put into the building up of that kingdom which is righteousness, joy, and peace in human hearts, into the comforting of sorrows and the lightening of darkness he could but deeply feel as he passed on?

All the while, in distant provinces, hundreds of miles farther north and west, a beginning was being made. Strange and new as was the presence of foreign ladies in the great inland cities they now called home, it was no more so than the experiences that were coming to them. Full of interest were the letters Mr. Taylor was receiving, though the preoccupations they told of left little time for writing. One of the women, Mrs. Nicoll wrote:

> For nearly two months past I have daily seen some hundreds of women. Our house has been like a fair. Men also have come to hear the Gospel in as large numbers. They are spoken to in the front part of the house; the women I see in the guest hall and the yard before it, for the room is soon filled....Often while getting one crowd out at the front door, another has found its way in at the back.

How much she needed help may be imagined; for, without a Christian woman anywhere within reach, the only person she could fall back upon was a member of their household who, being an old man, was tolerated among the guests in the inner courtyard. As the summer wore on, she had to get up at three o'clock in the morning to obtain quiet for Bible study or letters. The busy day that followed rarely brought opportunity for rest, and more than once she fainted from weariness in the midst of her visitors, returning to consciousness to find the women fanning her, full of affection and concern.

Among many well-to-do women who were her friends was one elderly lady who cared for her like a mother. From time to time, knowing how weary she must be, this lady would send round her sedan chair with an urgent request for Mrs. Nicoll to return in it immediately. If she succeeded thus in getting her away from the mission house, she would put her on the most comfortable bed in her own apartment, send out all the younger women, and sit down herself to fan her until the tired missionary was fast asleep. Then she would prepare an inviting meal and on no account let her go home until she had taken a good dinner.

That was the surprise, the unexpected encouragement that everywhere awaited these first women who went—the people were glad to see them, were often eager to hear their message, and showed not only natural curiosity and interest, but real heart sympathy.

But such service was not without its cost. While there was much to encourage—for by the end of 1880 the pioneers were rejoicing in sixty or seventy converts, gathered into little churches in the far inland provinces—there was much also to call for faith and patience and the spirit of those who overcame "by the blood of the Lamb" and "loved not their lives unto the death" (Rev. 12:11). First to go to the women of western China, Emily King was the first also to be called to higher service. But before her brief course ended—the one precious opportunity in which she had given her all—she had the joy of seeing no fewer than eighteen women baptized on confession of their faith in

Jesus. Dying of typhus fever in her far-off home, this it was that raised her above the sorrow of leaving her husband desolate, and their little one but five weeks old without a mother. The Man of Sorrows was seeing of "the travail of his soul" (Isa. 53:11) among those for whom He had waited so long! And she was satisfied.

This it was that strengthened the mother's heart by a little lonely grave, when in that same month of May, Mrs. George Clarke went on from Kwei-chow, in which she had been the only woman missionary, to the still more distant and difficult province of Yün-nan. The sisters who had come to her help were able by that time to carry on the work, and the precious child who had filled her hands as well as her heart had been taken to a safer, better land. The father wrote:

> The Lord has been leading us by a painful path. Doubtless He saw best to take our dear boy to Himself, to send us to Yün-nan, for if he had been spared we should not have thought of leaving Kwei-chow. Now, where is the married couple who can go as well as we?

Forty days' journey westward lay the city in which a house was waiting, and Yün-nan, with its twelve millions, was without a resident missionary, or anyone at all to bring to its women and children the glad tidings of a Savior's love. Kneeling beside that little grave, the mother consecrated herself afresh to God for this work, and went on to the loneliness and privations she knew so well, to do in a second great province of western China what she had already been doing in Kwei-chow. And though only two and a half years later she too was called to her reward, the fruit of that life, the answer to her many prayers, lives on.

"I seem to have done so little," she said to her husband toward the end. "I seem to have done less than any woman in China."

It was two years and more since she had seen a sister missionary or had anyone save her husband to share the prayers and tears over what, in those days and for long after, was a hard and fruitless field. But faith rose above discouragement.

"Others will come after us," she said when her brave task was nearly done. "Others will come after us."

The harvest is white to the reaping now, in that province where her life was the first to be laid down. From the snowcapped mountains that reminded her of her own Switzerland, on which she loved to watch the sunset glow, the long-neglected tribespeople are coming, coming in their hundreds to the Savior she so truly loved and served. More than eight thousand baptized believers form the present membership of a church in Yün-nan and Kwei-chow, and it is growing beyond the power to overtake it, because of those who long and pray for fellow workers, called by God, to garner the precious sheaves. Who will come while the Master still tarries, and share both in the present toil and in the endless joy of harvest home?

The Seventy

"Are the itinerations of the C.I.M. really valuable from a missionary point of view? Are they not unproductive and aimless wanderings? Can we hope for much good from the journeys themselves, and will they lead to more definite and settled work?" Such were some of the questions Mr. Taylor felt it desirable to answer in a paper for *China's Millions* early in 1881. It was now four and a half years since the Chefoo convention had thrown open the gates of the west, and pioneer journeys had been made in all the then-unoccupied provinces. Was it too early to discern the trend of the movement, or to speak of spiritual results? It was surely not little to be able to point, even then, to seventy baptized believers in those regions before that time destitute of the Gospel, and to settled work in no fewer than six important centers in five provinces, in all of which women missionaries were to be found as well as men. When one records the name of Pastor Hsi as among those first converts, it will be seen how well worthwhile the labors were that had brought such a man out of darkness into God's marvelous light. He was already receiving opium smokers into his home, to cure them of their craving and lead them to Christ, and was one of those whose faithfulness under persecution, and zeal in making known the one and only Savior, filled Mr. Taylor's heart with joy and led him to ask in his turn the question, "While the Lord so cheers us in our work, will we hesitate to continue, nay to go forward?"

But Mr. Taylor's was not the only pen that by this time was found to advocate the line of things he and his fellow workers had felt led to adopt.

"They are opening up the country," wrote A. Wylie of the L.M.S. as early as 1880, "and this is what we want. Other missionaries are doing a good work, but they are not doing *this* work."

That following summer was memorable for the personal sorrow it brought to Mr. and Mrs.

Taylor in the death of both their beloved mothers within a few weeks of each other. In the midst of much sickness and trial of various kinds this bereavement was specially felt and made the parting all the harder in October 1881, when Mrs. Taylor's return to England could no longer be delayed. The three years she had been in China had brought her so fully into the work that for Mr. Taylor it meant losing his right-hand helper. But it was clearly her duty to return to home responsibilities, and he could not be free for months to come. He wrote ten days after she had left:

> God is helping us very much, and not less by our trials than by our joys. I am sure you have been longing for me, as I for you. At the right time, by the right way the Lord will bring us together again. Let us seek to live all the more with Him, to find Him a satisfying portion.

Traveling up the Yangtze in November to attend a conference, he was more than ever confirmed in a position of quiet trust in the Lord, and in the conviction—tested in many ways—that in the main the mission was on the right lines before Him:

> You are plowing the Mediterranean, I hope, and will soon see Naples. I am waiting here (on the landing stage at An-king) for a steamer to Wu-chang. I need not, cannot tell you how much I miss you, but God is making me feel how rich we are in His presence and love....He is helping me to rejoice in our adverse circumstances, in our poverty, in the retirements from our mission. All these difficulties are only platforms for the manifestation of His grace, power and love.

And from Wu-chang four days later, when the conference had begun:

> I am very busy at work here.... God is giving us a happy time of fellowship together and is *confirming us in the principles on which we are acting.*

That one little sentence, taken in connection with the crisis to which they had come, lets in a flood of light upon the important sequel to those days of fellowship at Wu-chang. For unconsciously, perhaps, to the younger members of the mission, it was a crisis, and more was hanging in the balance than Mr. Taylor himself could realize. After years of prayer and patient, persevering effort, a position of unparalleled opportunity had been reached. Inland China lay open before them. At all the settled stations in the far north, south, and west, reinforcements were needed, whole provinces as large as kingdoms in Europe being at last accessible to resident as well as itinerant missionary work. Not to advance would be to retreat from the position of faith taken up at the beginning. It would be to look at difficulties rather than at the living God. True, funds were low—had been for years—and the workers coming out from home were few, while several retirements had taken place in China. Difficulties were formidable, and it was easy to say, "All these things are indications that for the present no further extension is possible." But *not* to go forward would be to cripple and hinder the work, to throw away opportunities God had given, and to close, before long, stations that had been opened at great cost. This, surely, could not be His way for the evangelization of inland China.

What then was to be done? What answer must be given to the pioneers who were writing and eagerly looking for help? There are several different ways of working for God, as Mr. Taylor reminded the little company.

> One is to make the best plans we can and carry them out to the best of our ability. This may be better than working without plan, but it is by no means the best way of serving our Master. Or, having carefully laid our plans and determined to carry them through, we may ask God to help us and to prosper us in connection with them. Yet another way of working is to begin with God: to ask His plans, and to offer ourselves to Him to carry out His purposes.

This, then, was the attitude taken up. Day by day the needs of the whole work were laid before the Lord, guidance being sought as to His will in connection with them. Mr. Taylor continued:

> Going about it in this way, we leave the responsibility with the Great Designer, and find His service one of sweet restfulness. We have no responsibility save to follow as we are led, and we serve One who is able both to design and to execute, and whose work never fails.

It was only gradually it came to them—for it seemed too big a thing for faith to grasp. Walking over the Serpent Hill in the midst of Wu-chang, Mr. Taylor was counting up with one of his fellow workers, Mr. Parrott, how many men and women it would really take to meet the most pressing claims. Station after station was considered, their thoughts quickened meanwhile by the scene outspread before them—the homes of no fewer than two million people being gathered at that confluence of the mighty Yangtze with the Han. Thus it was the thought dawned, overwhelming almost in its greatness. Fifty to sixty new workers? Why, the entire membership of the mission was barely a hundred! But fifty or sixty, at the lowest computation, would be all too few. "Other seventy also," came to Mr. Taylor's mind: "the Lord appointed other seventy also, and sent them..." (Luke 10:1).

But it seemed too much to ask, not in view of the great, waiting field, but in view of wholly insufficient resources. Just then, as they walked, Mr. Parrott's foot struck against something hard in the grass.

"See," he said, stooping to pick up a string of cash, "see what I have found! If we have to come to the hills for it, God is well able to give us all the money needed!"

But they did not run away with the new idea all at once. Several prayer meetings and quiet consultations were held before they came to feel liberty and confidence in asking the Lord for seventy new fellow workers.

"I quite believe that Mr. Taylor prayed the prayer of faith tonight," wrote Mr. Parrott of one of those meetings; and of another: "There was a great spirit of expectancy."

This was the spirit, indeed, that characterized the whole transaction—definite expectation that God would answer definite prayer in the name of Jesus.

"If only we could meet again," said one, "and have a united praise meeting when the last of the Seventy has reached China!"

Three years had been agreed upon as the period in which the answer should be looked for, as it would hardly be possible to receive and arrange for so many new workers in a shorter time.

"We will be widely scattered then," said another with a practical turn of mind. "But why not have the praise meeting now? Why not give thanks for the Seventy before we separate?"

This happy suggestion commending itself to all, the meeting was held, and those who had joined in the prayer joined in the thanksgiving also, with which the answer was received—in faith.

Fired with new faith and refreshed with spiritual blessing, the little party scattered from Wuchang. What a message was theirs to take and send throughout the mission! On his way downriver, Mr. Taylor wrote:

> The Lord has been with us indeed. We have been guided, I believe of Him, to ask for "other Seventy also" (Luke 10:1), and if He tarry He will send them I am sure. I am now on my way to Chinkiang, where I hope to have some meetings for spiritual blessing.
>
> God is faithful, and expects us to walk by faith....We have our definite lines of working: we must not leave them, nor grow weary in them. If any leave us on account of them, they, not we, are the losers...God remains faithful. Do not be cast down if you meet with difficulties at home. All things are working together for good, as in due time we shall see. Pray much for me...Satan is a terrible reality, so is the flesh, but more is He who is within us. If God be for us, who, what can overcome us?

The meetings at Chinkiang early in December were fully as encouraging as those at Wu-chang had been. All the members of the mission present agreed to pray daily for the Seventy until they should be given. When Mr. Taylor left, several of the young men went down with him to the steamer.

From that time on it was a constant joy to Mr. Taylor to see how the prayer for reinforcements was taken up throughout the mission. No one knew better than he did what it meant to his fellow workers not to be willing only, but earnestly desirous that the staff of the mission should be so largely increased, when funds were and had long been low. But he knew too that it is a safe thing to launch out upon a course of obedience, no matter what testing may be involved.

In the scene of his early labors at Ningpo, Mr. Taylor drafted an appeal to the home churches, which in due course was signed by seventy-seven members of the mission in China. The sense of responsibility that lay behind it, as well as its quiet confidence in God, may be judged from the following extracts:

> Souls on every hand are perishing for lack of knowledge; more than a thousand every hour are passing away into death and darkness....Provinces in China compare in area with kingdoms in Europe and average between ten and twenty millions in population. One province has no missionary; one has only one, an unmarried missionary; in each of two other provinces there is only one missionary and his wife resident; and none are sufficiently supplied with laborers. Can we leave matters thus without incurring the sin of bloodguiltiness?

After requesting prayer for more workers "in connection with every Protestant missionary society on both sides of the Atlantic," the needs of the C.I.M. were specially referred to.

> A careful survey of the spiritual work to which we ourselves are called...has led us to feel the importance of immediate and large reinforcements, and many of us are daily pleading with God in agreed prayer for forty-two additional men and twenty-eight additional women, called and sent out by God, to assist us in carrying on and extending the work already committed to our charge. We ask our brothers and sisters in Christ at home to join us in praying the Lord of the Harvest to thrust out this "other seventy also" (Luke 10:1). We are not anxious as to the means for sending them forth or sustaining them. *He* has told us to look to the birds and flowers, and to take no thought for these things, but to seek first the kingdom of God and His righteousness, and that all these things shall be added unto us (see Matthew 6:25–33). But we *are* concerned that only men and women called of God, fully consecrated to Him, and counting everything precious as dross and dung "for the excellency of the knowledge of Christ Jesus my Lord" (Phil. 3:8), should come out to join us, and we would add to this appeal a word of caution and encouragement, to any who may feel drawn to offer themselves for this blessed work. Of *caution,* urging such to count the cost; to wait prayerfully on God; to ask themselves whether they *will* really trust Him for *everything,* wherever He may call them to go. Mere romantic feeling will soon die out amid the toilsome labor and constant discomforts and trials of inland work, and will not be worth much when severe illness arises and perhaps all the money is gone. Faith in the living God alone gives joy and rest in

such circumstances. But a word also of *encouragement,* for we ourselves have proved God's faithfulness and the blessedness of dependence on Him. He is supplying and ever has supplied all our need. And if not seldom we have fellowship in poverty with Him who for our sakes became poor, shall we not rejoice if the Day prove that we have been, like the great missionary apostle, "poor, yet making many rich; as having nothing, and yet possessing all things" (2 Cor. 6:10)? He makes us very happy in His service, and those of us who have children desire nothing better for them, should the Lord tarry, than that they may be called to similar work and similar joys.

What should we not expect from 1882 after this beginning, with the prayer for the Seventy being taken up in such a spirit throughout the mission? Should we not confidently look for a rising tide of spiritual blessing both at home and in China, and expect that Mr. Taylor especially, as representing the movement, should be led on from strength to strength? Perhaps a deeper knowledge not only of the "acts" but of the "ways" of God would modify such expectations and lessen the surprise with which one finds the reality to have been very different. For in England, as in China, difficulties did not lessen. Working to the limit of his powers, Mr. Broomhall was not able to report any decided increase either of funds or of service. Eleven new workers were sent out, but three only of the number were men, when five times as many had been hoped for. So great was the trial as to shortness of supplies that Mr. Taylor could scarcely wonder at the retirement of one and another from the mission whom he knew to be loosely attached to its principles. And, most sorrowful of all, as he moved from place to place, the work in some important stations seemed to be going back rather than forward.

Faith was thus thrown into the crucible in many ways, and the reality behind outward seeming, both as to Mr. Taylor's own position and that of others, was tested as never before. Weaknesses were brought out with startling clearness—need of spiritual power, of organization, of leaders of more caliber. With answered prayer on the one hand as to the opening up of inland China, and a growing faith for large reinforcements on the other, they were forced to a realization of the utter inadequacy of existing arrangements to carry on the work even as it was. And in and through it all, Mr. Taylor himself was assailed by extreme depression, loneliness, and foreboding, due in part to illness; thus it was that Hudson Taylor held on—hard pressed in faith and circumstances, sustained, borne down at times, but strengthened—thus it was that he was brought out victorious.

Meanwhile, Mr. Taylor had paid another visit to the district in which he had found so much to discourage a few months previously. Then he had written of his efforts being all or "nearly all in vain, so far as this part of the work is concerned." Now, baptized afresh with a spirit of love, he was enabled to find his way to hearts that had seemed closed against him, and a work of grace was the result that was not only to save valuable workers from being lost to the mission, but was to set them in its front rank as regards fruitfulness in soul-winning.

It was at Chefoo that the later months of the year were spent and some of its most important work accomplished, and there Mr. Taylor began to see his way at length to returning to England. In this matter, too, faith was encouraged by definite answers to prayer in the matter of funds. Early in October, for example, they were looking with special expectancy for the home remittance, autumn journeys having to be provided for those who were going up-country, to whom Mr. Taylor would have been glad to entrust extra supplies for their own and other stations. He recalled:

> We were at table when we received our letters (the home mail), and when on opening one of them I found, instead of seven or eight hundred pounds for the month's supplies, only ninety-six pounds, nine shillings, and five pence, my feelings I shall not soon forget!
>
> I closed the envelope again, and seeking my room, knelt down and spread the letter before the Lord, asking Him what *was* to be done with less than ninety-seven pounds—a sum it was impossible to distribute over seventy stations in which were eighty or ninety missionaries, including their wives, not to speak of about a hundred native helpers, and more than that number of native children to be fed and clothed in our schools. Having first rolled the burden on the Lord, I then mentioned the matter to others of our own mission in Chefoo, and we unitedly looked to Him to come to our aid; but no hint as to our circumstances was allowed to reach anyone outside.
>
> Soon the answers began to come—kind gifts from local friends who little knew the peculiar value of their donations, and help in other ways, until the needs of the month were all met without our having been burdened with anxious thought even for an hour. We had similar experiences in November and again in December, and

on each occasion, after spreading the letter before the Lord and leaving the burden with Him, we were "helped." Thus the Lord made our hearts sing for joy and provided, through local contributions in China, for the needs of the work as never before nor since.

Above All That Is Asked

Paris and Easter: how little had either Mr. or Mrs. Taylor in their long separation imagined such a setting for the reunion that came at length! Even the day or two spent at Cannes had seemed long when the traveler learned who was coming to meet him. Before leaving China he had been much impressed with the prophecy of Zephaniah, especially the closing chapter with its wonderful revelation of the heart of God: "The LORD thy God in the midst of thee is mighty; he will save, he will rejoice over thee with joy; he will rest [or 'be silent'] in his love, he will joy over thee with singing" (Zeph. 3:17). Mr. Taylor said:

> The whole passage had been made a great blessing to me, but it was not until I reached Paris that I learned the full preciousness of this clause. For there I was met by my beloved wife (after a separation of fifteen months), and as we sat side by side in the cab, though she had so much to say and I had too, I could only take her hand and be silent—the joy was too deep for words. Then it came home to me: if all this of earthly affection is but the type, what must it be when He is silent in His love? And that love is drawn out by our trust. Oh, it is such a pity to hinder!

Reaching home at the end of March 1883, Mr. Taylor was in good time for spring and summer meetings, and soon had cause to notice the new position accorded to the mission in the esteem of the Christian public. The eight years of Mr. Broomhall's unwearied labors had told especially in the direction which was his forte—that of inspiring confidence and making friends. Then, too, the achievements of the pioneers, women as well as men, in effecting a settled residence in almost all the inland provinces, had called forth thanksgiving to God. In many parts of the country people were wanting to hear how the seemingly impossible had been brought to pass; how, without appeals for money or even collections, the work had been sustained; and how, in the most distant parts of China, little groups of converts were being gathered. Meetings, therefore—meetings in all directions—soon claimed the leader of the mission, the unobtrusive man so sure of his great God!

The correspondence of the next two years, the period of Mr. Taylor's stay in England, is deeply interesting from this point of view. To him who had never sought it had come the loving appreciation of high and low, rich and poor, old and young, to a remarkable degree.

"If you are not dead yet," was the charming communication of a child at Cambridge to whom "Hudson Taylor" was a household word, "I want to send you the money I have saved up to help the little boys and girls of China to love Jesus."

"Will you do me the kindness," urged Canon Wilberforce of Southampton, "to give a Bible reading in my house to about sixty people...and spend the night with us? Please do us this favor, in the Master's name."

"Much love to you in the Lord," wrote Lord Radstock from the Continent. "You are a great help to us in England by strengthening our faith."

From Dr. Andrew Bonar came a hundred pounds, forwarded from an unknown Presbyterian friend "who cares for the land of Sinim." Spurgeon sent his characteristic invitations to the Tabernacle, and Miss Macpherson to Bethnal Green.

"My heart is still in the glorious work," wrote Mr. Berger, with a check for £500. "Most heartily do I join you in praying for seventy more laborers—but do not stop at seventy! Surely we will see greater things than these, if we are empty of self and only seeking God's glory and the salvation of souls."

There are letters from the nobleman inviting Mr. Taylor to his castle, and from the old family servant, sending a gift for China after his departure. And there are letters, above all, telling of blessing received in the meetings, not through Mr. Taylor's addresses only, but through his personality and spirit.

Meanwhile, out in China the need for reinforcements was increasingly felt. Five only had been sent out in the first quarter of the year, but fifteen sailed in the months that followed, and many fresh candidates were in touch with the mission.

But if 1883 was memorable, with its many causes for encouragement, what will be said of 1884 and the movement into which these young men came? It was a rising tide indeed of spiritual power and blessing; a year of intense activity, in which Mr. Taylor seemed to do the work of ten; a year of incessant meetings, and the flowing in of sympathy and gifts as never before; a year of harvest in the matter of new friends and workers; and above all a year of close and constant dependence upon God. It was the last of the three years in which the Seventy were to be given, according to the faith that had received them from the Lord, and given they were in royal fashion—most of the large party that sailed toward the end of October being over and above the number. Forty-six in all were sent out during the twelve months, and it was not only the number but the caliber of the workers that was remarkable. Often must Mr. Taylor have been reminded of the prayer going up from many hearts that the Seventy might be god-sends as well as God-sent to China.

And here attention may well be drawn to some of the outside influences that contributed to the developments of this wonderful year and the years that followed, chief among which was the second visit of Messrs. Moody and Sankey to the United Kingdom. The foundations of the C.I.M. were laid, as we have seen, at a time when the spiritual life of the churches had been marvelously quickened by the great revival of 1859. Moody's first visit in 1873 had brought to the front again the supreme duty of soulwinning, preparing the way for many a forward movement, including the appeal for the eighteen and the opening up of in-land China, and now, when a fresh advance was to be made in missionary enterprise, the heart of Christian England was being stirred to its depths by a practical, overwhelming demonstration of the power of the Gospel. Who will say how much the worldwide work of foreign missions owes to these devoted evangelists?

Then there was a book, equally simple and God-honoring. Published many years before, *China's Spiritual Need and Claims* had about it a living power. Edition after edition had been called for, and always the same deep spiritual influence seemed to flow from its pages. Steeped in prayer from the first, it had been used by God continually to call forth consecration in His service, and now enlarged and brought up to date, it was to have a new lease of life in the attractive edition of 1884.

But still it was in prayer the work was really done. Quietly, at the back of everything, the spiritual life was maintained at the heart of the mission. Never had the daily and weekly prayer meetings been more full of power.

In the midst of these experiences, Mr. and Mrs. Taylor were facing another long separation. The outgoing of so many new workers urgently called for his presence in China, and she could not be spared from home. He too seemed needed in England—never more so, with doors opening on every hand, candidates applying, and friends ready to help. Yet it was in China the fight had to be fought and the new recruits got into line. So the parting had to come, and Hudson Taylor went forward in the spirit of Livingstone's entry in his journal for one of his last, lonely birthdays in central Africa: "My Jesus, my King, my Life, my All—again I dedicate my whole self to Thee."

Sending Mr. McCarthy on ahead to deal with the most pressing matters, and leaving Mr. Stevenson to stand by Mr. Broomhall and the council for a while at home, Mr. Taylor was preparing to set out early in January with a party of young men when the unexpected happened, and God's purposes broke in upon these well-laid plans with an overflowing fullness that carried all before it.

It came about very naturally, and apart altogether from design or effort. In his *History of the Church Missionary Society*, Mr. Eugene Stock speaks of "the extraordinary interest aroused in the autumn of 1884 by the announcement that the captain of the Cambridge Eleven and the stroke oar of the Cambridge boat were going out as missionaries." When the news reached Edinburgh, it deeply stirred a group of medical students who for some months had been burdened about the indifference to spiritual things in the university, especially among their fellow medicals. A series of remarkable meetings had just been held at Oxford and Cambridge in which Mr. Taylor and several of the outgoing party had won the sympathies of the undergraduates for foreign missions as never before. But they were too much occupied with preparations for an early departure to be able to follow up even such promising openings. Then it was that, providentially, Reginald Radcliffe came upon the scene—that fervent evangelist whose parish was the world and whose aim nothing less than that the Gospel should be preached "to every creature" (Mark 16:15). Loving Scotland with a special love, he longed to bring the outgoing band into touch with her university life. But first, on obtaining Mr. Taylor's permission, he wrote to Professor Simpson to suggest that Studd, known for his prowess on the cricket-field, but more importantly for his love for the Redeemer, and Stanley Smith should visit Edinburgh.

Coming just at the time when those medical students were earnestly seeking guidance as to how to bring the claims of Christ before their fellows, the suggestion was hailed with thankfulness, and the student gathering with these men was a success in interesting many students, not before concerned with such things, in mission work. But that was not to be the end of it. During the campaign with Mr.

Radcliffe the students had seen the possibilities of such work and had unfolded a plan for further meetings. Invitations had been urgent to return to Scotland, especially from Edinburgh students, and in spite of the early date fixed for the sailing of the party, it was hoped that Mr. Taylor might accompany them.

"Could you come," wrote Mr. Stanley Smith to the beloved leader of the mission, "and if not, may we go?"

By this time it was becoming clear to Mr. Taylor that the hand of God was in the movement, and greatly must he have longed to make the most of his share in it. He had been very conscious of the power of the Holy Spirit with those who had helped him in his meetings, and had seen the influence of their joyous consecration not over students only, but over leaders of Christian life and thought. The whole thing was beginning to stand out before him: the uniqueness of the opportunity and of the band of fellow workers who had been given to him; the evident purpose of the Lord of the Harvest to use them along lines that had always been his own ideal—through the deepening of spiritual life among His people, to thrust out many fresh laborers into His harvest. How his heart was in it all; how he would have rejoiced to stay and help! But, for him, duty clearly pointed in another direction.

Thus, then, it was arranged: Mr. Taylor going on ahead to get through important matters awaiting his attention in Shanghai, and Mr. Radcliffe undertaking, with Mr. Broomhall and others, the campaign that was to be so far-reaching in its results. One notable meeting Mr. Taylor had at Exeter Hall, when all the outgoing party were present—a meeting which in measure prepared him for Mr. Eugene Stock's comment:

> The influence of such a band of men going to China was irresistible. No such event had occurred before, and no event of the century had done so much to arouse the minds of Christian men to the tremendous claims of the field and the nobility of the missionary vocation.

But it was not in public gatherings that these men were knit to their leader and the mission with which they had cast in their lot. It was behind the scenes, in quiet hours when the work was done, and chiefly in times of prayer at Pyrland Road, as on the last day of 1884. There was no disguising on these occasions the poverty, as far as material resources were concerned, of the mission that had closed its latest balance sheet with only ten pounds in hand—"ten pounds and all the promises of God." But how small a matter this seemed when the presence of the Lord Himself was so consciously felt! It never had been Mr. Taylor's way to minimize the trials that awaited young workers in China, especially if they desired to identify themselves with the people along the lines of the C.I.M.

When Mr. Taylor left London three weeks later, some of the party were again in Scotland, rejoicing to tell of all the wealth they were finding in deeper fellowship with Christ, which so far outweighed anything of worldly advantage they were laying down. And in a blinding snowstorm, as he crossed France alone, the traveler's heart was full of praise for news received only that morning from the northern capital:

"Two thousand students last night—wonderful times! It is the Lord."

Nearing Shanghai some weeks later, the sense of responsibility in connection with all that lay before him was very great. An absence of two years, at a time of unparalleled growth and extension in the mission, meant that many problems would await him for which he had neither wisdom nor strength. Mr. Taylor wrote from the China Sea in February 1885:

> Soon we shall be in the midst of the battle, but the Lord our God in the midst of us is mighty, so we "will trust, and not be afraid" (Isa. 12:2). "He will save" (Zeph. 3:17): He will save all the time, in everything.

For himself, Mr. Taylor was not expecting to be long detained in China, there being much of importance to require his presence at home. He hoped to give effect, on this sixth visit, to the plans for organization that had been maturing in his mind, and to see something of the work in the interior, especially in the province of Shansi. The time had come when superintendents were needed to give help and guidance to the largely increased number of recruits, and someone who could be associated with himself as deputy director, in view of his necessary absences from the field. A China council also was desirable, to assist the director or his deputy, as the London council had long helped Mr. Taylor at home, and it was important to establish training centers for the study of the language, in which new arrivals, men and women respectively, could have experienced help in preparing for their lifework.

Seen in the light of subsequent developments, it was to be expected that the great Adversary would leave no stone unturned to hinder, and if possible frustrate, these purposes. "Our wrestling is not against flesh and blood, but against the principalities, against the powers, against the world rulers of this darkness, against the spiritual hosts of wickedness in the heavenly places." (See Ephesians 6:12.) Wonderful things had been happening in connection with the mission, wonderful things were yet to happen, and the Enemy seems to have been prepared at every point to oppose and hinder. Month after month went by, and at the close of 1885, Mr. Taylor wrote:

> A year ago I thought to be back in England ere December was out, but I seem to be as far from it as on landing. Not that nothing has been done! A great deal, thank God, has been accomplished, and not a little suffered—but He knows all about that. Such a hand-to-hand conflict with the powers of darkness as I have seldom known has been no small part of the work of the year; but "hitherto the Lord hath helped us" (see 1 Samuel 7:12), and He *will* perfect that which concerns us, whatever that perfecting may mean or involve.

Only to Mrs. Taylor could he unburden his heart, and as the separation lengthened, many were the revealing passages in his letters:

> Oct. 15: Great trial, great blessing are very present. My only rest is in God. But He is more than ever all to me, and I am resting in Him.
>
> Nov. 1: I have it much impressed on my heart to plead mightily for a special outpouring of the Holy Spirit on those who cause most concern. This is what they need; this would put all right, and nothing else will. So long as the motto

practically is, "Not Christ but I," our best organization will never give the victory over the world, the flesh, and the Devil. The motto *must* be changed.

Nov. 11: I am sure you will pray hard for us. The conflict is heavy indeed. Satan harasses on all sides, but the Lord reigneth, and shall triumph gloriously....It is easy enough to fancy we are weaned children when we don't mind much the thing we miss, but at other times and about other things we are less in danger of making this mistake.

Nov. 14: I believe we are on the eve of great blessing, perhaps of great trial too. The Lord our God in the midst of us is "mighty to save" (Isa. 63:1); let us trust Him. Flesh and heart often fail: let them fail! He faileth not. Pray very much, pray constantly, for Satan rages against us. But God uses this most diligent though unwitting of His servants to refine and purify His people and to bring in the greatest blessings—witness the Cross.

One thing that had tried Mr. Taylor a good deal throughout 1885 had been the frustration, again and again, of his purpose to visit the northern provinces. Reasons of importance seemed to require his presence in Shansi without delay, yet endless complications detained him at Shanghai or called in other directions. More than once he had been on the point of starting, and it was not until the time really came—twelve months and more after it had been expected—that he began to see how wisely even the hindrances had been planned, for they had allowed him the chance to visit stations that he might not otherwise have been able to visit. He then was able to arrange for more workers, especially women, to settle in such stations and make the evangelization of them their lifework.

Days of Blessing

It had come at last—the opportunity so long looked forward to! For seven years Mr. Taylor had been planning to visit Shansi. Once he had even set out, only to be recalled by claims at the coast. But now, the better organization of the mission permitting an absence of several months from Shanghai, he hoped to strengthen the work not only in Shansi but in other regions lying farther inland. For many desires were on his heart in connection with this journey. Each station to be visited had its problems, but greatest of all was the question of how to evangelize the vast population to which the missionaries now had access. To bring help and encouragement to these lonely toilers was his chief object, and to confer with them about the organization of the native church, which in some places was growing rapidly. It was also his hope to establish a Church of England district in the great western province of Szechwan, a matter which had long been under consideration. In the Rev. W. W. Cassels, the mission had for the first time one qualified to take the lead in such an enterprise, and Szechwan with its sixty-eight million had as yet only two centers in which Protestant missionaries were to be found. Mr. Cassels with others of the Cambridge party had been gaining experience in Shansi, where they were eagerly awaiting Mr. Taylor's coming, and he was looking forward with no less pleasure to seeing them in the midst of their work.

But first of all the desired province had to be reached, over the vast plains of Chih-li and the mountain passes beyond. Such traveling was strange to Mr. Taylor, who was accustomed to the endless waterways of central and southern China. Springless carts and northern roads, consisting of unmade tracks over sun-baked or rain-flooded country; rivers to be crossed without bridge or ferry; and dangerous passes braved in litters swinging from the backs of mules very prone to stumble; these by day, and big, noisy inns at night, together with northern speech, food, and manners, all made large demands upon strength and patience. While a native junk on a canal or river may leave much to be desired, it is at any rate a shelter you can call your own, but to exchange the weariness of a cart in which you have been jolted and shaken for hours for a brick bed shared with others in a close, not to say filthy room, the minor occupants of which may be numbered by hundreds if not thousands, is quite another matter.

The district in which they found themselves was that of Mr. Hsi, the ex-Confucian scholar, and his friends Chang and Ch'ü of the Buddhist temple and little city of Ta-ning among the Western Hills. On either side of the Fen river these men, full of their first love and zeal, were sounding out the glad tidings of salvation far and wide. Seventy-two baptisms at the spring gatherings a few months earlier had doubled the membership of the Ping-yang church and made the need for wise and careful supervision all the more apparent. The time had come for setting apart some of the Chinese leaders as deacons and elders in the village gatherings and for recognizing the God-appointed ministry of Hsi and others who were doing pastoral work. But before going on to the native conference at which these ordinations were to take place, Mr. Taylor was thankful for the quiet days in Tai-yuan-fu, the capital of the province, for united waiting upon God.

Days of Blessing—how truly the title of the book in which a record of these meetings has been preserved expresses what they were in reality! As one turns the pages, the fragrance of the Lord's own presence cannot but be felt. He never could be hid, and from first to last it was His fullness in which those waiting hearts rejoiced. Face to face with the overwhelming need around them and the insufficiency within, it was good to remember, as Mr. Taylor put it, that it is not a question of the supply at all, but of the Supplier. "He (the Lord Jesus) is enough for Shansi, from the Great Wall to Ho-nan. We have a grander Savior than we realize!"

The Hundred

Profoundly impressed by all he had seen of the accessibility and need of the northern provinces, Mr. Taylor had come by boat a thousand miles down the Han, bringing with him the little daughter of one of the Han-chung missionaries, whose parents saw that nothing but a change of climate could save her life. Only five years old, little Annie could speak no English; though, when not too shy, she could prattle away in Chinese prettily enough. Strange to say, she was never shy with Mr. Taylor. It had been hard for the mother to part with her, frail as she was from months of illness, but once on the boat in Mr. Taylor's care, she wonderfully brightened up. It speaks much for the confidence with which fellow workers regarded him that Mr. and Mrs. Pearse had no hesitation about the arrangement, save on the ground of giving Mr. Taylor trouble. They knew there would be no woman in the party, and that for a month or six weeks he would be the only one to see to little Annie's food and clothing, as well as to care for her by day and night. They were quite satisfied that the child would not suffer, however, though even they might have been surprised at the comfort Mr. Taylor found in her companionship:

> My little charge is wonderfully improving and is quite good and cheerful. She clings to me very lovingly, and it is sweet to feel little arms around one's neck once more.

Hard as it was to be so long absent from home and loved ones, the way was not yet clear for Mr. Taylor's return to England. Nearly two years had passed since he had come out in advance of the Cambridge Party, but great as had been the progress in many directions, the recently developed organization needed strengthening before he could think of leaving China.

The year (1886) was drawing to a close, and the chief object before him was the formation of a council of experienced workers to help Mr. Stevenson in his new capacity as deputy director. The latter had also returned from his inland journey, full of enthusiasm over what he had seen in the northern provinces. He had spent several weeks with Pastor Hsi after Mr. Taylor had left, visiting widely scattered groups of converts, and was more than ever impressed with the vitality and possibilities of the work. His heart was overflowing with joy in the Lord, the joy that is our strength, and coming freshly into responsibilities Mr. Taylor had been bearing for years, he brought with him no little accession of hope and courage.

In this spirit, then, the superintendents of the various provinces gathered for their first meeting, at An-king in the middle of November. Several were detained in their own stations, and one or two were at home on furlough, but a little group of leaders, including Mr. McCarthy, spent from two to three weeks with Mr. Taylor and Mr. Stevenson. Before the council was convened at all, a whole week was given to waiting upon God with prayer and fasting (the latter on alternate days), so that it was with prepared hearts they came to the consideration of the questions before them.

Upon the conclusions of that council meeting, important as they were, we must not dwell in detail. A little gray book, embodying the chief results, soon found its way to all the stations of the mission—a little book breathing the spirit of the Master, as well as packed full of wise and helpful suggestions. There were instructions for special officers, the treasurer, the secretary in China, and the superintendents; instructions for senior and junior missionaries, lady evangelists and probationers, all based upon a thorough understanding of conditions in China. A course of study in the language, carefully prepared by Mr. Stevenson, Mr. Baller, and others, was adopted for use in the training homes, and the principles and practice of the mission were restated and somewhat amplified for younger workers. In a concluding letter, Mr. Taylor wrote:

> It is hoped that all our friends will have seen from the foregoing that what is sought is to relieve and help each one, and only to conduce to that harmonious cooperation without which the

working of a large and scattered mission would be impossible. Those at a distance must be helped by those near, and this can only be done as those near know the extent to which they can depend on the cooperation of those at a distance.

The principle of godly rule is a most important one, for it equally affects us all. It is this—the seeking to help, not to lord; to keep from wrong paths and lead into right paths, for the glory of God and the good of those guided, not for the gratification of the ruler. *Such rule always leads the ruler to the Cross*, and saves the ruled at the cost of the ruler....Let us all drink into this spirit; then lording on the one hand and bondage on the other will be alike impossible....When the heart is right it loves godly rule and finds freedom in obedience.

But there is something more important than the gray book which must be traced to the meetings of this first China council, and that is the spirit of faith and expectancy which launched the mission at this time upon new testings of the faithfulness of God. Up in Shansi it had begun, when Mr. Stevenson had written from the capital:

> We are greatly encouraged out here and are asking and receiving definite blessings for this hungry and thirsty land. We are fully expecting at least one hundred fresh laborers to arrive in China in 1887.

It was the first suggestion of the Hundred. Ardent as he was and full of confidence in God, he kept the matter to the front on his return to Shanghai and in the council meetings, but Mr. Taylor seems at first to have shared the general impression that this was going rather too fast. A hundred new workers in one year, when the entire staff of the mission was less than twice that number—why, even if the men and women were forthcoming, think of the additional expenditure involved!

"Yes," urged the deputy director unperturbed, "but with needs so great, how can we ask for less?"

That was difficult to answer, for fifty central stations and many outstations in which resident missionaries were needed, not to speak of China open from end to end, made a hundred new workers even in one year seem but a small number.

And so, little by little, they were led on, until, in the council meetings, such was the atmosphere of faith and prayer that the thought could strike root. Begun with God, it could not fail to be taken up by hearts so truly waiting upon Him, and before leaving An-king, Mr. Taylor was writing home quite naturally:

> We are praying for one hundred new missionaries in 1887. The Lord help in the selection and provide the means.

A little later at Ta-ku-tang, amid the quiet of lake and mountains, he was working at accounts, etc., with a view to leaving for England as soon as possible, when an incident occurred that fanned expectancy to a flame. Mr. Taylor was dictating to his secretary, walking up and down the room as was his custom, when he repeated in one of his letters what he had written above: "We are praying for and expecting a hundred new missionaries to come out in 1887." Did he really mean it? Mr. Stevenson saw the secretary, a young man who was himself to be one of the Hundred, look up with an incredulous smile. "If the Lord should open windows in heaven," that look seemed to say, "then might this thing be." Mr. Taylor saw it too, and immediately caught fire. Mr. Stevenson recalled:

> After that, he went beyond me altogether. Never shall I forget the conviction with which he said,
>
> "If you showed me a photograph of the whole hundred taken in China, I could not be more sure than I am now."
>
> Then I sent out a little slip throughout the mission: "Will you put down your name to pray for the Hundred?" and cabled to London, with Mr. Taylor's permission: "Praying for a hundred new missionaries in 1887."

Thus the step was taken, and the mission committed to a program that might well have startled even its nearest friends. Yet it was in no spirit of rashness or merely human energy. Far too deeply had Mr. Taylor learned the lessons of experience to embark upon such an enterprise without the assurance that he was being led by God, without much forethought as well as faith, and the determination to see it through by unremitting toil, no less than unceasing prayer. He wrote to Mrs. Taylor early in December:

> The accepting and sending out of the Hundred will require no small amount of work, but the Lord will give strength; and no little wisdom, but the Lord will guide. There is all-sufficiency in Him, is there not?...We are ready to receive say fifty at once and shall be ready for others shortly.

It was this vision, this spirit of joy that upheld him through all the wonderful and strenuous days of 1887. But what a year it was! Preceded by two days of prayer because one was not enough, it ended with the last party of the Hundred on their way to China—all the work accomplished, all expenses met—and with a fullness of blessing that was spreading and to spread in ever-widening circles.

The story of the Hundred has often been told—it belongs to no one mission or land. We know how, with growing courage, Mr. Taylor and those associated with him were led to pray for ten thousand pounds of additional income, as necessary to meet the increased expenses, and that it might be given in large gifts, so that the home staff should not be overwhelmed with correspondence. We know that no fewer than six hundred men and women offered themselves to the mission that year for service in China; that one hundred and two, to be exact, were sent out; and that not ten but eleven thousand pounds of extra income was received, no appeal having been made for financial help. And we know, most wonderful perhaps of all, how definite prayer was answered as to the very form in which the money came; the whole being received in just eleven gifts, involving little or no extra work for the office staff of the mission. But such a story bears retelling, to the glory not of man or methods, but of God.

Mr. Taylor was back in England, and what an example he set by his unparalled labors throughout the year! It was about the beginning of November when he had the joy of announcing to the friends of the mission that their prayers were fully answered—all the Hundred having been given and the funds supplied for their passages to China. In later meetings, therefore, he had to tell of the response of a faithful God to the prayers of His believing people, and of the way in which His "exceeding abundantly" (Eph. 3:20) was being given.

Two days before the close of the year Mr. Taylor returned to London, the great work accomplished which, though wrought in faith and deep heart rest, had taxed both him and those associated with him to the uttermost. To Mr. Stevenson he wrote:

> I have assured the friends that there will be a big hallelujah when they, the crowning party of the Hundred, reach Shanghai! It is not more than we expected God to do for us, but it is very blessed, and to see that God does answer, in great things as well as small, the prayers of those who put their trust in Him will strengthen the faith of multitudes.

Twelve months previously, a veteran missionary in Shanghai had said to Mr. Taylor, then on the point of leaving for home:

"I am delighted to hear that you are praying for larger reinforcements. You will not get a hundred, of course, within the year, but you will get many more than if you did not ask for them."

Thanking him for his kindly interest, Mr. Taylor replied, "We have the joy beforehand, but I feel sure that, if spared, you will share it in welcoming the last of the Hundred to China."

And so it proved. For among those who gathered to receive that last party with thanksgiving, no one was more sympathetic than the white-haired saint who, a few weeks later, was called to his reward.

What Is Between Christ and Me

Among many visitors to Pyrland Road toward the close of the year of the Hundred came Mr.

Henry W. Frost of America. He came, he believed, because he was called by God to talk with Mr. Taylor about the establishment of an American council that would work as a feeder of men and money for China, on the same principles of faith on which the C.I.M. operated. But though this first visit resulted in an abiding friendship, it seemed to the one who was building much upon it to have failed in its object. His interest in the mission was warmly appreciated and his desire to work with it welcomed, but Mr. Taylor could not see his way to the establishment of an American branch. It would be, he suggested, far better for Mr. Frost to start a fresh organization on the lines of the C.I.M. if he pleased, but something that would be native in its inception and development, for a transplanted mission, like a transplanted tree, would have difficulty in striking root in the new soil. Needless to say, this was a great disappointment.

> On reaching my lodgings, I had one of the most sorrowful experiences of my life. At the threshold of my room, Satan seemed to meet me and envelop me in darkness....I had come over three thousand miles only to receive to my request the answer, No. But this was not the worst of it. I had had positive assurance that the Lord had Himself guided me in my prayer, and had led me to take the long journey and make the request that had been made, but now I felt I could never again be sure whether my prayers were or were not of God, or whether I was or was not being guided of Him.

Only those who have passed through similar experiences can know what such a test of faith meant, and how real was the victory when the one so tried was enabled to trust where he could not understand. This restored "something of soul rest," and Mr. Frost went back to America leaving the issues with the Lord.

But the matter did not end there. Mr. Frost had learned that Mr. Taylor was returning to China before long, and that if invited to do so he might travel by way of America. This he made known to the conveners of the Bible study conference at Niagara-on-the-Lake and to Mr. D. L. Moody, whose summer gatherings at Northfield were already a center of much blessing, with the result that invitations began to reach Mr. Taylor to visit the great New World.

Meanwhile in England, the latter was unremitting in his labors. The widespread interest aroused by the outgoing of the Hundred brought more openings for meetings than he could possibly accept, and very stimulating to faith were the facts he had to tell. He wrote to Mr. Stevenson early in 1888:

> What a wonderful year it has been, both for you and me! Satan will surely leave no stone unturned to hinder, and we must not be surprised at troublesome difficulties coming up, but greater is He who is for us than all who can be against us.

The certainty of opposition, definite and determined, from the powers of darkness seems to have been much before him, and the question of funds for the largely increased work was one that could not be ignored. But with regard to both the one and the other, his mind was kept in peace.

It was a summer day toward the end of June when the SS *Etruria* put out to sea, carrying among her "intermediate" passengers, Mr. Taylor, his son, and a secretary. Outward discomfort mattered little to Mr. Taylor, but he was finding, almost with surprise, that parting from those he loved best did not become any easier. A long while might elapse before he could return, and the very uncertainty was painful. He wrote to Mrs. Taylor from Queenstown:

> As I walked the deck last night, I found myself singing softly, "Jesus, I am resting, resting in the joy of what Thou art"—such a comfort when feeling desolate, and feeling your desolation! No one comforts like He does.

"Few know what is [between] Christ and me," wrote the saintly Rutherford, and little can Mr. Taylor's fellow passengers on that Atlantic voyage have realized what lay behind the quiet exterior of the missionary on his way for the seventh time to China. Yet the sweetness was felt, and the power, and by no one more than the young American who was on the New York landing stage to meet them. For there was about Mr. Frost's spiritual nature a quality that responded in an unusual way to much of which he could be, as yet, but dimly conscious in the life of Hudson Taylor.

It was with joy at any rate that he received the party, including Mr. and Mrs. Reginald Radcliffe, and escorted them to his father's home on Madison Avenue where there was ample accommodation and the warmest of welcomes. How gracious was the hospitality that encompassed them, the visitors could not at the time fully realize.

Of the three months that followed it is difficult to write, not for lack of information, but because of the very fullness of the records and the importance of events that took place. For who could have foreseen that, arriving in America in July, little known and with no thought but to take part in a few conferences on his way to China, Mr. Taylor would leave again in October, widely loved and trusted, laden with gifts, followed by prayer, and taking with him a band of young workers chosen out of more than forty who had offered their lives for service in the mission? If the going out of the Hundred in the preceding year had been a striking evidence of the hand of God working with him, what will be said of this unexpected movement, deeply affecting Christian life in the eastern states and Canada, and rousing Toronto, from which the party finally set out, to an enthusiasm rarely equaled?

As to bringing forward the work of the mission with a view to developing an American branch, nothing was further from his thoughts. Had he not told Mr. Frost only a few months earlier that he had no guidance in that direction, sending him back from England perplexed and disappointed? And if it was not in Mr. Taylor's purpose, still less was it anticipated by those to whom his personality and message came as so new a force that summer at Northfield. The student conference was in full swing when he and his companions arrived and, met by Mr. Moody himself, were driven out to his beautiful home in the middle of the night. It was a strangely new experience to the English visitors, and one full of interest. Four hundred men from ninety different colleges filled the seminary buildings and overflowed in tents on the far-reaching campus backed by hills and woods. The afternoon was kept entirely free for recreation; morning and evening the spacious auditorium was filled for devotional meetings and Bible study—the open doors admitting birds as well as breezes, and the summer dress of the students giving a rainbow effect in the blending of soft colors.

It was an inspiring assembly, including many pastors, professors, Y.M.C.A. secretaries, and leading philanthropists. The corps of speakers was able and representative, and Mr. Moody, who presided, was at his best. But it was in the young men themselves that the inspiration lay—such power, such possibilities! Mr. Taylor could not but be moved by such an audience, and to him the students seem to have been attracted in a special way. It was written of the impact he had at this conference:

> What impressed us undergraduates was not merely the spirituality of Mr. Taylor, it was his common sense. One asked him the question: "Are you always conscious of abiding in Christ?"
>
> "While sleeping last night," he replied, "did I cease to abide in your house because I was unconscious of the fact? We should never be conscious of not abiding in Christ."
>
> When asked, "How is it that you can address so many meetings?" he said to us: "Every morning I feed upon the Word of God, then I pass on through the day messages that have first helped me in my own soul."
>
> "You can work without praying, but it is a bad plan," was another of his sayings, "but you cannot pray in earnest without working." And, "Do not be so busy with work for Christ that you have no strength left for praying. True prayer requires strength."
>
> It was not, however, the words only of Mr. Taylor that helped us, it was the life of the man.

He bore about with him the fragrance of Jesus Christ.

And this was the impression wherever he went.

But of this and subsequent happenings Mr. Taylor knew nothing. After speaking twice at a conference at Niagara-on-the-Lake and visiting Chicago, he had gone to Attica, New York, where Mr. Frost, senior, and his son had their summer homes. The son was expected on the midnight train from Niagara, and Mr. Taylor was at the station to meet him—eager to hear more of the conference, but little thinking of the news Mr. Frost had to bring.

For unexpected developments had taken place at the Niagara meetings after Mr. Taylor's departure. Disappointed at not hearing more from him on the subject of foreign missions, the conference all the more welcomed the addresses of Mr. Radcliffe and Mr. Robert Wilder, for which the way had been well prepared. Burning words were spoken by the veteran evangelist and the young volunteer on the responsibility of each succeeding generation of believers to obey the Great Command, "Go ye into all the world, and preach the gospel to every creature" (Mark 16:15). After these words were spoken and were followed by prayer and singing, young men and women consecrated themselves to service in the C.I.M., and money came in without advertisement or urging on the part of any. This experience was surpassed the next day when the conference reassembled. Gifts and pledges of money sufficient for the support of two missionaries had been given the previous evening to Mr. Frost, who wrote:

> As I reached the pavilion, I found that people had become intoxicated with the joy of giving, and that they were seeking another opportunity for making freewill offerings for the Lord's work in China. A number were standing up, pledging themselves to give a certain amount toward the support of a missionary....Again promises and money came flowing in, until, this time, I had scarcely a place to put them. There I stood in the midst of the assembly—without ever wishing it or thinking such a thing could be—suddenly transformed into an impromptu treasurer of the China Inland Mission. And afterwards, upon counting what had been given, I found enough to support not two missionaries but actually *eight*, for a whole year, in inland China.

Returning to his room that summer morning, Mr. Frost could not but remember the sorrowful experience through which he had passed in London, when he had wondered whether he could ever know that prayer was really answered, or be assured of the guidance of God again. The faith that had sustained him then was being exchanged for sight, and as he poured out his heart in wondering thankfulness, he realized how safe and good it is not only to wait upon God, but also to wait for Him.

This, then, was the story he had to tell, when upon reaching Attica at midnight he found Mr. Taylor on the platform to meet him. He continued:

> I kept my secret, however, until we reached my father's house and Mr. Taylor's bedroom. Then, fully and joyously, I described to him how after his departure from Niagara the Spirit had swept over the conference; how the offerings had been given and put into my hands to pass on to

him; and how they had been found to amount to a sum sufficient to support *eight* missionaries for a year in China.

Quietly he listened, and with such a serious look that I confess, for once in my life, I was disappointed in Mr. Taylor. Instead of being glad, he seemed burdened. If I remember rightly, he did just say, "Praise the Lord," or "Thank God," but beyond this there was nothing to indicate that he accepted the news as good news, as I had anticipated. For a few minutes he stood apparently lost in thought, and then said, "I think we had better pray."

Upon this we knelt beside the bed, and he began to ask what the Lord meant by all that had taken place. It was only as he went on pleading for light that I commenced to understand what was in Mr. Taylor's mind. He had realized at once that this was a very marked providence, and that God had probably brought him to America for other purposes than simply to give a few addresses on his way to China. He had inquired from me how the money was to be used, and I had replied that it was designated, by preference, for the support of North American workers. From this he saw that the obligation was laid upon him of appealing for missionaries from North America—a heavy responsibility, in view of all that it involved....It was becoming clear to him, as to me, that my visit to London and appeal for a branch of the mission to be established on this continent had been more providential than was at first recognized.

Unexpectedly a crisis had arisen, fraught, as Mr. Taylor could not but see, with far-reaching results. He was glad to be returning to Northfield shortly for the general conference, when he would have the opportunity of consulting Mr. Moody and other friends. For the problem that faced him, after little more than three weeks in America, was no simple one, and as yet the man at his side, young and reserved as he was, had not been recognized as the providential solution.

The conclusion to which Mr. Taylor was thus being led was strongly confirmed on his return to Northfield. Mr. Moody advised his appealing at once for workers and introduced him to some of his own students who were feeling called to China. But even then it was with fear and trembling he went forward. The mission had always been interdenominational, but there had been no thought of its becoming international, and twenty-one years of experience had made its leader cautious. But once his mind was made up, the appeal was a strong one:

> To have missionaries and no money would be no trouble to me, for the Lord is bound to take care of His own: He does not want me to assume His responsibility. But to have money and no missionaries is very serious indeed. And I do not think it will be kind of you dear friends in America to put this burden upon us and not to send some from among yourselves to use the money. We have the dollars, but where are the people?

One by one, in ways we must not attempt to detail, prepared men and women responded to the call, until Mr. Taylor was assured that it was indeed the Lord's purpose for him to take on a band to China. When the first three were accepted, he began to be relieved about the funds in hand. Their passages had been promised independently, but their support for the first year would use a considerable part of the money contributed at Niagara "if things went smoothly." But from this point of view, things did not go at all smoothly. Parents, friends, or the churches to which they belonged claimed the privilege of sustaining these workers. When as many as eight had been accepted, the original fund was still untouched, and the further they went, the less chance there seemed of getting to an end of it. Consecrated money, Mr. Taylor remarked, was something like the consecrated loaves and fishes; there was no using it up.

* * * * *

Mr. Taylor came to America once again after leading the first North American group to China in 1888. His chief object in coming over being the settlement of the work upon a permanent basis, he gave much time to meetings with the new council. The number of the latter was increased, and Mr. Frost was invited to assume the sole responsibility as treasurer and secretary, making his home in Toronto. It was with concern that Mr. Frost saw the days and weeks slip by of Mr. Taylor's visit, which was too short. Much helpful fellowship they had together as they traveled from place to place, Mr. Taylor addressing over forty meetings in eighteen different centers during the five weeks he was in America. Four days at Northfield completed the program and brought the mission again before many friends of the previous summer. Mr. Moody's interest was so much deepened that he offered the beautiful and spacious "Northfield Hotel" during the winter, as a training home for the candidates of the mission, undertaking himself to give a course of one month's Bible lessons.

Cheered and strengthened by many tokens for good, Mr. Taylor left America in August to carry out a full program of meetings, which included a visit to Sweden before the close of the year. So pressing and constant were his engagements that he found it difficult to obtain the time needed for remembering all his fellow workers daily before God. Well he knew that to relax prayer was to open the way for the Enemy to come in like a flood, and as he traveled from place to place, he literally had to buy up every opportunity for this unseen but important work.

The burden on Mr. Taylor's heart all through this Swedish visit, if burden it could be called, was the deeper apprehension that had come to him of the meaning of the divine command, "Go ye into all the world, and preach the gospel to every creature" (Mark 16:15). For more than forty years that command had controlled his life, and he had responded to it with unquestioning obedience. What had he not done and suffered; how had he not helped and inspired others in seeking to carry it out! Surely if there were a man anywhere who might feel that he had discharged his responsibility in this matter, it was Hudson Taylor.

And yet, on a quiet Sunday by the sea, how new the conception that had dawned upon him of the Master's meaning in those long-familiar words! It was Mrs. Taylor's birthday (October 6, 1889), and they were spending it at her father's home at Hastings. Did it recall that other memorable Sunday, on the sands at Brighton, when he had met the crisis of his life and had yielded himself to God for the evangelization of inland China?

What he saw now, in the light of the Holy Spirit's teaching, was a meaning so great, so comprehensive, in those few simple words—among the last that fell from the ascending Savior's lips—that it seemed as if he heard them for the first time. He wrote a few months later:

> I confess with shame that until that moment the question, What did our Lord *really mean* by His command, "Preach the Gospel to every creature"? had never been raised by me. I had labored for many years, as have many others, to carry the Gospel further afield, had laid plans for reaching every unreached province and many smaller districts in China, without realizing the plain meaning of our Savior's words.

"To every creature"? And the total number of Protestant communicants in that great land was only forty thousand. Double the number, triple it, to include adherents, and suppose each one to be a messenger to eight of his fellow countrymen—even so, only one million would be reached. "To every creature": the words burned into his very soul. But how far was the church, how far had he been himself from taking them literally, as intended to be acted upon! He saw it now, however, and with Hudson Taylor there was but one course—to obey. He wrote that very day:

> How are we going to treat the Lord Jesus Christ with reference to this command? Shall we definitely drop the title Lord as applied to Him, and take the ground that we are quite willing to recognize Him as our Savior, so far as the penalty of sin is concerned, but are not prepared to own ourselves "bought with a price" (1

> Cor. 6:20), or Him as having any claim to our unquestioning obedience? Shall we say that we are our own masters, willing to yield something as His due, who bought us with His blood, provided He does not ask too much? Our lives, our loved ones, our possessions are our own, not His; we will give Him what we think fit and obey any of His requirements that do not demand too great a sacrifice? To be taken to heaven by Jesus Christ we are more than willing, but we will not have this Man to *reign* over us?
>
> The heart of every Christian will undoubtedly reject the proposition, so formulated, but have not countless lives in each generation been lived as though it were proper ground to take? How few of the Lord's people have practically recognized the truth that Christ is either *Lord of all*, or is not *Lord at all!* If we can judge God's Word instead of being judged by that Word, if we can give to God as much or as little as we like, then we are lords and He is the indebted one, to be grateful for our dole and obliged by our compliance with His wishes. If, on the other hand, He is Lord, let us treat Him as such. "Why call ye me, Lord, Lord, and do not the things which I say?" (Luke 6:46).

So, all unexpectedly, he came to the widest outlook of his life, the purpose that was to dominate the closing decade of its active service. With hair fast turning gray and fifty-seven years of experience behind him, he met the new sense of responsibility with the old faith and confidence. Oh, the fresh appeal of the old incentives; the uprising of soul before the old ideals; the faithfulness to early vision, to the first calling; the undimmed power of the one, the ever-supreme Love! It is all there—all the purpose of youth without abatement, without compromise, despite the stern realities of twenty-four years of the grinding mill as leader of the Inland Mission. It was fine, fine flour now, but none of it was lost. "None other name" (Acts 4:12), none other sufficiency! Christ and Him crucified, the one, the only remedy for the sin and need of the world; God, changeless, inexhaustible, behind His commands and promises; divine, constraining love, the motive-power—it is all there, first as last and last as first.

Chapter 13

To Every Creature

Not a mere human project but a divine command was what Mr. Taylor saw in the words, "to every creature," that autumn day by the sea. They came to him with all the urgency of a royal mandate that brooks no delay. It was a question of duty, and no time was to be lost. "If we begin at once," he realized afresh with straitened heart, "millions will have passed away ere we can reach them."

But begin what? Begin a definite, systematic effort to do just as the Master said—to carry the glad tidings of salvation to every man, woman, and child throughout the whole of China. Was not that His order? Did He not intend it to be obeyed? Nothing if not practical, Mr. Taylor set himself forthwith to consider, not whether the attempt should be made, but simply—how? And as he thought and prayed he came to see, first of all, that it could be done. There was no impossibility about the matter. Armies of scores of thousands could be sent to the ends of the earth for the sake of material conquest, and the church had at her command resources fully equal to the obligations laid upon her.

Very simply it occurred to him, about the vast population to be reached: a million is a thousand thousands; given a thousand evangelists, each one teaching two hundred and fifty people daily, in a thousand days, two hundred and fifty million would have the offer of divine mercy. Surely a task that could, at this rate, be accomplished in little over three years should not be thought of as fanciful or beyond the resources of the Christian church.

Many objections, he knew, could be raised to this calculation. To begin with, some might think it impossible for an individual worker to reach as many as two hundred and fifty people daily, or that, if they could, such an offer of the Gospel would accomplish little. Mr. Taylor could not but remember, however, the work he had done himself in early years, and especially the many months spent with the Rev. William Burns in thorough, systematic evangelization in districts in which there were no settled missionaries. They had not found it difficult to reach five hundred to one thousand people daily, preaching in all the streets of a given town or city and entering every shop with books and tracts. As night came on they would repair to a previously announced tea shop where interested hearers could meet them for conversation, and any who wished to learn more were invited to their boats for further talk and prayer. How he had loved the work; how often he longed to be in it still! And as to results, he in common with many others could recall that among the brightest converts they had ever known were more than a few who had truly given their hearts to Christ the first time they ever heard of redeeming love.

His calculation, moreover, did not take into account the help to be given by the missionaries already in China—of whom there were considerably over a thousand--nor the immense and invaluable contribution to be made by native Christians. Forty thousand church members, not to speak of inquirers, would make the proposition a very different thing from what it could be without them. He had seen enough already, even in the newly opened provinces, to know that Chinese Christians were ready to lead as well as follow in such an enterprise.

It might be said, however, that our Lord's injunction was not only to "preach the gospel to every creature" (Mark 16:15), but also to baptize and instruct, "teaching them to observe all things whatsoever I have commanded you" (Matt. 28:20), hence the schools, settled churches, and much besides, in which the large majority of missionaries were engaged. This Mr. Taylor recognized, and none can have longed more than he to see such agencies multiplied. It was not the suspension or neglect of any existing work he was considering, but the great unmet need beyond. "There is that scattereth, and yet increaseth" (Prov. 11:24) was a principle he had found deeply true in this connection, and, after all, a thousand additional workers could not give themselves for five years to a widespread evangelistic campaign throughout the whole of China without fitting themselves all the more fully for the settled work that was sure to follow.

Thus it was that in the December *China's Millions* an earnest, practical paper entitled, "To Every Creature," made its appearance, outcome of the deep soul exercise of that October day. Its plea was for immediate action, first in the realm in which every believer may have power, the realm of prayer. What part the C.I.M. might take in the forward movement Mr. Taylor did not attempt to determine. It was the united, simultaneous action of all the societies that alone could put one thousand evangelists in the field without delay. His recent visits to

America satisfied him that on that side of the water fully half the required number could be found.

Deepening the Channels

Mr. Taylor continued to travel and gain support for his call to spread the Gospel "to every creature." Trips to Australia and Scandinavia brought new workers to China and opened the hearts of the people of these countries to the work of the Inland Mission. Yet with all this growth and encouragement, seldom had there been a time of more serious and widespread danger for foreigners in China, or of greater strain for Mr. Taylor as leader of the mission, as there was in the early 1890s. Riots began to break out all along the Yangtze valley, and in place after place mission premises were destroyed. Though the fury of the people was especially directed against the Roman Catholics, all foreigners were more or less imperiled. Even in Shanghai it seemed uncertain whether the authorities would be able to restrain looting and violence, and little sleep was to be had on more than one hot summer night because a riot was expected before morning.

For five long months in 1891, the excitement continued, notwithstanding an imperial proclamation which had a good effect. With few exceptions, C.I.M. workers were enabled to remain at their stations, none in which rioting actually occurred, though many were seriously threatened. Prayer for rain in June was wonderfully answered, and it was again in October when the council meetings were adjourned in order that all in the mission house at Shanghai might unite in waiting upon God for deliverance. The summer had been intensely hot, and nothing was so likely to quiet the people as steady, continuous rain, which was much needed. Prayer was earnest and definite, therefore, in this connection, and three weeks later a letter from Mrs. Taylor recorded the definite answer: "Rain has been coming down almost all this month." The effect was just what was hoped for: crowds were scattered, gradually the antiforeign feeling died down for the time being, and normal conditions were restored.

* * * * *

A thousand missionaries were asked for next, and by 1895 Mr. Taylor was thankful to be able to state that not a thousand only, but 1,153 new workers had been added to the missionary staff in China during the previous five years—a wonderful answer to prayer that could not but call forth widespread thanksgiving. And yet, as he pointed out, it was far from final, in the sense of having attained the end in view. A great step forward had been taken, but it left the primary duty—that of making known the Gospel "to every creature" in China, in obedience to the Master's Great Command—still unfulfilled. The addition of even this large number hardly affected the situation in the great waiting world of inland China, because many of the societies to which many of these new workers were sent were working on or near the coast. It was for these unreached millions Mr. Taylor pleaded still, and with renewed urgency.

As the years went by, the work for Mr. Taylor did not lessen. He continued in his direction of the mission and the council for as long as his health would permit. Even after he appointed Mr. D. E.

Hoste as his successor, Mr. Taylor continued his loving support of the mission he had founded. Times of trial continued through the last years of his active work, one of the worst being the Boxer Rebellion (1900). At the time of this rebellion, Mr. Taylor was recovering from ill health in Switzerland, where he had been wonderfully restored some years previously. There it was that the blow fell, and telegram after telegram was received telling of riots, massacres, and the hunting down of refugees in station after station of the mission—until the heart that so long, in joy and sorrow, had upheld these beloved fellow workers before the Lord could endure no more and almost ceased to beat. But for the protection of the remote valley where news could, in measure, be kept from him, Hudson Taylor would himself have been among those whose lives were laid down for Christ's sake and for China in the oversweeping horror of that summer. As it was, he lived through it, holding on to God.

"I cannot read," he said when things were at their worst; "I cannot think; I cannot even pray; but I can trust."

His Way Is Perfect

In 1902, Mr. Taylor finally felt that the time had come for laying down responsibilities for which he was no longer equal. Many problems were pressing in connection with the reconstruction and rapid development of the work. Opportunities were wonderful, and the seed sown in tears and watered with blood was giving promise of an abundant harvest. The blessing of God had notably rested on the appointment made two years previously, and knowing he had the full concurrence of all the directors and councils, Mr. Taylor felt only thankfulness in resigning to Mr. Hoste the full direction of the mission. The change had come about so gradually that to many it was hardly felt, Mr. and Mrs. Taylor remaining in all but name as closely connected with the work as ever, but to Mr. Hoste it meant a heavy increase of responsibility.

Hudson Taylor's last years with his wife were spent together without the separations that had defined most of their married life together. Mrs. Taylor's death in 1904 happened after a long illness, and for Mr. Taylor, right after her death, the desolation was unutterable. On the wall of the little sitting room hung a text, the last purchase they had made together, and many a time during the days that followed did he look up through his tears to the words in blue, shining out from their white background:

"Celui qui a fait les promesses est fidèle."[2]

"My grace is sufficient" (2 Cor. 12:9) had been almost her last words to him, and then—"He will not fail." Upon this certainty he rested now in the desolation he had so little strength to endure, remembering her constant joy in the will of God, and that, as he recalled again and again, "she never thought anything could be better."

* * * * *

It was Friday, May 26, 1905, during Mr. Taylor's last trip to China, when his party reached

---

[2] "Faithful is He who made the promises." (See Hebrews 10:23.)

Hankow once more, the thirty-ninth anniversary of the sailing of the *Lammermuir*. In the train on the way down they had had precious times of prayer. After a quiet Sunday in Hankow, Mr. Taylor decided to go on by steamer to Chang-sha, capital of the province of Hunan, which he had never visited. First of the far inland provinces the mission had attempted to enter, it had been the last in which settled residence had been obtained, and for more than thirty years Mr. Taylor had borne it especially upon his heart in prayer. Only since the troubles of 1900 had it been fully opened, and he greatly desired to see the work of Dr. Keller and others in the capital, described with graphic interest by Dr. Harlan Beach in a recent number of *China's Millions*.

As they crossed the far-reaching lake and steamed up the river, passing well-built cities, beautiful pagodas and temples, rich plains covered with ripening crops, and noble mountain ranges near and distant, they could not but think of all the toil and prayer of years gone by, of buried lives and dauntless faith, richly rewarded at last in the change that was coming over the attitude of the people. Until eight or nine years previously there had not been one Protestant missionary settled in the province. None had been able to gain a footing. No fewer than a hundred and eleven missionaries were to be found there now, connected with thirteen societies, working in seventeen central stations and aided by a strong band of Chinese helpers. Of Mr. Taylor, it was written:

> It was Thursday afternoon the first of June when we reached the capital (Chang-sha) and were welcomed by our dear friends Dr. and Mrs.

Keller and Dr. Barrie. Twenty minutes in chairs brought us to the mission house, in which we felt quite at home already, having carefully studied Dr. Harlan Beach's ground plan and article. Of the two days that followed, how can I write? They were so calm and peaceful, so full of interest and encouragement, so rich in love and sympathy and the tender care that surrounded our beloved one, that our hearts overflow on every remembrance of the Lord's goodness up to the very end.

Friday was a quiet, restful day. It rained all the morning and we could not go out. After lunch, chairs were called and we visited the T'ien Sin Koh, a lofty building on the highest point of the city wall. Father was delighted with the wonderful view of mountains, plain, and river, surrounding the city outspread at our feet. He climbed to the second story without being overtired, and afterwards went to see the site for the new hospital—several acres of land in a good situation that the governor hopes to give for the work of our medical mission.

On Saturday, Father did not come down to breakfast but was dressed and reading when we carried up his tray. He was to speak to the Chinese friends that morning, so as soon as the daily service was concluded he went to the chapel and said a little through interpretation. They were deeply interested in seeing him, many of them having just read the *Retrospect* translated by Mr. Baller into Chinese. Mr. Li the evangelist responded, expressing the love and joy with which they welcomed him to Chang-sha.

That afternoon a reception had been arranged to give all the missionaries in the city an opportunity of meeting Mr. Taylor, and before the time appointed he came down seasonably dressed in a suit of shantung silk.

It was cool and pleasant in the little garden on to which the sitting room opened, and tea was served on the lawn, surrounded by trees and flowers. Father went out and sat in the midst of the guests for an hour or more, evidently enjoying the quiet, happy time, and interested in the photographs that were being taken.

After all had left, Howard persuaded him to go upstairs, and as we were busy sending our things to the steamer (we were to walk down ourselves on Sunday evening after the service), Dr. Barrie remained with him for half an hour. It was a still evening, and while they were talking Father rose and crossed the room to fetch two fans. One of these he handed to Dr. Barrie, who exclaimed, "Oh, why did you not let me bring them?"

"I wanted to get you one," was the reply, in a tone which deeply touched his companion.

Speaking of the privilege of bringing *everything* to God in prayer, Dr. Barrie said that he was sometimes hindered by the feeling that many things were too small, really, to pray about.

Father's answer was that he did not know anything about it—about such a distinction, probably. Then he added,

"There is nothing small, and there is nothing great; only God is great, and we should trust Him fully."

When the evening meal was ready, Mr. Taylor did not feel inclined to come down, and a little later he was preparing to go to rest when his son brought him his supper. While waiting for him to be comfortably settled, his daughter-in-law spent a few minutes alone on the little roof platform which is such a pleasant addition to many Chang-sha houses.

> Twilight had fallen then, and darkness veiled the distant mountains and river. Here and there a few glimmering lights dotted the vast expanse of gray-roofed city. All was silent under the star-lit sky. Enjoying the cool and quietness I stood alone awhile, thinking of Father. But oh, how little one realized what was happening even then, or dreamed that in less than one half hour our loved one would be with the Lord! Was the golden gate already swinging back on its hinges? Were the hosts of welcoming angels gathering to receive his spirit? Had the Master Himself arisen to greet His faithful friend and servant? What was happening, oh, what was happening, even then, over the sleeping city?
>
> Knowing nothing, realizing nothing, I went down. Dear Father was in bed, the lamp burning on the chair beside him, and he was leaning over it with his pocketbook lying open and the home letters it contained spread out as he loved to have them. I drew the pillow up more comfortably under his head and sat down on a low chair close beside him. As he said nothing, I began talking a little about the pictures in the *Missionary Review* lying open on the bed. Howard left the room to fetch something that had been forgotten for supper, and I was just in the middle of a sentence when dear Father turned his head quickly and gave a little gasp. I looked up, thinking he was going to sneeze. But another came, then another! He gave no cry and said no word. He was not choking or distressed for breath. He did not look at me or seem conscious of anything.

I ran to the door and called Howard, but before he could reach the bedside it was evident that the end had come. I ran back to call Dr. Keller, who was just at the foot of the stairs. In less time than it takes to write it he was with us, but only to see dear Father draw his last breath. It was not death—but the glad, swift entry upon life immortal.

"My father, my father, the chariot of Israel, and the horsemen thereof" (2 Kings 2:12; 13:14)!

And oh, the look of rest and calm that came over the dear face was wonderful! The weight of years seemed to pass away in a few moments. The weary lines vanished. He looked like a child quietly sleeping, and the very room seemed full of unutterable peace.

* * * * *

Tenderly we laid him down, too surprised and thankful to realize for the moment our great loss. There was nothing more to be done. The precious service of months was ended. Mr. Li and other Chinese friends went out to make arrangements, but we could hardly bring ourselves to leave that quiet room. All the house was still, hallowed by a serenity and sweetness that hardly seemed of earth. Though he was gone, a wonderful love and tenderness seemed still to draw us to his side. Oh, the comfort of seeing him so utterly rested. Dear, dear Father, all the weariness over, all the journeyings ended—safe home, safe home at last!

One by one or in little groups the friends who were in the house and the dear native Christians gathered round his bed. All were so impressed with the calm, peaceful look that lingered on his face, and many touching things were said, showing that even in these short days, the sweetness and simplicity of his life had won their hearts.

"*Oh Sï-mu,*" whispered one dear woman as she left the room, "*ts'ien ts'ien wan-wan-tih t'ien-shi tsieh t'a liao!*" (thousands and myriads of angels have welcomed him)—and in a flash one almost seemed to see it.

Last of all a dear young evangelist and his wife, a bride of eighteen, came up. They had journeyed in from an outstation on purpose to meet us all, and especially Father, whose *Retrospect* they had been reading. Arriving in the afternoon while tea was going on, they did not like to ask to see him, and when the guests had left he was tired. So they put it off till morning, as we were to spend Sunday with them all. And then, suddenly, they heard of his departure to be with the Lord.

Full of sorrow, they sent in to ask if they might come and look upon his face. Of course we welcomed them, telling them all that had happened and how grieved we were that they had not seen him earlier in the day. Together they stood beside the bed in silence, until the young man said, "Do you think that I might touch his hand?"

Then he bent over him, took one of Father's hands in his and stroked it tenderly, while to our surprise he began to talk to him just as if he could hear. He seemed to forget us and everything else in a great longing just to reach the one who still seemed near and make him feel his love and gratitude.

"*Lao Muh-sï, Lao Muh-sï,*" he said so tenderly (Dear and Venerable Pastor), "we truly love you. We have come today to see you. We longed to look into your face. We too are your little children—*Lao Muh-sï, Lao Muh-sï*. You opened for us the road, the road to heaven. You loved us and prayed for us long years. We came today to look upon your face.

"You look so happy, so peaceful! You are smiling. Your face is quiet and pleased. You cannot speak to us tonight. We do not want to bring you back, but we will follow you. We shall come to you, *Lao Muh-sï*. You will welcome us by and by."

And all the time he held his hand, bending over him and stroking it gently, his young wife standing by.

Downstairs, meanwhile, another touching scene was taking place. Mr. Li and others who had been out to make arrangements returned, bringing a coffin and bearers and everything necessary for the last journey. They had hoped when first they learned of dear Father's home call that he would be buried in Hunan and had rejoiced to think that in this way they might keep him among them still. But when it was explained that we must leave at once for Chinkiang, as his family grave was there, and he had always wished to be laid beside his loved ones should he die in China, they set aside their own desire and did all they could to forward our departure.

When everything had been brought to the house they sent word to my husband asking if they might speak with him. He went at once and was touched by the many evidences of their thought and care. Then, gathering round him, they said that they had wished to obtain a more beautiful coffin but had been obliged to be satisfied with the best they could find ready-made; that he need not ask the price, for it was their gift, the gift of the church; for if they could not be allowed to keep the Venerable Chief Pastor in Hunan, they must at any rate do everything for him at their own expense.

It was a great surprise, but they would take no denial. Had not the Lord brought their beloved father in the faith to Chang-sha, and permitted them to look upon his face? From their midst had he not been translated? Hunan Christians had been the last to hear his voice, to receive his blessing. Theirs must be the privilege of providing for his last needs.

Yes, it was beautiful and right. It meant a large sum to them, and they would feel it. But the joy of sacrifice was in their hearts, and we could not but stand aside and let them do as they would. So Hunan hands prepared his last resting place, Hunan hearts planned all with loving care—one little company of the great multitude his life had blessed. Not in vain, ah, not in vain the faith and toil and suffering, the ceaseless prayer and soul travail of fifty years. Inland China open everywhere to the Gospel proclaims the faithfulness of God, and these strong Hunan men with hearts as tender as children's, these women with tear-dimmed eyes helping in the last ministries of love, attest the gratitude of a redeemed and blood-washed company no man can number.

By the mighty river at Chinkiang they laid him, where it rolls its waters two miles wide toward the sea. Much might be said of the love and veneration shown to his memory; of memorial services in Shanghai, London, and elsewhere; of eulogies in the public press; of sympathetic resolutions passed by missionary and other societies; and of personal letters from high and low in many lands. From the striking tribute of a high church bishop in *The Guardian* to the tender reminiscences of fellow workers, many were the written and spoken words that showed him to have been not only "the heartbeat felt throughout the mission," but a vital force of life and love in every part, one might almost say, of the body of Christ. But the voices that linger longest are those he would have loved the best—the voices of Chinese children singing sweet hymns of praise as they laid their little offerings of flowers upon his resting place.

"Thus one by one the stars that are to shine forever in God's firmament appear in their celestial places, and the children of the kingdom enter upon the blessedness of their Father's house which is not made with hands."

Prayers Yet to Be Answered

Prayers yet to be answered—how rich the inheritance Hudson Taylor left to the land he loved, to the church of God in China for which his life was given! In one sense, the prayers of that lifetime had indeed been answered.

But in another sense, do not those prayers lie beyond us yet, marking out wide possessions upon which the foot of faith has trodden, possessions still to be possessed?

Nothing could have been more definite than Mr. Taylor's own conviction as to the thoughts that had come to him in 1889. Once he had seen it, he could never doubt again the Master's will and purpose that "every creature" in China should hear the glad tidings of salvation. Through all the years that followed, though hindered again and again, and postponed for a time by the Boxer crisis, his original purpose never wavered. He said at the C.I.M. conference in 1890:

> This work will not be done without crucifixion, without consecration that is prepared *at any cost* to carry out the Master's command. But, *given that*, I believe in my inmost soul that *it will be done.* If ever in my life I was conscious of being led of God, it was in the writing and publication of those papers, the first of which came out in November of last year.

"The sun has never risen upon China without finding me at prayer," Mr. Taylor could say of long years of his labors in that land, and perhaps no part of those labors had more to do with the results we see today. But he not only prayed. The foregoing pages have revealed a little of what lay behind those prayers. "I do want to give up myself and you too, darling, for the life of the Chinese and of our fellow workers," he wrote to Mrs. Taylor in one of their many separations, and, "Notice, in 1 Corinthians 1:18, the connection of the Cross with power. Do not many lives lack power because they do not love the Cross? May your life be full of the power of God, and mine."

The needs that moved him, the command that revealed the yearning of the heart of Christ whom we, too, call Master and Lord—remain the same years after Hudson Taylor's death. Great changes have come and are coming in China. New methods are needed in missionary work to meet the new conditions, and they are being prayerfully developed and applied. But the great underlying facts remain the same. Idolatry has not lost its hold. Writing from the far northwest (June 1918), a member of the mission tells of guilds in one city numbering thousands of men and women sworn to regular worship at stated times. In one of these some fifteen hundred women are pledged to go to a certain temple on the second and sixth of every month, "where they kneel upright on the verandahs and in the courtyard, each holding a stick of incense between the two hands raised to the level of the forehead. This position has to be maintained and prayers recited until the stick of incense has burned away—quite a long process." And offerings of money must be made on every one of the stated worship days, which go to the building and beautifying of temples and making fresh idols. And this is only one city out of hundreds that have as yet no resident missionary. Do the people need light in their darkness? Do they not care about the unknown future and what becomes of the soul? Is it for them too that the precious blood was shed which alone can cleanse from sin and bring us nigh to God? And what will be said of the responsibility that rests upon us if, knowing these things, we are not doing our utmost—whether by prayer or gifts or personal service—to bring to them, too, the knowledge which is life eternal?

Much is being done, but much more is needed if the present opportunity—perhaps the most glorious that has ever come to Christian men and women—is to be dealt with faithfully. "When China is moved," Napoleon used to say, "it will change the face of the globe." China *is* moved, is moving; will it not be home to the heart of God?

If the one whose steps we have followed through a life of toil and sacrifice, yet of radiant joy in fellowship with Christ, could speak to us today from the "exceeding and eternal weight of glory" (2 Cor. 4:17), would he not say again as he said in the midst of the fight:

> There is a needs-be for *us* to give *ourselves* for the life of the world—as He gave His flesh for the feeding of the lifeless and of living souls whose life can only be nourished by the same life-giving Bread. An easygoing, non-self-denying life will never be one of power.
>
> Fruit-bearing involves cross-bearing. "Except a corn of wheat fall into the ground and die, it abideth alone" (John 12:24). We know how the Lord Jesus became fruitful—not by bearing His Cross merely, but by dying on it. Do we know much of fellowship with Him in this? There are not two Christs—an easygoing one for easygoing Christians, and a suffering, toiling one for exceptional believers. There is only one Christ. Are you willing to abide in Him, and thus to bear much fruit?
>
> Would that God would make hell so real to us that we cannot rest; heaven so real that we must have men there; Christ so real that our supreme motive and aim shall be to make the Man of Sorrows the Man of Joy by the conversion to Him of many concerning whom He prayed, "Father, I [long] that [those]...whom thou hast given me, be with me where I am; that they may behold my glory" (John 17:24).